FORTHCOMING TITLES

James A. Caporaso
Challenges and Dilemmas of European Union

☐ ☐ ☐

David S. Mason
Revolution in East-Central Europe, Second Edition

☐ ☐ ☐

Thomas G. Weiss
Humanitarian Action, Intervention, and World Politics

☐ ☐ ☐

Janice Love
Southern Africa in World Politics

DILEMMAS
OF INTERNATIONAL
TRADE

■ ■ ■

Bruce E. Moon
LEHIGH UNIVERSITY

WestviewPress

A Division of HarperCollinsPublishers

Dilemmas in World Politics

Copyright © 1996 by Westview Press, Inc., A Division of HarperCollins Publishers,
Inc.

Published in 1996 in the United States of America by Westview Press, Inc., 5500
Central Avenue, Boulder, Colorado 80301-2877, and in the United Kingdom by
Westview Press, 12 Hid's Copse Road, Cumnor Hill, Oxford OX2 9JJ

Library of Congress Cataloging-in-Publication Data
Moon, Bruce Edward, 1950-
    Dilemmas of international trade / Bruce E. Moon.
        p.   cm. — (Dilemmas in world politics)
    Includes bibiliographical references and index.
    ISBN 0-8133-1844-0 (hardcover: alk. paper).—ISBN
0-8133-1845-9 (pbk.: alk. paper)
    1. International trade.   I. Title.   II. Series.
HF1379.M66 1996
382—dc20   95-46998
                                                                    CIP

The paper used in this publication meets the requirements of the American National
Standard for Permanence of Paper for Printed Library Materials Z39.48-1984.

10   9   8   7   6   5   4   3   2   1

Contents

□ □ □

Tables and Illustrations

Tables

Cartoons

Boxes

□ □ □

Acknowledgments

It is impossible to adequately acknowledge all those who have contributed to this volume, and I shall not attempt to do so. However, special mention must be made of the contributions of my students at Lehigh University, who have read and commented upon several drafts of this work. Their indispensable efforts are gratefully acknowledged.

This book would not have been written without the enthusiasm and support of Jennifer Knerr and George Lopez. I thank them for displaying a good deal more confidence in this project than I could frequently muster. My colleague and friend Rajan Menon contributed his usual careful reading, helpful comments, and wise advice.

As always, I owe more to one who has not read the manuscript than to all the others: My wife, Beverly, has provided more support than anyone has a right to ask.

Bruce E. Moon

Acronyms

CAP	Common Agricultural Policy
CGE	computable general equilibrium
CUSTA	Canada–United States Trade Agreement
DM	Deutsche mark
EC	European Community
ECSC	European Coal and Steel Community
ECU	European currency unit
EEC	European Economic Community
EFTA	European Free Trade Association
EIB	European Investment Bank
EMS	European Monetary System
ERM	Exchange Rate Mechanism
ESC	Economic and Social Committee
ESF	European Social Fund
EU	European Union
EURATOM	European Atomic Energy Community
FDI	foreign direct investment
FTC	Federal Trade Commission
GATT	General Agreement on Tariffs and Trade
GDP	gross domestic product
GNP	gross national product
H-O	Heckscher-Ohlin (theory)
IBRD	International Bank for Reconstruction and Development (World Bank)
IMF	International Monetary Fund
ISI	import-substituting industrialization
ITO	International Trade Organization
LDCs	less developed countries
MFA	Multi-Fiber Agreement
MFN	most favored nation
MITI	Ministry of International Trade and Industry (Japan)
MOF	Ministry of Finance (Japan)
MPs	members of Parliament

NAFTA	North American Free Trade Agreement
NICs	newly industrializing countries
NTBs	nontariff barriers
OECD	Organization for Economic Cooperation and Development
OMAs	orderly marketing arrangements
PRC	People's Republic of China
PRI	Mexican Partido Revolucionario Institucional
SII	structural impediment initiative
TRIM	trade-related investment measures
TRIP	trade-related aspects of intellectual property
VAT	value-added tax
VIE	voluntary import expansion
VERs	voluntary export restraints
VRAs	voluntary restraint agreements
WTO	World Trade Organization

ONE

□ □ □

Trade and Trade Issues

This book has two missions. The first is to explain the fundamental dilemmas that surround international trade and trade policy issues. How we respond to these trade dilemmas will not only shape our economy but also determine the kind of society in which we will live. Too often, trade is treated purely as an economic phenomenon that is—or ought to be—divorced from politics. In fact, because the political and the economic components of international trade are intertwined, neither can be understood without the other. I examine the dilemmas of trade in the context of several contemporary controversies, especially the Japanese-American trade relationship, the **European Union** (EU), the **North American Free Trade Agreement** (NAFTA), and the **Uruguay Round** of the **General Agreement on Tariffs and Trade** (GATT).

The second mission is to introduce the basic principles of international political economy by examining how politics and economics interact to shape trade policies. To provide historical and theoretical perspective, I discuss nineteenth-century British trade policy and the evolution of the **Bretton Woods** international economic system of the modern era.

THE THEMES OF THE BOOK

Whenever people purchase products made abroad, they unknowingly act in accord with one set of interests, values, and theories concerning international trade but in discord with another set. This book demonstrates that the consequences of these individual choices pose fundamental policy dilemmas for governments. States seek many outcomes from trade—full employment, long-term growth, economic stability, power, security, and

1

friendly external relations—yet discover that these desirable outcomes are frequently incompatible. The resulting dilemmas can be seen with clarity only when the standard economic theories of international trade are un-derstood to be partial and incomplete. They must be augmented with treatments rooted in the perspective of international **political economy**.

Since the nineteenth century, **economic liberalism** has been the dominant theoretical perspective on international trade. Liberal economic theorists maintain that free markets establish prices that result in the most **efficient allocation of factors of production,** such as land, labor, and **capital**. Thus, from the time of Adam Smith (1723–1790), they have concluded that **free trade** is the surest path to economic prosperity and growth. Consequently, they have urged that governments refrain from interfering with private en-trepreneurs and free markets in international trade. Yet in the intervening two centuries, virtually no national government has followed this advice.

This book probes the reason for this curious disparity between accepted economic theory and established political practice, rejecting the interpreta-tion proffered by some economists that the discrepancy results from irra-tional or corrupt policy. Instead, the book's political economy perspective acknowledges that governments seek to influence trade because markets generate multiple consequences, many of which exceed the boundaries of economic theory yet touch the fundamental responsibilities of govern-ment. For example, just as trade affects the prices of individual products, global markets influence which individuals and nations accumulate wealth and political power. They determine who will be employed and at what wage. They determine what natural resources will be used and at what environmental cost. They shape opportunities and constraints in for-eign policy. Because trade affects such a broad range of social outcomes, conflict among alternative goals and values is inevitable. As a result, gov-ernments, which seek to balance all the interests and values of society, con-front dilemmas that require painful choices.

In this book I describe the dilemmas resulting from the distributional consequences of trade, the competing values affected by trade, and the impact of trade on the concerns of the state. I also explain how various governments (and individuals) respond to these dilemmas and why.

The Meaning of Economic Liberalism

The term "economic liberalism" is *not* to be confused with the ambiguous way that the term "liberal" is applied in American politics. Economic liber-alism is wary of government interference with the market, whereas those called liberals often advocate it.

THE IMPORTANCE OF TRADE AND THE TRADE BALANCE

Most economists and policymakers believe that expanded levels of trade provide substantial benefits for individual nations and the global economy as a whole. Exports are valued because they produce jobs for workers and profits for corporations. They also earn revenue that can be used to purchase imports. The very fact that individuals choose to import implies that some products produced abroad are of higher quality or lower price than could be obtained from domestic producers. Thus, import expansion implies an increase in welfare for the citizens of the nation because they can acquire more for their money. Of course, some imported products are not available from domestic sources at all. Thus, governments are frequently advised to adopt policies that will maximize the volume of trade.

Trade has become an important element in the economies of all developed nations, but there is considerable variation both across nations and over time. In Table 1.1, which shows the importance of exports in selected nations in 1970 and 1992, two patterns can be seen within that variation. First, larger nations, which have sizable domestic markets of their own, tend to rely less on trade than smaller nations. The United States, for example, with exports constituting only a little over 10 percent of its **gross national product** (GNP), is less reliant on trade than virtually any other country in the world. Even Japan, with its reputation as a great trading nation, is much less dependent on trade than any European nation. Despite its shortage of natural resources, the sheer size of Japan's economy, second only to that of the United States, enables it to meet most of its own needs

TABLE 1.1   Exports as a Percentage of Gross National Product

Nation	1970	1992
United States	6.8	10.6
Japan	11.3	10.1
Germany	22.6	33.4
Canada	22.9	27.7
Mexico	6.7	12.8
United Kingdom	21.9	23.6
South Korea	14.0	29.5
France	15.8	23.3
Netherlands	45.0	52.4
Belgium	43.5	70.6

SOURCE: Based on data for exports of goods and nonfactor services from World Bank, *World Tables 1991* and *World Tables 1994* (Baltimore: Johns Hopkins University Press, 1991, 1994).

and to consume most of its own production. Smaller nations, such as Belgium and the Netherlands, as well as most Third World countries, must engage in greater levels of trade because they can neither supply goods to meet all their own needs nor provide a market sizable enough for many industries to produce in the large volumes required to be efficient.

Even if we allow for those differences in size, however, trade has been more significant for European economies than for those of North America. Part of the explanation is that their relative proximity to one another lowers transport costs, but part also lies in government policy, especially the establishment of regional organizations like the European Union that facilitate trade within Europe. The precedent set by the EU encouraged the creation of a North America Free Trade Agreement designed to allow a similar growth of trade among the United States, Canada, and Mexico. Together with the advent of an East Asian group centered around Japan, these developments may foreshadow a world of **trade blocs** in which free trade may prevail within each bloc but trade between blocs is restricted.

The second pattern revealed by this table is the greater role that trade has assumed, increasing from 1970 to the early 1990s more than 50 percent in the United States as a percentage of GNP, for example. With such heavy reliance on jobs in the export sector and on foreign products to meet domestic demand, it is evident why trade issues have become so politically explosive in recent years. With exports now constituting about a quarter of the economy in most countries and well over half in some, any major reduction in trade would require a vast economic restructuring that would entail huge welfare losses. Table 1.1 also helps to explain why the trade issues that have occupied Europe for decades have entered the policy agenda in the United States only quite recently. Though American trade reliance has increased dramatically, it has still not reached the level that was common in Europe decades ago.

Liberal economic theory claims that trade benefits all nations because it permits each consumer to buy the most desirable products and each **entrepreneur** to invest resources in the most productive way. As a result, consumption is maximized by the **efficient allocation of resources,** and both the global economy as a whole and each nation within it are better off. Considerable evidence supports the view that trade improves productivity, consumption, and therefore welfare. The growth of the global economy has been most rapid during periods of trade expansion, especially after World War II, and has slowed when trade levels have fallen, especially during the **Great Depression** of the 1920s and 1930s. Periods of national growth have also coincided with trade expansion, most notably in Germany, Japan, and Korea. There is some uncertainty about whether trade leads to growth or growth leads to trade, but there is little doubt

STICKER SHOCK

Hidden costs. Danziger—*The Christian Science Monitor*

that most governments believe that trade expansion improves living standards.

Whereas nearly all nations have sought trade expansion, they have generally tried to avoid an excess of imports over exports, which is known as a deficit in the **balance of trade**. The consumption of imports permits foreigners to enjoy employment and profits from production that might otherwise benefit citizens of the home country. For example, the high levels of unemployment in Detroit have been ascribed partially to annual sales of nearly 2 million Japanese cars in the United States. This would be of little concern if these imports were balanced by exports that produce employment and profits from American products sold abroad, but during a **trade deficit** they are not.

Further, such deficits cannot be sustained for very long without compensating capital outflows that are usually seen as undesirable. Table 1.2 demonstrates that the United States has had persistent balance-of-trade deficits since the early 1970s, though for a time they were small enough to be balanced easily by the income from previous foreign investments. Since the middle of the 1980s, however, the annual deficits have been huge. To put in perspective these vast sums—$166.36 billion in 1994—imports exceeded exports by about $600 per American, over 3 percent of the American GNP in that year. (At the estimated rate of 20,000 jobs lost for every $1 billion in trade deficit, this corresponds to more than 3 million

TABLE 1.2 U.S. Balance of Trade, 1972–1994 ($ billion)

	Exports	Imports	Trade Balance
1972	49.38	55.80	−6.42
1973	71.41	70.50	.91
1974	98.32	103.83	−5.51
1975	107.08	98.18	8.90
1976	114.75	124.22	−9.47
1977	120.80	151.91	−31.11
1978	142.06	176.00	−33.94
1979	184.47	212.01	−27.54
1980	224.27	249.77	−25.50
1981	237.09	265.08	−27.99
1982	211.20	247.64	−36.44
1983	201.81	268.89	−67.08
1984	219.90	332.41	−112.51
1985	215.93	338.09	−122.16
1986	223.36	368.41	−145.05
1987	250.28	409.77	−159.49
1988	320.33	447.19	−126.96
1989	361.70	477.38	−115.68
1990	388.71	497.55	−108.84
1991	416.95	490.74	−73.79
1992	440.14	536.28	−96.14
1993	456.90	589.48	−132.58
1994	502.69	669.05	−166.36

SOURCE: Based on data for merchandise trade in billions of current U.S. dollars from World Bank, *World Tables 1991* and *World Tables 1994* (Baltimore: Johns Hopkins University Press, 1991, 1994).

jobs lost to the deficit.) Throughout the 1980s much more money flowed *out* of the American economy in the form of dollars to pay for imports than flowed back *into* the economy through payments for American goods purchased by foreigners. The obvious question is, What are foreigners *doing* with those dollars?

One answer is that they are investing them in the United States to generate future income. For example, the U.S. federal government **budget deficit**—in the magnitude of $200 billion annually since the early 1980s—has been financed partially by the selling of **Treasury bonds** to foreigners, especially Japanese investors. When the government sells Treasury bonds, it borrows money and agrees to pay interest on the debt. Thus, some of the money sent abroad to pay for imports has been borrowed back at interest rates that will keep the United States paying for this balance-of-trade deficit for years to come. Some has also returned to the United States in the form of investments in new plant and equipment—funded by the profits of Japanese auto firms—such as the Honda plant in Marysville, Ohio. New auto plants produce American jobs, of course, but the profits are earned by Japanese corporations, which will presumably return them to Japan one day. Such **repatriation** of profits again implies that paying for trade deficits can be postponed, but the burdens of such a deficit must eventually be faced.

Economists disagree about whether these developments ought to raise alarm. After all, this balance-of-trade deficit is allowing American citizens to consume more today than they are currently producing; thus, they enjoy a higher standard of living than would otherwise be possible. Furthermore, some economists emphasize that the willingness of foreigners to invest in the United States is an indication of confidence in the strength of the American economy. However, there are signs from international **currency markets** that the persistent balance-of-trade deficit is eroding that confidence. The demand for dollars by foreigners—to purchase products or investments from the United States—is now smaller than the supply of dollars created by Americans purchasing foreign products and investments. As a result, the value of the dollar, once equivalent to 360 Japanese yen (or nearly 4 German Deutsche marks [DM]), declined in 1995 to under 100 yen (and under DM1.50). The declining purchasing power of the dollar means, for example, that the 1 million-yen cost of a Japanese automobile would translate into a dollar price of about $2,800 at the old exchange rate (360 yen per dollar) but more than $10,000 at the current one (under 100 yen per dollar). Because balance-of-trade deficits tend to lead to such currency declines (and price rises), they imply that future consumption will be reduced and standards of living will fall. In short, a trade deficit engineers a shift in welfare from the future to the present.

If economists are uncertain about some of the negative effects of these developments, the public is not. For example, in 1988 (during the Cold War), Americans were asked, "Which poses the greatest threat to our national security, a military adversary like the Soviet Union or economic competitors like Japan?" Almost twice as many Americans answered the latter.[1] During the 1992 presidential campaign, Bill Clinton charged that President Bush had endangered national security by mismanaging the economy. About 50 percent of the public believed that the U.S economy was "slipping dangerously when compared to other industrialized nations," and 68 percent believed that Japan was a very strong competitor in the global economy; only 32 percent thought of the United States in that way.

THE DILEMMAS OF INTERNATIONAL TRADE

In seeking to achieve the benefits from trade expansion while avoiding the costs associated with trade deficits, nations must weigh three sets of dilemmas. The first concerns the distribution of income and wealth created by international trade. Simply put, some individuals and groups gain from trade while others lose. As a result, trade is inevitably politicized. Standard economic theory tends to deemphasize these distributional effects in its focus upon the impact of trade on the economy as a whole. Because these distributional consequences have such obvious political implications, however, the state is much more attentive to them than economic theorists are.

The most visible distributional effects are usually sectoral because trade policy often protects or promotes one industry or sector of the economy at the expense of others. For example, **tariffs** on imported steel protect the domestic steel industry by making foreign-produced steel more expensive, but they also harm domestic automakers who must pay higher prices for the steel they use. As in this case—where car buyers face higher prices—most barriers to trade benefit some sector of the economy at the expense of consumers.

Just as trade policy redistributes costs and benefits from one sector to another, it also benefits some classes and regions at the expense of others. For example, the elimination of trade barriers under the EU forces some British manufacturing workers into direct competition with Spanish workers who earn a markedly lower wage. Unless British wage rates decline, production may shift to Spain and British jobs will be lost. However, if that competition drives down wage rates in Britain, the profits earned by the owners of British business might be maintained at the expense of the standard of living of workers in those industries. The losses from such wage competition will be greatest for workers in high-wage countries employed in industries that can move either their products or their production facilities most easily across national boundaries. Others, particularly more affluent professionals such as doctors, lawyers, and university professors, who face less direct competition from abroad, stand to gain from trade because it lowers prices on the goods they consume. Trade opportunities thus pose the **distributional dilemma**: Whichever trade policy the government chooses will harm someone.

The second dilemma arises because the same economic changes that enable a nation to secure the benefits of trade may imply a compromise of other societal values. Trade places greater competitive pressure on firms even while it opens up greater opportunities for them to profit. As the stakes rise, domestic firms place increasing pressure on governments to ease restrictions that limit their ability to compete with foreign industries.

But these restrictions—environmental regulation, health and safety requirements, and many others—were designed to meet other legitimate national goals. Environmental regulations, for example, may add to production costs, but surely the pressures of international trade need not require that we abandon all other values.

The competitive pressure of trade also drives companies to lower their labor costs and pressure the state to alter policies that keep them from doing so. Lower wages could be paid if the minimum wage was eliminated and collective bargaining and labor unions were outlawed. The abolition of seniority systems and age-discrimination laws would enable companies to terminate workers when their efficiency declined (or at the whim of a boss). Eliminating pensions, health care, vacations, and holidays would also lower company labor costs. But such actions entail a compromise with very fundamental values about the kind of society in which we want to live. We prefer that workers have security and a decent standard of living, that income gaps among citizens be moderate, and that the attendant class conflict remain muted enough to sustain social harmony.

If trade competitors do not share these values, however, it may prove difficult for the United States to maintain them—without restricting trade, accepting deficits, or designing state policies to alleviate the most dire consequences, especially the concentration of winners and losers among certain economic sectors, geographic regions, and social classes. Concentrated geographic unemployment, for example, brings a litany of social problems including inequality, crime, drugs, urban violence, and, potentially, social collapse. Ripple effects cause trade issues to influence many other domains of social concern and public policy because geographic concentrations often imply disproportionate effects on particular ethnic groups and sectoral concentrations often imply disproportionate effects on women or teenagers.

Economists can show that the most efficient approach to many of these problems, in theory, is to earn the benefits of free trade and use the proceeds to compensate the losers. Actually achieving that mix is a good deal more difficult than it sounds, however, so government officials usually prefer to restrict trade instead even though that also requires that the benefits of trade be sacrificed.

Moreover, continuing to trade with nations that permit shabby treatment of workers—or even outright human rights abuses—poses a difficult moral dilemma. Should we purchase cheap foreign goods even though they may have been made with child labor—or even slave labor?

A nation committed to trade also faces pressures from other nations seeking favorable treatment for its firms, which can be expected to object to any trade barrier that restricts their access to markets. They may also regard any circumstance that provides a cost advantage for domestic firms

Values dilemma. Danziger—*The Christian Science Monitor*

as an unfair barrier to trade, such as labor laws and health care systems. Yet nations have many interests that seem to justify trade restrictions. For example, it is often argued that some sectors must be spared foreign competition because of their importance to the economy (e.g., banking or steel). Other areas are said to require special state supervision to protect consumers that could not be effective if foreign firms were involved (e.g., insurance or pharmaceuticals). Additional sectors are said to be privileged by considerations of national defense (e.g., American microelectronics) or culture (Japanese rice) or national pride (French wine). Imported goods may undermine national identity. For example, many nations decry the creeping imperialism of American culture introduced by jeans, rock music, Hollywood films, and McDonald's hamburgers. The decision to trade or not thus poses the **values dilemma**: Whichever choice is made, some values will be compromised to achieve others.

A third dilemma concerns the effect of trade on the goals of states, especially in foreign policy. Purely economic theories are not adequate to understand these issues because state actions are motivated by power and autonomy as much as by growth and efficiency. As nations come to rely upon trade, their ambivalent attitude toward the resulting dependence upon others produces behavior that can be explained only with the help of theorists of international relations. Some nations become subordinate and their freedom of action diminishes in the face of trade. Others become dominant and expand the scope of their power and influence. All find that they must anticipate the reactions of others much more frequently and tailor their actions accordingly. Tensions develop, resentments build, and conflicts arise. American relations with Japan are often mentioned as a contemporary instance, and the violence of the 1930s and 1940s is cited as an awful historical precedent. Canadian fear of the economic dominance of the United States has long colored relations between the two and delayed a free trade agreement that was proposed as early as 1851. Britain remains ambivalent about closer ties with Europe because of fear that **national sovereignty** must be sacrificed to achieve them.

But theorists of **interdependence** also remind us that trade can force nations to recognize the need to coexist and the opportunity to "coflourish" through cooperation. The Bretton Woods international economic system created at the end of World War II is an example at the global level. Both the European Union and the North American Free Trade Agreement are examples of these same principles of cooperation pursued at the regional level. This dilemma raises a theoretical question: Under what conditions does trade lead to conflict and when does it generate peaceful cooperation? It also presents a policy challenge: How do we find one path and avoid the other? Economic theories that focus only on macroeconomic growth do not recognize the **state goals dilemma**: Any trade policy will affect some aspect of the state's ability to achieve one or another of its goals. Thus, the policy advice that emanates from them is, at best, incomplete.

CHOICES FOR THE INDIVIDUAL

These dilemmas are posed most directly at the level of individual citizens as they act in multiple roles when contemplating any purchase. Economic theory explains consumer behavior as the maximization of material interests. But a citizen also assumes the role of a moral agent responsible for the chain of outcomes set in motion by the consumer choice. The motivation behind the **Buy America** bumper sticker, for example, is not the logic of best product and lowest cost but an appeal to other considerations entirely.

In fact, every day each individual must—explicitly or implicitly—assume a stance on the dilemmas previously identified. Is it patriotic to purchase domestic products? Should a Japanese consumer buy a foreign car, knowing it means unemployment for a Japanese worker? Do we owe greater obligations to domestic workers and corporations than foreign ones? Should one purchase a product that is cheap because it was made with slave labor or by workers deprived of human rights? Should one choose transportation that requires the importation of foreign oil, knowing it encourages a costly American military presence in the Middle East? Should one lobby the government to restrict the sales of American

Trade dilemma for the individual. Danziger—*The Christian Science Monitor*

forestry products abroad because they compromise environmental concerns? Should a French citizen support the end of farm subsidies that would threaten traditional life in the French countryside? Answering these questions requires normative judgments as well as a keen understanding of the empirical consequences of trade—the motivations for this book.

In particular, trade affects the individual in six different roles, each of which requires him or her to weigh somewhat different values, interests, and perspectives:

1. As a consumer, it is rational to prefer free trade because it makes imports cheaper. (But if the absence of protection drives domestic firms out of business and gives a **monopoly** to foreign firms, future prices could rise.)
2. As a worker, it is usually wise to prefer free trade if one is employed in a sector that exports goods or imports raw materials but to prefer **protectionism** if employed in a firm that competes with imports.
3. As a member of an economic class, it is usually reasonable for a worker to prefer policies that favor labor and for a business owner to prefer policies that favor capital. Since the early 1970s, American labor has generally supported protectionism and American business has supported free trade.

4. As a resident of a community, it is sensible to prefer policies that benefit local industries even if one is not directly involved in that sector. For example, most residents of Detroit prefer protection against auto imports because it contributes to the general prosperity of the region, and residents of agricultural states prefer **export promotion** policies, which increase farm prices.

5. As a citizen of a nation, it is natural to prefer policies that strengthen the nation as a whole. Because it is not always obvious what policies will accomplish that goal, one must analyze the impact of trade on the foreign policy relations between nations as well as the economic gains from trade.

6. Finally, an individual must weigh all of these considerations in the context of one's own personal sense of values and obligations. It is not the purpose here to judge whether one's obligation to the interests of the nation should outweigh one's individual interest or to stipulate whether economic interests should dominate more ethereal ethical concerns. It is possible, however, to clarify those consequences of trade and trade policy that individuals should consider when making their own ethical choices.

POLICY ALTERNATIVES

National governments have traditionally sought to avoid balance-of-trade deficits while expanding the volume of trade. Their policy actions, which raise the issues and dilemmas that are the motivation for this book, fall within four basic approaches. Each is discussed briefly in the following sections.

The first approach consists of efforts to increase exports by improving the overall international **competitiveness** of a nation's economy. The second, called **industrial policy**, consists of efforts to engage in export promotion by subsidizing particular industries. The third seeks to enlarge exports by removing the trade barriers imposed by the policies of other nations, either through **bilateral** negotiations or in the arena of regional or global institutions. The fourth approach is to reduce imports through protectionist measures such as tariffs and quotas. The first and third are essentially **liberal** approaches that place greater reliance upon the free reign of markets; the other two, which are usually referred to as **mercantilist**, involve government actions to influence or displace the market.

THE SEARCH FOR COMPETITIVENESS

One trade policy approach seeks to avoid a trade deficit by solving social problems and eliminating government policies that drive up the costs of all domestic firms. (If the factors that burden import-competing or export firms are unique to those sectors, the government may target them directly with a so-called industrial policy, which is discussed in the next section.) This strategy to enhance international competitiveness provides an especially vivid illustration of the dilemmas that trade presents, particularly with respect to the distributional effects of trade and the tension between alternative values.

The following brief discussion of factors that affect competitiveness demonstrates that trade issues cannot be separated from the remainder of the public agenda and that competitiveness cannot be treated in a vacuum. In some cases, competitiveness problems cannot be solved without sacrificing other values; in other cases, a focus on competitiveness may be useful in bringing to public attention problems that would require action even if they did not pose a threat to competitiveness.

First, most American corporations carry the burden of health care coverage for their workers. For example, the U.S. auto industry now spends more for health care than it does for steel. Because American health care costs are the highest in the world—overall, Americans spend about 13 percent of GNP on health care—this burden undermines the competitiveness of all American firms. Those who address this issue—whether or not their principal motivation is to improve American competitiveness—cannot avoid contact with some of the toughest issues in American politics: trust in government bureaucracies versus private insurance bureaucracies, breadth of coverage for all citizens versus quality care for some, and the possibility of explicitly rationing health care.

Second, since World War II, American expenditures for defense have been many times higher than those of nations with which we compete. Ironically, much of that money has been spent directly protecting the very nations against which our competitiveness has slipped, especially Germany, Japan, and Korea. These expenditures erode the competitiveness of American business by requiring higher tax levels, they constrain the funds available to spend on other items that could enhance competitiveness, and they divert a substantial share of American scientific and technological expertise into military innovation and away from commercial areas. The trade-off between competitiveness and defense may be judged differently by different individuals, but it can be ignored by none. Giving up global leadership or national security may be a wise choice, but it is not without costs of its own.

Third, the quality of American education, once the best in the world, has eroded. Although the global division of labor now places a premium on skilled labor, many other countries now have a better-educated citizenry and a better-trained workforce—which may explain why the growth in American economic productivity since the 1960s is among the lowest in the industrial world. Because both the American school day and school year are now among the shortest in the world, fixing education may require a substantial increase in cost, compromises with cherished traditions, and flexibility on the part of parents, teachers, and children. Like defense and health care, this problem acquires more urgency in the context of a competitiveness issue, but there are very good reasons for wanting to improve education that do not involve the balance of trade.

Fourth, the decline of America's infrastructure—decaying roads and bridges and overburdened water, sewer, and mass-transit systems—costs American business daily. Because the provision of infrastructure is largely a function of government, this competitiveness issue is intertwined with questions of taxation, government effectiveness, and citizen trust. Infrastructure problems are unexciting—and thus unpopular as a locus of innovation or spending among politicians—but it is evident that trade competitiveness cannot be sustained without government no matter how vibrant the private sector may be.

Fifth, very high debt levels, including personal credit card debt, corporate debt, and the federal budget deficit, require that savings be used to fund past consumption rather than to invest in the future. Furthermore, because the American personal savings rate is the lowest in the industrial world, U.S. interest rates must be kept higher in order to induce foreigners to supply the investment funds from their savings that Americans do not provide. But these higher interest rates—what economists would call the higher cost of capital—become an additional expense for American businesses that must borrow money for expansion. This illustrates exactly how close to home competitiveness issues can come: The family budget is a matter of national security!

Sixth, other social problems, including crime and drugs, contribute in indirect ways to increased costs for American business. Richard Lamm estimates that "American business spent $51 billion in 1986 for private anti-crime measures such as alarms, iron bars, video cameras, and security guards."[2] American tax dollars support more than 550,000 inmates, eleven times the figure in Japan. Even ecological problems affect business because the deteriorating environment diminishes the health and productivity of workers, forces higher costs for health care, and complicates the choice of business location.

Finally, some have blamed corporations themselves for fixating on the short term and ignoring long-term competitiveness. Expenditures on research and development occupy a much smaller portion of corporate spending in the United States than in Japan or Germany, for example, and the pay of top corporate executives is much higher in America than in its chief competitors.

Some proposed solutions to the competitiveness problem violate the definition of competitiveness laid out in a report from the President's

Commission, "the degree to which a nation, under free and fair market conditions, produces goods and services that meet the test of international markets *while simultaneously maintaining and expanding the real incomes of its citizens*."[3] The last clause of this definition disqualifies from consideration such proposals as the abolition of the minimum wage, Social Security, workplace safety regulation, pensions, sick leave, workman's compensation, unions, vacations, holidays, and so on.[4] This list exemplifies the dangers of affording competitiveness concerns too high a priority on the national agenda: Cutting wages and benefits for workers would surely make American corporations more profitable and better able to compete, but the attempt would be self-defeating from the standpoint of national welfare. National policy should seek to make corporations more competitive in order to improve the lives of its citizens, not compromise citizen welfare in order to improve competitiveness.

EXPORT PROMOTION AND INDUSTRIAL POLICY

A second trade policy approach seeks to achieve a favorable trade balance through export promotion, usually in conjunction with what is called an industrial policy. By industrial policy is meant a set of government actions designed to encourage the growth of particular industries, usually those believed to be especially important for the future of the economy. Most nations that engage in aggressive industrial policy—Japan is the most frequently cited example—target the export sector because of the growth prospects offered by the global economy.

Export promotion is accomplished through a variety of techniques. The simplest is a direct export **subsidy** or bounty, a government payment for each good exported from the target industry. The result is that a domestic firm has the incentive to export goods even though it may not have a cost advantage in comparison with competing firms in other nations.

Such a policy has at least three aims. First, increased production in the chosen industry will likely lead to employment growth, perhaps enough for the government to enjoy the political benefits of having reduced the unemployment rate. Second, these firms will gain a greater share of foreign markets, which might give them greater leverage to increase prices (and profits) in the future. Third, increasing exports will improve the balance of trade, thus avoiding some of the problems discussed earlier.

This policy also yields distributional effects—and the political controversies they engender—because of its impact on prices. For example, the domestic consumer will see the price of the good in question rise by the amount of the subsidy, since otherwise firms would prefer to export the product in order to earn the export bonus. Furthermore, the revenue to pay for that bounty would have to be raised through taxes. The domestic consumer would thus appear to be a double loser while the exporting firm gains, but there may also be complex intertemporal distributional effects. For example, the sacrifices of the current generation of consumers may benefit future ones if this subsidy eventually transforms an **infant industry** into a powerful enterprise that can repay the subsidies through cheaper prices or greater employment.

Another form of industrial policy is simply to provide subsidies to particular firms or industries that appear to have long-term export potential whether or not they are presently exporting. Such subsidies might be direct cash payments, special tax advantages, help in attracting investment, or relief from regulations that might otherwise constrain the industry. Export subsidies are not always easy to see. The United States, which explicitly rejects industrial policy, nonetheless engages in behavior that yields the same outcome. For example, American military expenditures often have spillover effects into civilian production, especially for export. The Boeing B–52 bomber introduced many elements that led to the highly successful Boeing 707 passenger jet. American agriculture has benefited from the activities of the Agricultural Extension Service and other subsidies of agricultural research. Grants to universities for research yield benefits for industry. Some nations promote their exports by lending the sale price to importing nations; in the United States, these export credit subsidies are handled by the Export-Import Bank.

Such industrial policies are controversial both in the nations that enact them and in those with whom they trade. Liberal theorists contend that they don't really work or that their costs usually outweigh their benefits, a position generally accepted in the United States, especially by the Republican Party. Moreover, export-promotion policies attract the opposition of other nations because they place competing nations at a severe disadvantage. The U.S. steel industry has been particularly outspoken in its denunciation of steel imported from foreign firms that are heavily subsidized by their governments. They contend that American jobs and American profits are being undercut by this unfair competition. They call for the U.S. government to guarantee "fair trade" either by prohibiting the importation of such subsidized goods or by levying heavy taxes on them (so-called **countervailing duties**). Industrial policy has interesting distributional implications, however. For example, it benefits the consumers of countries into which subsidized products are imported, at least in the short-term.

LOWERING GLOBAL TRADE BARRIERS

The third method employed to maintain a desirable volume and balance of trade emphasizes the expansion of exports by facilitating the efficiency of markets and by lowering the trade barriers imposed by other nations. This approach to trade policy includes both direct bilateral negotiations to change specific policies of other nations and more general efforts to create and maintain international institutions that facilitate trade.

The outstanding example of institutions at the global level is the Bretton Woods trade and monetary regime, created under the leadership of the United States at the end of World War II. The Bretton Woods regime, centered around the institutions of the General Agreement on Tariffs and Trade and the **International Monetary Fund** (IMF), has governed international trade and finance for nearly fifty years, though it has evolved and changed markedly in that time. The IMF has sought to expand trade by guaranteeing stability in monetary affairs and providing mechanisms to finance imports and adjust trade imbalances. The GATT has provided a setting for nations to resolve trade disputes and to negotiate reductions in barriers to trade. Because both involve some restrictions on the policies of nations, they pose the dilemma of exchanging the gains of trade for some loss of **national autonomy**.

The European Union represents the most extensive and most successful effort to achieve free trade at the regional level. However, to achieve the fair competition necessary to sustain it requires a leveling of the playing field that threatens also to level cultural and political differences among nations. Furthermore, the logical end point of the desire to fully exploit the benefits of free trade and to cope with the resultant interdependence is the creation of a regional political community that would replace nation-states. The EU illustrates the degree to which truly free trade requires, in practical application, much more than formal economic theory recognizes. And in the process, it poses in particularly stark form the fundamental dilemmas discussed previously, especially those involving national autonomy.

The EU is also an illuminating precedent for NAFTA, designed to expand trade among the United States, Canada, and Mexico. That agreement conceives of regional integration in a very different way, reflecting a different resolution of the trade dilemmas involved. In particular, it reserves much greater autonomy for the national governments involved, but at the cost of not addressing some of the other dilemmas posed by trade, such as its distributional consequences and its impact on the environment.

FORMS OF IMPORT RESTRICTIONS

The fourth approach to trade policy is protectionism, which limits imports directly. Its origins in the mercantilism of early England is the subject of an extensive case study in Chapter 2, but it has been very common historically. There are many forms of import restrictions, all of which are designed to limit the purchases of goods from abroad so that the domestic import-competing industries can capture a larger share of the market.

The simplest of these mechanisms is the **quota**, a government restriction that places a fixed limit on the quantity or value of goods that can be imported. This is usually accomplished by requiring that importers obtain import licenses that are strictly rationed by governments. The usual effect of a quota is to raise the domestic price of the commodity by limiting the number of lower-priced products that can be imported. This allows domestic producers to gain a larger market share but requires that consumers pay a higher price. Both domestic and foreign producers are able to maintain higher prices because of this artificial restriction of supply.

Prohibitions are a special case—namely, they set a quota at zero. This form of trade barrier is relatively infrequent today, but it was common in an earlier age. In fact prohibitions were the major source of protection in early England, though they were often not absolute prohibitions but conditional ones that were triggered by a particular situation. For example, in 1815 wheat imports were prohibited whenever wheat prices fell below 80 shillings per quarter. This conditional prohibition assumed that domestic producers could compete with imported grain if it was priced above 80 shillings but could not if the price was lower.

Tariffs (or import duties) are the most traditional import barrier. They come in two forms. Most are ad valorem, calculated as a percentage of the value of the good imported. American ad valorem tariffs average about 4 percent in the mid–1990s, about the same as most developed nations. Specific tariffs are applied to a particular quantity of an imported good; for example, the United States imposes a fixed tariff of $3 on every barrel of imported oil.

Many forms of protectionism have increased since the early 1980s as governments have responded to the pleas of industries threatened by foreign competition. Tariffs are no longer, however, the main form of protectionism. In fact, declining from their peak in the 1930s, tariff levels throughout the world are generally very low. In the United States the average tariff rate reached a modern high of 59 percent in 1932 under the Smoot-Hawley Act, a remarkably irresponsible tariff law that has been widely credited with triggering a spiral of restrictions by other nations that helped plunge the global economy into the Great Depression of the 1930s. The average tariff level had previously reached 70 percent in 1813 and about 60 percent in the "tariff of abominations" of 1828 but remained between 40 percent and 50 percent from the Civil War until the turn of the century. It was reduced to 25 percent after World War II and declined to about 5 percent after the Tokyo Round of GATT negotiations concluded in 1979. Average ad valorem import duties reached their high in Britain in the 1820s at more than 50 percent, retreating to about 5 percent at the height of the British free trade era in 1880 before spiking again in the 1930s at about 50 percent.

Probably the most controversial remaining tariffs are the duties imposed by the EU in the context of the **Common Agricultural Policy** (CAP). These tariffs sustain higher food prices in Europe than would prevail if cheaper American grains were admitted without barrier. Because the higher prices of European producers leave them unable to compete on global markets, the revenue derived from the tariffs is used to subsidize exports. Both elements of the CAP have infuriated the United States in recent years: its restrictions on American exports to Europe and the advantage its subsidies provide to European agricultural producers wherever they compete with American exporters.

In the place of tariffs, a variety of **nontariff barriers** (NTBs) has arisen. An early version was the 1969 **voluntary restraint agreement** (VRA) with Japan and the **European Community,** which was designed to reduce steel imports into the United States. Since that time **voluntary export restraints** (VERs) have become common. The most famous case of VERs is that in which Japanese automakers in 1981 "voluntarily" agreed to limit exports to the United States. (Had Japan refused, a quota that would have been more damaging to Japanese automakers would have been imposed in place of the VER.) The original agreement restricted imports to 1.68 million cars, then to 1.85 million in 1984. Since then Japan has voluntarily remained under that target.[5] The Federal Trade Commission (FTC) has estimated the cost to U.S. consumers at about $1 billion per year in the form of higher prices for autos. Not only does the restricted supply of Japanese autos cause their prices to rise because of the artificial shortage but it also enables American manufacturers to maintain higher prices in the absence of this competition. A VER is essentially a quota system that is managed by the exporter rather than by the importing nation. Like all quotas, it is considerably more beneficial to the exporter than an equivalent tariff because it allows the exporter to retain the additional revenue that results from the artificial restriction of supply. Under a tariff system, that revenue goes to the importing government. VERs are even more advantageous to the exporting nation than quotas, however, because they allow the exporting government to allocate the exports among its own firms as it sees fit. These bilateral restrictions have a **multilateral** cousin, **orderly marketing arrangements** (OMAs) such as the Multi-Fiber Agreement in which the share of textiles imported into the United States is divided among twenty-two nations.

Other protectionist measures include local content regulations that restrict imports by imposing a burden on purchasers of intermediate goods to make sure that imports do not exceed a prescribed fraction of their total purchases. Another form is government procurement policies, which often favor domestic firms. For example, the EU requires that government contracts be open to all bidders, but they permit governments to give a 3 percent "preference margin" to European firms or to exclude entirely any product produced largely outside of Europe.[6] Other regulations, such as product-safety standards, can have a protectionist effect even though their motivation may be open to interpretation.

CONCLUSION: CHOOSING A TRADE POLICY

A principal mission of this book is to explain why nations select the policies they do. At the broadest level, that means explaining why they would choose to emphasize either mercantilist or liberal strategies and focus either on the volume or on the balance of trade as the principal policy target. Thus, as a starting point, Chapter 2 describes the historical evolution of both mercantilism and liberalism. It will quickly become obvious that understanding the motivations and the assumptions that underlie these two broad families of approaches requires an appreciation of how they respond to the trade dilemmas discussed earlier.

The cases examined in the remainder of the book suggest that the trade policy choices of governments are partially predictable because they result from the interaction among prevailing theories of economics and social justice; the state of supply and demand conditions in markets; and the balance of political power among those who represent producers, consumers, and the state. I discuss each briefly in turn.

Trade policy is affected by both economic theory and ethical doctrines. We cannot divorce current attitudes toward international trade from the goals that we expect public policy to achieve or from the social and political values these goals express. Any trade policy choice rests upon one response to the dilemma posed by competing values; trade inevitably helps achieve some goals but hinders the pursuit of others. The importance accorded to maximizing national economic growth by contemporary debates over international trade is in part a reflection of the set of values that dominate modern Western society. But these values are not unchallenged, and thus the debates over trade policy contain within them a clash of values. We ask not only What trade policy will best achieve our goals? but also What should our goals be? So, too, did early British theorists and policymakers. Remembering the values dilemma—that all debates over trade policy are ultimately debates over alternative values—will help us understand why a nation selects the trade policy that it does.

The state of the market itself also affects the desirability of regulating that market. If a market appears disposed to yield a desirable outcome if left unregulated, it is far more likely that it will be allowed to run its course. We shall see that changes in attitudes toward trade policy directly parallel changes in estimates of the likely consequences of free trade. It is no coincidence that the industrialists of nineteenth-century England agitated for free trade only after the Industrial Revolution had left them with a major advantage against their foreign competitors. Similarly, it is no coincidence that many American trade unions (notably the AFL-CIO) abandoned their free trade position in favor of protectionist sentiments just as American heavy industry began to be seriously challenged by foreign competitors. Of course, in assessing market performance, one must carefully weigh the distributional dilemma of trade—that all debates over trade policy are also ultimately debates over who will win and who will lose.

Finally, whereas prevailing theory and values interact with market conditions to shape attitudes toward trade, it is the balance of political power among various groups that determines how these attitudes are translated into public policy. The dilemmas posed by trade are typically resolved by appeals to theory, to values, and to market conditions, but the theory, values, and conditions cited by proponents of one position are usually very different than those cited by advocates of another. The winning side need not have the best arguments if it has the political power to prevail.

TWO

□ □ □

The Theoretical and Historical Origins of Trade Issues

Two competing visions have dominated discussion of international trade for more than two centuries. These ideas, which linger beneath the surface of most contemporary issues, can be seen with greatest clarity in the context of the historical periods that spawned them.

LIBERALISM AND MERCANTILISM

One vision is that of economic liberalism, which has been dominant in theoretical circles since the very advent of systematic thinking about economics. Economic liberalism was first articulated in precise form by Scottish political economist Adam Smith (1723–1790) in his brilliant masterpiece of 1776, *An Inquiry into the Nature and Causes of the Wealth of Nations*. This school of thought, which was advanced by a long line of British theorists including David Ricardo (1772–1823) and John Stuart Mill (1806–1873), now numbers most contemporary economists among its membership. Economic liberalism is often summarized by the answer it offers to government seeking advice on how to deal with the market: **laissez-faire** (from the French "allow it to act" or "leave it alone").[1] Thus, liberalism holds that international trade should be conducted by private actors largely free of government control.

The second perspective derives from mercantilism, a body of thought that originated with the mercantile policy (i.e., commercial or trade policy) of European nations, especially England, from the sixteenth century to the middle of the nineteenth. Though the practice of mercantilism long

23

predated liberalism, the best-known text in the mercantilist tradition is Friedrich List's *The National System of Political Economy*, written in 1841, half a century after Smith's death. List's counterattack against Smith's liberalism is better known than the original doctrine he defends, because the sophistication of Smith and Ricardo's analysis elevated the rigor of subsequent economic debate beyond that of the narrow and piecemeal writings left by the early pamphleteers who supported mercantilist policies.

Even today, mercantilism is not so much a theory as a bundle of ideas centered around the conviction that governments must regulate trade in order for it to further the **national interest**. Perceptions of that national interest have varied from time to time, from place to place, and from author to author, but most variants of mercantilism have emphasized the goals of national self-sufficiency, a favorable balance of trade, the vitality of key industries, and the promotion of the power of the state, especially in foreign policy. Because the national interest encompasses a multitude of different goals that must be judged by each nation in its particular circumstances, no universal policy advice is offered by mercantilism, but protection against imports and the promotion of exports is common to most versions.

Much of the early writing of both mercantilism and liberalism concerned the controversies surrounding the English **Corn Laws**, a series of protectionist measures that regulated the trade of agricultural goods, especially grain, between the fifteenth and nineteenth centuries.[2] Their repeal in 1846 ushered in a period of free trade that represented the triumph of economic liberalism over mercantilism, which had dominated both economic theory and political practice in England for most of the previous three centuries.

However, the history of international trade reveals that the mercantilist inclination to regulate trade, particularly in order to protect domestic producers, has been somewhat more commonly adopted by nations than has the liberal policy of free trade. Perhaps it is more accurate to say that no nation has ever completely accepted or completely rejected either view. Instead, governments have sought to encompass elements of both in fashioning their trade policies. This is understandable because both theories are "true." But neither is universally so, since the policy advice of each is rooted in a different set of values, interests, and priorities. For that very reason, these compromises must always contain tensions that reflect the fundamental dilemmas posed by trade.

In this chapter, I examine the debate over the Corn Laws because it so closely parallels contemporary contests between free trade and protection and because the lessons of this period help us to understand some of the puzzles of our own era.

MERCANTILIST TRADE POLICY

Early English mercantile policy involved three major elements: the promotion and protection of industry, the **Navigation Acts**, and the Corn Laws. All involved restricting the scope of markets in international trade.

The motivations for the promotion and protection of industry—we would call their modern counterparts "industrial policy"—continue to inspire advocates of trade limitations down to the present day. One goal was the creation of industries that would foster self-sufficiency and economic development. This drive was manifested in a variety of actions dating to the time of Queen Elizabeth's reign (1558–1603), including exclusive patents (legal monopolies) to develop domestic industries that could substitute for imports: sugar refining, salt production, glass manufacturing, soap production, and others. Many industries were also introduced into England by government policy encouraging the immigration of foreign workers with special skills. Once initiated, these industries were then sustained by import restrictions in the hope that eventually they would develop sufficiently to be capable of exporting. Support for infant-industries is an integral part of all modern mercantilist policies, including the **import-substituting industrialization** (ISI) common to most of Latin America in the 1950s and 1960s and the postwar industrial policy of Japan.[3] Self-sufficiency and economic development were goals given greater urgency by the concern that Elizabethan England lagged behind such continental rivals as the Dutch and the French in industrial development.

Exports were encouraged in part because they produced an inflow of **treasure**—gold or silver—to pay for them. Today, we would refer to this net inflow as a balance-of-trade surplus. The revenue earned from exports could be used to purchase goods from abroad that could not be manufactured at home, such as wine, tea, and spices. Treasure could also be accumulated for use at a later time. Given the crude monetary system of the age, the inflow of precious metals was also necessary to maintain the domestic money supply, especially as the nation shifted from an elementary agricultural economy dominated by barter exchanges and self-sufficiency to a more complex modern economy in which money and credit were needed to facilitate transactions. Exports were also desirable because once established they could be taxed to generate revenue that would support national interests (such as maintaining the navy) or state interests (such as sustaining the power of the Crown against domestic challengers). Requiring exporters to secure government licenses also gave government officials the ability to earn revenues while playing favorites among contenders for export licenses.

Moreover, exports provided employment for workers and profits for industrialists, both of which fostered the growth of the economy as a whole. Rising employment increased the demand for food and thus benefited the agricultural sector. The export trade helped to strengthen the merchant marine, which trained seamen for service in the navy, a vital factor in maintaining the power and security of an island nation like Britain. For all these reasons, exports were promoted, sometimes by bounties (subsidies) and sometimes by encouraging the cheap importation of raw materials necessary to manufacture goods for export.

At the same time, however, import restrictions were imposed on most goods. Trade regulations were designed to protect domestic manufacturing industries and their workers from a very early time. The first beneficiary in England, textile production, was protected as early as the thirteenth century, but a parliamentary law of 1337 is the first classic package of infant-industry protection. It included an **embargo** (i.e., prohibition) on the exportation of raw wool to prevent the textile industries of other nations from acquiring this important raw material to compete against English weavers. It also encouraged the emigration of clothworkers from abroad in order to build an English industry that would be capable of exporting finished cloth.[4] Most important, it added a prohibition against the importation of foreign cloth.

Import restrictions of this sort were designed for several purposes. First, they protected the employment of laborers and the profits of owners, considerations that motivate the bulk of import restrictions in the current era. Typical was the act of 1700 in which Parliament restricted the importation of silk textiles from India on the grounds that it would directly endanger the jobs of 250,000 employees in the English woolen-textile industry and indirectly lower the price of wool, threatening the prosperity of the landed interests supported by sheep grazing. Modern-day analogues include the Multi-Fiber Agreement (MFA) and its predecessors, which have protected the U.S. cotton textile industry since 1961.

Second, import restrictions typically took the form of tariffs, which provided a substantial amount of government revenue. This consideration is less relevant in the modern age among developed countries, but it remains central to many less developed countries for the same reason as in early England: Revenues were difficult to raise through general taxation because of the relatively low level of taxable domestic activity and the logistical problems of collection.[5] The importance of this consideration is shown by the necessity of reintroducing the income tax as a part of the package of import duty reductions between 1841 and 1846, which culminated in the repeal of the Corn Laws. Even in 1994, final U.S. Senate passage of the long-awaited Uruguay Round trade agreement was held up by the need to find $14 billion to replace the import tax revenue that would be lost when tariffs were reduced.

Third, import restrictions were used as a tool of foreign policy both in order to induce other nations to open their markets to British industries and to harm enemies while helping friends. For example, when Jean-Baptiste Colbert raised French tariffs to levels that effectively prohibited the export of English cloth to France in 1667, Parliament retaliated with tariffs and prohibitions on French goods in England. A 1703 commercial treaty imposed a lower tariff on Portuguese wine than on French wine, thus diverting the lucrative wine trade away from France, which was England's greatest political, military, and commercial rival. Retaliatory tariffs designed to bring other nations to the bargaining table are now commonplace; in 1992's "beer war" the United States imposed a 50 percent duty on Canadian beer to protest Ontario's environmental tax on aluminum cans and warehouse charges for U.S. beer. Tariffs are still frequently used as a carrot and stick in other foreign policy areas, such as the U.S. policy of threatening to withdraw the preferential tariff rate known as **most favored nation** status from China in order to induce progress on human rights.

Domestic producers were also favored by another mechanism of protection, the domestic preference sentiment, whose modern expression is found in the Buy America program and the propensity of Japanese consumers to purchase domestic rather than imported products. Then as now, domestic preference was partly a matter of public sentiment and partly a matter of government policy. For example, there was a period in which woolen clothing was mandated for some occasions, including burial, in order to sustain the production of the domestic textile industry. The consumption of herring to sustain the fishing industry was encouraged by mandated "fish days." For a time the importation of Indian fabrics was prohibited by law; at another point, English textile workers took matters into their own hands by throwing acid on women who wore clothing made of Indian calicos.[6] The latter scene anticipates the symbolic destruction of Japanese cars by Detroit autoworkers two centuries later. It also presents a vivid picture of the kinds of distributional trade-offs that liberal theorists remind us always attend import restrictions: The protection of English workers was paid for by English consumers because the price of English woolens was about eight times higher than that of foreign textiles.

The national interest was also protected by the Navigation Acts, which date from 1381. Because defense of an island nation and, later, the maintenance of a far-flung empire required a strong navy, the Navigation Acts required that English grain be carried only by English ships. This prohibition was designed to stimulate shipbuilding and sustain the merchant marine, which, like the fishing industry, trained sailors in seafaring skills useful to the navy. The Navigation Acts were only one part of an extensive system of government control designed to strengthen naval power. For example, to guarantee that wood supplies for shipbuilding would be available, a 1558 act prohibited timber cutting for use in iron smelting within fourteen miles of the coast. Monopolies were granted by royal letters patent to encourage investment and innovation in the production of munitions and in the mining and smelting of metals required for their production. Thus we see that mercantilist trade policy complimented domestic policy; both were formulated in the pursuit of such nationalistic values as defense and national power.

However, neither the protection and promotion of manufactures nor the Navigation Acts were as controversial as the Corn Laws, which best illustrate both the arguments that sustained mercantilism and those of economic liberalism and free trade that eventually defeated them. The Corn Laws were a complex series of mercantilist trade regulations enacted by Parliament over a period of several centuries in order to control the price of grain. Depending on domestic supplies and prices, both exports and imports of grain were restricted at various times. Sometimes they were discouraged with quotas or taxes, sometimes promoted with bounties or subsidies, and sometimes outright prohibited—but seldom was the market permitted to freely determine prices or trade volumes.

The Corn Laws were initially designed largely to protect consumers. For example, when poor harvests caused a supply shortage and high prices, grain exports were prohibited. Whereas consumers required shielding from market forces, government policy recognized the need to protect producers as well. As early as 1463, for example, the importation of low-priced grain from abroad was restricted and producers were allowed to dispose of a surplus through foreign trade. Generally, exports were permitted only when prices were relatively low (thus signaling that supplies were adequate to demand and that domestic consumers were protected from shortages and "unjust" prices) and often only when licensed by the state. This power was contested by the Crown and Parliament, with the Crown preferring regulations that earned it revenue and protected consumers and Parliament tending to the protection of landowners and producers.[7] Prior to 1660, the predominant beneficiaries of government policy were the Crown and consumers, but the Restoration of 1660 increased the power of the landowners in Parliament and the Revolution of 1689 established the dominance of Parliament over the Crown. With these changes in the political balance of power, government policy shifted in favor of producers and against consumers.[8]

Over the next 150 years, the Corn Laws were contested terrain both in academic debates and in practical politics. Parliament dealt with them nearly annually as weather-related fluctuations in supply drove prices to levels that threatened either producers or consumers. When prices for grain rose, consumer riots were often directed against the Corn Laws, which were thought to be exacerbating supply shortages by keeping out imports and encouraging exports. When prices fell, farmers who rented land would frequently find themselves producing at a loss and landowners would be obliged to lower rents at considerable loss to their principal source of income. Parliament generally tried to strike a balance. On behalf of consumers, exports were prohibited or heavily taxed when domestic supplies were limited. On behalf of producers, plentiful domestic supplies would trigger not only a prohibition or heavy tax on imports but also a bounty (today we would call it an export subsidy) on exports. In this way, producers were encouraged to employ peasants and keep acreage in production in anticipation of years when such capacity might be needed to meet domestic demand.

Thus, an elaborate system of price regulation was maintained with tariffs and export subsidies triggered at a price meant to define the lower boundary acceptable to producers; import subsidies kicked in at a price meant to be the ceiling acceptable to consumers. This cumbersome system was frequently changed by Parliament in response to both annual market conditions and the intense political activity of landowners and peasants— with the petitions of the former being generally more effective than the riots of the latter. However, until the nineteenth century no one seriously advocated the abandonment of the mercantilist market-regulating approach altogether by allowing free imports and exports.

The desirability of maintaining self-sufficiency in such a critical area as food production was the most consistent argument used by protectionists. Of course, this concern with national security was imbedded deep in the characteristic perspective of mercantilism. Thus, it is ironic that this argument was best stated in succinct form by Adam Smith, whose writing on behalf of free trade made him not only the foremost exponent of economic liberalism but also a much-quoted opponent of the Corn Laws. He noted, simply and eloquently, that "defense is of more importance than opulence."[9] Protectionists frequently applied Smith's reasoning to support the Corn Laws even though these words were written in support of the Navigation Acts, which he regarded as necessary for the defense of the realm. (He opposed the Corn Laws, since he did not regard self-sufficiency in food as essential for national security.)

The widespread fear that abandoning agricultural protection would exchange self-sufficiency for a dangerous reliance on imports was founded in the economic and political conditions of the day. Because grain prices were often lower on the continent than in England, tariffs were thought necessary to protect English producers from European imports. Though cheap imports would benefit consumers in the short term, they would mean misery for English agricultural interests and could have detrimental effects for the nation as a whole in the long term. If English grain producers were not guaranteed a steady market, they would begin to shift their production away from these import-competing products or abandon investment in their land altogether. Indeed, a steady increase in sheep pasturing did impinge on the acreage held in grain production. Moreover, many landowners began to devote more time and wealth to investment opportunities in industry and commerce than to improvements in agricultural output. If this trend were to continue over time, protectionists feared, England would come to rely on foreign imports of grain not just in years of a bad English harvest but on a regular basis.

In this period, it is not surprising that such foreign reliance should make mercantilists nervous. It would leave the nation dangerously sensitive not only to weather and other harvest conditions in Europe but also to any disruption of trade. Further, the threat of disruption would reduce the freedom of action that the government of a self-sufficient nation could enjoy in conducting foreign relations.

It was feared that politically motivated disruption of trade could become an instrument of statecraft (or war) that would put England at a severe disadvantage in conducting its foreign policy. Certainly, Elizabeth had been well aware of the advantage possessed by England in its war with Spain: England was self-sufficient in food at that time, but Spain was not.[10] More recently, England's great rival, France, had sharply controlled the export of its grain when it was in short supply at home. Although this was done principally in order to protect French consumers (as was common in England and most other nations), it was feared that such control might also be exercised in order to force foreign policy concessions from England under the threat of mass starvation. Thus, mercantilists sought self-sufficiency where possible. Further, for those products in which England could not achieve self-sufficiency, reliance upon trade with their own colonies, a trade not so sensitive to potential political disruption, was preferred to trade with rival continental powers.

The interruption of trade by large-scale war was also justifiably feared not only because England was at war with France during most of the period from 1793 to 1815 but also because war had been a frequent occurrence in Europe for centuries. Indeed, between 1562 and 1721 there were only four years in which all of Europe was at peace.[11] Moreover, England would not want to be put in a position of actually aiding an enemy. Sir Henry Parnell's support of the highly protectionist Corn Law of 1815 called attention to England's heavy importation of wheat and flour from France in 1810, which had enabled Napoléon to both quell an insurrection in southern France and collect heavy export duties that were used to strengthen the French war effort.

The protection of agriculture to keep prices and land rents high had another justification as well. The maintenance of a strong agricultural sector was synonymous with the preservation of a prosperous and peaceful rural community, which from time immemorial had been the heart of English society as well as the core of the economy. When debates required that a policy's effect on national prosperity be defined and measured, the usual method was to invoke the strength of the rural sector. In turn, this usually meant that the well-being of landowners—especially the level of land rents—was used as a criterion. John Locke gave expression to this widely accepted interpretation: "An infallible sign of your decay of wealth is the falling of rents, and the raising of them would be worth the nation's care, for in that . . . lies the true advantage of the landed man and with him of the public."[12]

Since the social ideals of the landed gentry dominated both Parliament and the national culture, it is hardly surprising that the vision of England that motivated national policy remained rooted in this traditional, romantic, and self-serving view. Similarly, the protection of rice production in contemporary Japan can be explained partly by its enormous symbolic significance for Japanese tradition and partly by the predominantly rural political power base of the long-ruling Liberal Democratic Party.

Still, given the material conditions at the time, equating national prosperity with the wealth of landowners had considerable merit. It was the income derived by landowners from ground rents that fueled the entire economy. Most investment originated in the savings of landowners, even that which built the manufacturing sector that eventually transformed the nation. Government revenues depended directly on the wealth produced by ground rents, since taxes were largely raised from these same landowners. Of course, definitions of national prosperity were inevitably to change as the economy became more reliant on manufacturing for profits, for savings and investment, for employment, and for taxable income. In the process, industrial development allowed capitalists to offer an alternative vision of England just as the advent of political democracy allowed the masses to suggest an alternative definition of what constituted national prosperity.

THE ROOTS OF MERCANTILISM

The mercantilist view that international trade should be sharply regulated cannot be understood in a historical vacuum. Indeed, far from an aberration, it is a natural outgrowth of perspectives on *all* markets that were then prevalent. Prior to the evolution of modern economic society, free markets were no more common in the domestic economy than they were in international trade. In fact, mercantilism thrived in an environment in which none of the three elements of economic liberalism identified earlier—individualism, private property, or the free market—were widely accepted in either theory or practice.

The absence of these three elements is best illustrated by the communal character of agriculture, the dominant sector of the economy, as it had been widely practiced in England for centuries.[13] The open-field system of production was marked by a collective "commons," joint labor, and production decisions made at the village level. In a typical village, an individual would own or rent several small strips of land, but they were seldom contiguous. Because they were so intermixed with the plots of others, because the boundaries between them were not fenced, and because the entire open field would be given over to communal pastureland after the harvest, independent decisionmaking—entrepreneurship—was impossible and collective cultivation was imperative. If individualism was thus limited, so too was the freedom to use private property as one saw fit. The overlapping network of obligations typical of feudal systems meant that land ownership was not absolute. Though economically inefficient, this system promoted equality and full employment among agricultural laborers while it served as the basis for social interaction. The well-ordered village was the ultimate expression of the values of the period: It was a stable collective maintained by an ethical system rooted in a strongly hierarchical conception of society. It was also more or less self-sufficient, with most local production consumed locally rather than being sold on a larger market.

Prior to the nineteenth century, reliance upon the unregulated market was also uncommon outside of agriculture. The reasons parallel the three factors introduced in Chapter 1 to explain the choice of foreign economic policy by any nation. First, ethical considerations that originated in medieval social and economic theory cast doubt on the justice of markets. Second, material conditions did not allow efficient markets to develop. Third, the most powerful actors of the period—the church, the Crown, and landowners—were satisfied with the regulated economic system.

In the medieval period, it was believed that commodities should be sold at just prices that would enable each man to "have the necessaries of life suitable for his station."[14] To engage in a transaction that did not meet that standard was to commit the sin of avarice, punishable by both the church and the state. For example, in order to guarantee just prices, the parliamentary act of 1552 severely regulated the activities of brokers or merchants, prohibiting supply manipulation designed to increase prices and the resale of grain at a higher price in the same local market.

This last regulation is a striking reminder that the ethical status of markets and the morality of activities that benefit from their operation was a highly controversial issue centuries before Marx's critique of capitalism.

Among the most visible manifestations of the moral outrage generated by market operations is the famous Rusby trial of 1800. During a period of grain shortage that had driven up food prices, riots were commonly directed against the brokers who were blamed for much of the price increase. John Rusby, a London jobber, was alleged to have purchased a lot of oats at a price of 41 shillings and to have resold a part of it later that same day for 43 shillings. This action, which today would be considered profitable and altogether legal brokerage, was regarded in the medieval tradition as unethical "regrating" and prohibited by local regulations throughout much of England long before it was codified in national law in 1552. These specific statutes were repealed in 1772 and 1791, but the offenses were still punishable under the common law. More important, they were still considered unethical—a violation of common morality—by the bulk of the population, especially when seen to contribute to prohibitive prices in a time of food shortage and economic desperation. Rusby was found guilty and heavily fined—and a London mob intent on lynching him destroyed his house. Similar riots in sympathy occurred throughout the nation.

According to medieval social theory, a divergence was generally acknowledged to exist between private interests and the public interest. Because this divergence made it a duty of government to protect the community from the harmful effects of the market, commerce and industry were also sharply regulated during the entire mercantilist period.[15] For example, in addition to restraints on brokers, market regulation to protect consumers also included a standard system of weights and measures for various consumer goods, especially food and cloth. Laws governing the size and composition of bread loaves had existed for centuries before being meticulously codified by the Tudors and Stuarts beginning in the sixteenth century.[16] In conformity with accepted moral law, it was said that "the most desirable course is that prices should be fixed by public officials, after making an enquiry into the supplies available and framing an estimate of the requirements of different classes."[17] To that end, prices were fixed for various commodities at various times, especially bread and coal but also sometimes cloth, ale, and tea, among others. The market might serve the private interest of the seller, but it was not trusted to yield the just prices that were deemed to be in the public interest.

Restrictions on financial and labor markets were even more severe. Moneylending at excessive interest rates was prohibited by **usury laws** that were not finally repealed until 1854. Indeed, not until 1545 was money lending at any interest rate sanctioned by Parliament. These laws merely codified accepted moral standards that go back to biblical times. Parliament also mandated that wages be fixed by local justices of the peace rather than established by the supply and demand for labor, though the practice does not seem to have been universally followed. Finally, a minimum-wage law to protect workers (in the woolen industry) first appeared in 1604.[18] Thus, the regulation of markets to guarantee justice and to protect both consumers and workers has been an established governmental obligation in the Anglo-American tradition for centuries.

Of course, government was not the only source of interference with markets, nor was the public interest the only motive. As early as the thirteenth century, skilled artisans formed craft **guilds** that developed standards of workmanship to protect the public from shoddy goods, but an elaborate system of apprenticeships also protected established artisans from the competition of newcomers and outsiders.[19] Modern economists would call these arrangements **oligopolies**, meaning markets dominated by a small number of suppliers who may collude to keep prices high. (By contrast, fully competitive markets with many suppliers tend to benefit consumers because the competition among suppliers creates lower prices.) Those who benefited most from such arrangements, established artisans, were naturally the most enthusiastic in supporting them.

It is undeniable that government regulation of the market was rooted in the ethical values that the church successfully transmitted from the early ages of Christianity. But the condition of markets during this period was also a significant spur to government action in support of those values. Limitations of transportation, the relatively low level of commercial activity, guild controls, and modest standards of living combined to generate markets that were, in the vernacular of our age, "thin." That is, limited supply and demand left prices unstable and easily manipulated by unscrupulous profiteers. Thus, government control was directed not so much at the competitive markets extolled by modern economic theory but at the monopolistic or oligopolistic markets then most common.

The absence of individualism and free markets was especially striking in the area of trade, where the interests of powerful actors were as much an explanation as prevailing theory or the condition of markets. Initially, towns attempted to maintain self-sufficiency in key products, an effort that was mirrored in the drive for national self-sufficiency in later centuries. Moreover, trade between towns was sharply controlled by local merchant guilds as early as the twelfth century. Members of the guild were able to prohibit nonmembers from engaging in trade or to tax them for the privilege of doing so. In exchange, guild members were required to permit other members to participate in any transaction that they arranged and to share its benefits.[20] Clearly, individual entrepreneurial activity was neither valued nor rewarded. Like in the agricultural system earlier described, there were few opportunities for individual enterprise. Unquestionably, economic liberalism could not thrive in such an environment; indeed, its principles could not even be clearly articulated.

Against this backdrop of suspicion of markets and their sharp regulation in the domestic sphere, it was natural that similar attitudes would prevail as trade expanded from the intertown to the internation arena. The East Indies and Hudson Bay trading companies exerted an oligopolistic control of trade with British colonies analogous to that of the merchant guilds: They excluded competitors from other nations but divided the profits among the partners. It can hardly be surprising, then, that international trade was also heavily regulated by the government in the mercantilist age.

In fact, mercantile trade policy represented a distinctive response to each of the three dilemmas with which this book began: those concerning competing values, distributional outcomes, and effects on the state. The government controlled markets, especially those in international trade, in order to affect specific distributional outcomes such as the protection of consumers and grain producers. Mercantile trade policy also pursued the values of social justice, national development, and self-sufficiency more consistently than the values of efficiency and profitability associated with

---

Mercantilist and Liberal Responses to Trade Dilemmas

Mercantilism	*Liberalism*
1. Value trade-offs	
Trade should be regulated to achieve social justice, national economic development, stability, and self-sufficiency.	Trade should be free to maximize efficiency, productivity, consumption, and freedom.
2. Distributional outcomes	
Trade should be regulated to shield consumers from high prices and to protect producers, landowners, and workers from foreign competition.	Trade should be free so as to benefit the most efficient (i.e., industrialists).
3. Effects on the state	
Trade should be regulated to achieve state power and wealth, national security and autonomy.	Trade should be free to achieve interdependence and peace.

liberal trade ideas. Finally, advocates of mercantilism saw unregulated trade more as a threat to state power, autonomy, and national defense than as a guarantor of international peace.

THE DEMISE OF MERCANTILISM
AND THE BIRTH OF LIBERALISM

This variant of mercantilism evolved in response to existing conditions in the economy and foreign affairs, in tune with prevailing currents of social and economic theory, and in recognition of the realities of the distribution of power. But even while mercantilist trade policy was dominant, the foundations on which it had been erected were crumbling. Initially, the rise of the market was driven by rapidly changing material conditions at the same time that the values impeding it fell into decline. Then, the advent of liberal theory justified government policies that further strengthened the role of markets, especially those in international trade. Finally, the rise of social groups that championed free trade dramatically shifted the balance of political power. By examining each of these in turn, we will see why mercantilism was seen as a curious anachronism by the middle of the nineteenth century and as ill suited to meet the modern challenge.

But be forewarned: In the next chapter, I also trace the demise of the very free trade system whose ascent is about to be chronicled. Although classical mercantilism is necessarily rooted in time and place, analogous factors have produced neomercantilist forces that influence economic policy everywhere. Thus, the changes that swept away mercantilism—especially the abandonment of the Corn Laws in 1846—should be seen as paving the way for the amalgam of mercantilism and liberalism that has emerged in our own time.

THE RISE OF THE MARKET

Rapidly evolving material conditions lie at the hub of economic, political, and social changes. The center of economic life was shifting from the countryside to the towns in response to the major improvements in machinery and factory technique that we refer to as the Industrial Revolution. The rapidly growing population, much of it increasingly located in industrial towns, fueled a large increase in demand for grain. Dramatic improvements in domestic transportation systems were also permitting a much longer range exchange of goods so that grain surpluses in one area could be more easily marketed elsewhere.[21] Improvements in transportation were making international trade easier as well, so that demand from abroad encouraged increases in production and the threat of supply from abroad motivated English producers to improve production techniques and lower costs.

The communal style of agriculture, which was so admirably suited to the milieu in which it arose, could not adapt to these changing needs because it was hopelessly inefficient. Thus, the **enclosure** movement, in which the open fields and commons were enclosed (i.e., privatized and permanently fenced), that had been under way as early as the late Middle Ages, accelerated dramatically and contentiously after 1765. By the early nineteenth century, the predominant form of agricultural production had become capitalist rather than communal; land was owned by individuals in much larger, more contiguous, and permanently demarcated plots and worked by either wage labor or tenants who paid rent.[22] The agricultural system became more attuned to the market and less reliant on communalism, accepted practice, and government control. Land was bought and sold on the open market much more freely than in the past, labor was hired at market-driven wages when needed and dismissed when no longer required, and production decisions concerning cropping and grazing were made by individuals with an eye toward maximizing profit. The result was a sharp boost in efficiency: Agricultural output increased and the labor required to produce it decreased.

But the enclosure movement produced enormous controversy and extensive violence. It did so precisely because it so vividly illustrates two of the dilemmas of relying upon markets, whether in international trade or in domestic agriculture. Free markets, though more efficient and productive, produce distributional consequences and compromise other values. Enclosure resulted in large-scale unemployment of agricultural laborers and their eviction from the land. The heart of the old society—the slowly changing, self-contained, communitarian village—was ripped apart. Social harmony was strained and public order was undermined by the riots that frequently accompanied enclosure. The attitude of the villagers toward forced enclosure expresses these dilemmas:

> True, our system is wasteful, and fruitful of many small disputes. True, a large estate can be managed more economically than a small one. True, pasture-farming yields higher profits than tillage. Nevertheless, . . . our wasteful husbandry feeds many households where your economical methods would feed few. . . . In our unenclosed village there are few rich, but there are few destitute, save when God sends a bad harvest, and we all starve together. We do not like your improvements which ruin half the honest men affected by them. We do not choose that the ancient customs of our village should be changed.[23]

At issue was a clash in ethical viewpoints. The traditional view regarded land ownership as principally a stewardship, an obligation to maintain a system that produced products for the public good and sustained gainful employment for the peasants who worked the land and constituted the village. The profit derived by the landowner was an important component of the whole organism—because he too had a right to the standard of living properly associated with his station—but the profit motive did not assume the primacy that it was to achieve in later liberal economics. The more modern view stripped from the ownership of property any obligation to use it for the public good and asserted that a fundamental right associated with the ownership of property—indeed, the very meaning of "property"—was the freedom to use it in whatever way its owner saw fit. It was not within the purview of society as a whole or the state in particular to judge whether that use was in the public interest.

These changes were symbolic of a larger transition in the realm of values and social theory from a largely religious conception of society built upon an ethics of duties and obligations to a more secular vision that emphasized an ethics of rights—especially property rights—originating in natural law. This attitude change, not surprisingly, was centered among the commercial and merchant classes. It substituted for the communitarian vision of social organization an individualist conception, which reached its height with the British liberal theorists John Locke (1632–1704), who exerted such a powerful influence on the American constitution, and John Stuart Mill (1806–1873), whose passionate defense of the freedom of a citizen from the government still stands as the foremost statement of liberal thought with respect to civil liberties.

These transformations in attitude were brought about in part by the diminishing influence of the church as it became subordinated to the government after the Reformation and in part by changes in religious doctrine and social ethics associated with the Reformation itself. In particular, many theorists, most famously Max Weber in his 1930 classic *The Protestant Ethic and the Spirit of Capitalism*, have ascribed the "triumph of the economic virtues" to the influence of Puritanism, which not only tolerated profit-maximizing behavior that had been condemned by more traditional religious teachings but elevated such practices to the status of moral virtue. Weber's Protestant ethic was not merely a commitment to hard work in pursuit of a calling in order to glorify God but a drive for achievement that included sharp business dealings and canny calculation of the means to achieve wealth. With these changes came greater tolerance for market outcomes in which those with greater bargaining power benefited at the expense of those with less.[24] Over time, of course, the justification for profit seeking came to be rooted much more deeply in the secular utilitarian ideas familiar to us today than in any religious precepts. With this evolution a separation developed between the realm of ethics and the realm of business, with organized religion ceasing to have much to say about the latter. It is no coincidence that the full elaboration of an economic theory relevant to the age arrived only after this division between ethical thought and economic management had become accepted.

Liberalism emphasized the expansion of productive output as its goal and reliance upon individual entrepreneurship and market forces as the means to achieve it. Both were too discordant with the older Christian tradition to have been tolerated in the earlier society, which was organized around its ethical precepts.

Of course, the enclosure movement proceeded not only because of the efficiency gains it promoted but because its distributional consequences were favorable to political forces that were on the rise. In particular, enclosure was beneficial to the landed gentry both because it produced greater profits and because it divorced the rights of landowning from its customary obligations to maintain stable employment for the peasantry. Because the Crown was more deeply committed to the values of the traditional village than to increasing agricultural production, the government at first opposed the commercialization of agriculture, the enclosure movement, and the transition from crops to pasture. However, with the coming to political power of the landed gentry after 1660, government policy began to change. As the Industrial Revolution shifted the demand for labor and food after 1765, public law strongly favored enclosure and the production changes it permitted.[25] These changes were both inevitable and, on balance, desirable: The huge improvements in living standards of the masses and the emergence of Britain as a world power would have been impossible without them.

Many of the same forces that led to greater reliance upon free markets in agriculture also brought about laissez-faire policies in other areas of the domestic economy. For example, domestic price regulation, which was opposed by increasingly powerful industrialists, had begun to fade by the middle of the seventeenth century. As early as 1437 Parliament moved to limit the interference with free markets by craft guilds.[26] The merchant guilds that controlled domestic trade disappeared long before their counterparts in international trade.

A critical factor was that the Crown, which had been the principal agent of market regulation, was too weak after the Restoration to maintain control of a complex, expanding economy. Merchants and industrialists were restive and intolerant of a government regulatory system that constrained their activities, created artificial monopolies in the interests of political favorites, and induced inefficiency and corruption. The limits of government control had been surpassed, perhaps most vividly in the Corn Laws themselves. The balancing act between keeping prices low enough for consumers but high enough for producers had always been difficult; the unwieldy system of prohibitions, sliding-scale duties and bounties, and trigger prices required frequent amendment and even more frequent temporary suspension in the face of changing market conditions. As increased demand and larger-scale trade induced even greater price fluctuations, it became evident that government could not control even this relatively simple market. Effective management of more complicated arrangements seemed unlikely, especially in labor markets, financial markets, and long-distance trade.

Thus, laissez-faire principles slowly came to eclipse government regulatory arrangements. Wage control was abandoned in the woolen industry, the core of the emerging industrial sector, in 1756. Employers were no longer required to maintain employment for workers during a depression. The apprenticeship system of the craft guilds was also rapidly in decline when finally abolished in 1835. Consumer-protection laws that regulated production standards for cloth disappeared.[27] It was in this environment that free trade theory emerged.

THE ADVENT OF FREE TRADE THEORY

In 1751, Charles Townshend wrote a pamphlet on the Corn Laws that foreshadowed later liberal arguments. He attacked import restrictions and export bounties that raised the price of grain not because of their impact on agriculture but on the then-novel grounds that they injured English manufacturing industries. He noted that when food prices increased, the wages paid to manufacturing workers had to increase in order to cover their "necessaries." The resulting price increases in finished goods made English industry uncompetitive with that of other nations. This was especially damaging because English import restrictions had exactly the opposite effect on nations with whom England competed: Preventing foreign farmers from exporting their grain to England tended to keep grain prices low abroad just as it kept grain prices high in England. This enabled foreign wages to remain relatively low and finished products, correspondingly cheap.

This basic argument, strengthened, as we shall see further on, by the later elaboration of Adam Smith, was central to parliamentary debate in 1791, which for the first time featured explicit arguments for free trade derived from theoretical ideas. It was also during this debate that the first major clash occured between the landed interests that dominated Parliament and the growing commercial and manufacturing cities of the Midlands and North. Prior to this, arguments for free trade lacked the gravity they would later attain due to the changing economic structure (especially the dominance of the manufacturing sector), social structure (especially the growth in size of the cities), and political structure (especially the importance of the capitalist class). Nor had the theoretical ideas themselves developed sufficient cogency until presented systematically by Adam Smith in 1776.

With agricultural interests still dominant in Parliament, the last highly restrictive Corn Law was adopted in 1815. This marked the high point of both agricultural protectionism and the class antagonism that was increasingly attendant to these issues. During the parliamentary debate of 1813 to 1815 fierce rioting against the proposed legislation occurred since most Londoners were convinced it would mean higher food prices. Further, the class bias in favor of landowners manifested so clearly in this bill was also evident in the debate surrounding it. As a result, all of the ire of the lower classes over food prices, which had long fallen on brokers such as Rusby, was now directed against the Corn Laws and the landed members of Parliament who supported them. It was against this law that the agitation for free trade was directed in the following thirty years, bequeathing to us such a rich literature of theoretical and practical considerations.

The arguments for free trade, which had surfaced in a less systematic way at least a century previously, became imbedded in the evolving theoretical edifice of economic liberalism, championed most visibly by Adam Smith and the English economic theorist (and member of Parliament) David Ricardo. Smith's argument for free trade rested on the concept of **division of labor** and drew a parallel with the argument concerning specialization in the domestic economy that was at the time better known and more widely accepted.

By the end of the eighteenth century, a reasonably extensive domestic division of labor had already developed: Individual peasants did not make their own shoes, grind their own grain, bake their own bread, weave their own cloth, or tailor their own clothing. With the growth of the town and specialized artisans, it became apparent that considerable savings could be achieved by concentrating one's efforts on producing that good which took advantage of the skills and productive resources at hand and by contracting through domestic trade for the other necessaries of life. For example, the skilled artisan was a better weaver than a peasant, owing to his more extensive tools, better access to quality materials, acquired skill, and advantages of specialization. It was more practical and profitable for all parties to enter freely into the division of labor—that is, to specialize and trade—than to maintain self-sufficiency.

This argument was key to gaining ethical acceptance for the role of the market. Liberal theory contended that free markets would serve the highest moral purpose by maximizing aggregate consumption and thereby maximizing the welfare of the entire society. This position was wholly compatible with the emerging materialist conception of welfare and utilitarian ethical standards, though it remained at odds with the prior ethical tradition.

Smith applied the division of labor logic more broadly. The birth of modern international trade theory can be traced to his memorable phrase, "What is prudence in the conduct of every private family, can scarce be folly in that of a great kingdom."[28] If local trade between the artisans of a town and the peasants of the surrounding countryside can benefit both, if interregional trade between the grain-producing regions of England and areas where the land is more conducive to sheep grazing can be mutually beneficial, why cannot international trade that capitalizes on the respective blessings of different nations be equally advantageous? Thus, nations, like families, should specialize in some products for sale (exports) while acquiring others through purchases (imports).

The important intellectual breakthrough supplied by liberal thought is its blurring of the distinction accepted in medieval economic theory between the public good and the private good. Indeed, liberalism in its rawest form virtually dissolves that distinction. In this famous passage, Smith maintains that the pursuit of maximum profit by individuals inevitably steers them—as if guided by the so-called invisible hand of self-interest—toward behavior that maximizes the benefit of the community as a whole:

> As every individual . . . endeavors as much as he can both to employ his capital in the support of domestic industry, and so to direct that industry that its produce may be of greatest value; every individual necessarily labours to render the annual revenue of the society as great as he can. He generally, indeed, neither intends to promote the public interest, nor knows how much he is promoting it. . . . He intends only his own gain, and he is in this, as in many other cases, led by an invisible hand to promote an end which was no part of his intention. Nor is it always the worse for society that it was not part of it. By pursuing his own interest he frequently promotes that of society more effectually than when he intends to promote it.[29]

Inherent in this logic is the assumption that because all individuals are best equipped to make production decisions concerning their own skills and circumstances, they will naturally specialize in the production of the good in which they have a competitive advantage. Applying the same principle to international trade, Smith thus contended that trade barriers limit not just the private benefits but the public benefits of the gains from trade that accrue to the nation as a whole.

The most elaborate expression of this gains-from-trade argument appeared in Ricardo's 1817 classic, *The Principles of Political Economy and Taxation*, written forty years after Smith's masterpiece and building considerably upon it. Ricardo's famous example of the gains to be achieved by trading British cloth for Portuguese wine remains a powerful statement of the liberal position for free trade.[30] He began with the supposition that the climates, lands, and skills of the people were different in England than in Portugal and that the requirements for successful production of goods such as wool and wine were thus better met in one than the other. Because of this combination of what Smith earlier had called "natural advantages" and "acquired advantages," England was an efficient producer of wool cloth and Portugal an efficient producer of wine. Ricardo observed that each has an advantage in the production of one of the two goods, which he expressed in the form of the amount of labor required to produce each good in each country.

The example displayed in Table 2.1 is in the spirit of Ricardo's original, though the numerical exposition has been simplified to ease the application. Suppose that given the climate, soil, and manufacturing capital available in England, a worker would be capable of producing either two yards of cloth or one gallon of wine per hour. Suppose further that a worker in Portugal could produce only a single yard of cloth but two gallons of wine in the same time. England would be said to have an **absolute advantage** in the production of cloth, and Portugal possessed an absolute advantage in the production of wine.

To see that trade between them would be profitable to both, consider the levels of production in the absence of trade, assuming that both countries chose to produce the same amount of cloth as wine. In England, 100 hours devoted to the production of cloth and 200 hours to the production of wine would produce 200 yards of cloth and 200 gallons of wine. In

TABLE 2.1   Gains from Trade with Absolute Advantage

Production Possibilities		Productivity per Hour	
	Labor Hours	Wine	Cloth
England	300	1	2
Portugal	300	2	1

Without Trade	Hours × Productivity		Production		Consumption	
	Wine	Cloth	Wine	Cloth	Wine	Cloth
England	200 X 1	100 X 2	200	200	200	200
Portugal	100 X 2	200 X 1	200	200	200	200

After Trade	Hours × Productivity		Production		Consumption	
	Wine	Cloth	Wine	Cloth	Wine	Cloth
England		300 X 2		600	300	300
Portugal	300 X 2		600		300	300

Portugal, that same production—200 units of each good—would require that 200 hours be devoted to cloth and only 100 to wine.

But suppose that each producer observed these relative advantages and chose to specialize in the production of only one good and to trade part of that production for the other. The English worker, specializing completely in cloth, could produce 600 units of cloth and the specialized Portuguese worker could produce 600 units of wine. If they then agreed to trade 300 units of one for 300 units of the other, each nation could consume 300 units of both goods, whereas in the absence of specialization and trade, each could consume only 200 units of each good. The gains from trade consist of the increased consumption made possible by each producer allocating his resources in the most efficient way.

But Ricardo saw beyond Smith's idea of absolute advantage, illustrated in Table 2.1. He observed that profitable trade could occur between the two countries even if the worker in one country was more efficient in the production of both goods than the worker in the other country. This idea, illustrated in Table 2.2, is Ricardo's enduring legacy to contemporary international trade theory: the theory of comparative advantage. Here, England is more efficient than Portugal in the production of both goods: An English worker can produce 3 units of wine and 6 units of cloth per hour, and the Portuguese worker's efficiency is the same as before—2 units of wine and 1 of cloth. Although England has an absolute advantage in the production of both goods, Portugal is said to have a **comparative advantage** in wine because its workers can produce more wine than cloth and the reverse is true in England. As a result, trade can still be profitable. In this case, incomplete specialization occurs: England shifts only 100 workers to the production of cloth from wine— to the product in which it holds a comparative (as well as an absolute) advantage and away from the product in which Portugal has a comparative advantage. Still, England consumes the same amount of wine and more cloth after trade than before. Portugal consumes more of both products after specialization and trade than when self-sufficient in both. Thus, we can see that trade can be profitable even if one country possesses an absolute advantage in both goods. (That does not mean that both nations profit equally, but assessing the relative gains requires far more sophisticated analytic tools than this example provides.)

This simple statement of the gains-from-trade argument remains the most vivid demonstration of Ricardo's theory of comparative advantage. And it is the theory of comparative advantage, itself merely a subset of the more general theory of economic liberalism, that gives such intellectual force to the drive for free trade. It is cited as frequently in the trade controversies of the late twentieth century as it was in the Corn Law debates more than a century and a half ago.

TABLE 2.2 Gains from Trade with Comparative Advantage

Production Possibilities	Labor Hours	Productivity per Hour	
		Wine	Cloth
England	300	3	6
Portugal	300	2	1

Without Trade	Hours X Productivity		Production		Consumption	
	Wine	Cloth	Wine	Cloth	Wine	Cloth
England	200 X 3	100 X 6	600	600	600	600
Portugal	100 X 2	200 X 1	200	200	200	200

After Trade	Hours X Productivity		Production		Consumption	
	Wine	Cloth	Wine	Cloth	Wine	Cloth
England	100 X 3	200 X 6	300	1200	600	900
Portugal	300 X 2		600		300	300

But the liberal argument for free trade is far from timeless: It depended for its force on particular historical developments of the modern age. For example, efficient allocation of resources among different economic sectors is not an idea that could arise in a relatively stagnant medieval economy with only one dominant sector. Similarly, it would have been imprudent to rely upon trade when transportation systems were technologically backward and politically fragile. But Ricardian theory is especially modern in its acceptance of a vision quite at odds with mercantilist ideas: that maximum aggregate consumption is the proper central goal of national policy. Liberals assume that national prosperity is the dominant element of the national interest and that it consists of the aggregated welfare of all the individuals that make up the nation. Welfare, in turn, is identical with consumption. Liberalism thus embraces a secular, materialist, individualistic conception of national welfare quite distinct from earlier emphases on a stable, organic, and collective social whole. It is implicitly far more attentive to the welfare of the masses than notions of national prosperity which emphasize the status of landowners or the power of the state. If it is not yet explicitly egalitarian or democratic, it uses a language that can more easily accommodate these more progressive ideas.

In another sense, too, liberalism was born to a moment: Although liberal theory had undeniable analytical merit, it was the changing balance of political power that was decisive in bringing about the demise of the Corn Laws.

THE POLITICAL CONFLICT OVER THE CORN LAWS

Indeed, Ricardo's brilliant theoretical ideas were translated into the free trade policies of the 1840s by somewhat surprising political forces. The trade policy preferences of various groups reflected their perceptions of the dilemmas of trade, but the resulting political alignments did not follow precisely the expectations one might derive from Ricardian theory. In particular, although liberal theory identifies the major beneficiaries of free trade as consumers, whose welfare improves when declining trade barriers allow imports to push prices down, the fight for free trade in grain was actually led by industrialists.

One reason, of course, is that industrialists were permitted to vote and the working class was not. Another was the special skill of the Anti–Corn Law League, which was headed by Richard Cobden and John Bright and centered among the manufacturing interests of Manchester. Through its influence on parliamentary leaders such as William Huskisson, William Pitt the Younger, and Sir John Peel, the Anti–Corn Law League was the principal architect of the drive for repeal from the end of the 1830s to eventual success in 1846. These industrial interests were motivated by both philosophical and practical considerations.

Philosophically, laissez-faire arrangements would give a great deal of freedom to capitalists who were becoming increasingly restive with the government regulations that constrained their entrepreneurial behavior. Unlike mercantilism, which placed the state at the center of economic development, Smith's "invisible hand of self-interest" analogy made it clear that a sound economy must be propelled by the creative activities of the capitalist entrepreneur. In liberal theory, it is the private individual—not the government—who discovers comparative advantage, invests in the export sector, and engages in trade. Government's only role is to stay out of the way. Such a doctrine would obviously have enormous appeal to an entrepreneur who not only welcomed the freedom from government control but no doubt appreciated that his profit-maximizing behavior—once castigated as the sin of avarice—could be portrayed as the act of a patriot.

Though liberal theory certainly held its intellectual attractions for industrialists, the repeal movement was largely motivated by practical opposition to the Corn Laws themselves. Hostility stemmed from the conviction that whatever their original rationale, these laws had long since degenerated into simple import barriers designed to protect landowners. This was correct: The provocative Corn Law of 1815 was openly designed to benefit the landed interests in utter disregard for its impact upon consumers. Unlike earlier versions dating back centuries, the 1815 law suspended all the restrictions on exports, which were designed to keep prices down, but imposed high tariffs on imports, which served to restrict grain supplies and drive prices up by keeping foreign grain out.

Capitalists feared that if grain-producing nations in Europe and America could not sell their products in England because of the Corn Laws, they would have no money to purchase English industrial products. They speculated that the repeal of the Corn Laws would stimulate demand abroad and that English manufacturers would benefit by capturing at least a portion of that expanding market. Following that logic, they also argued that nations unable to acquire British manufactures would launch industry of their own. Moreover, since British trade barriers would encourage them to erect retaliatory tariffs to protect these fledgling industries, such industries could eventually become global competitors. Repeal of the Corn Laws could avoid this scenario by encouraging other European nations to remain specialists in grain production in order to serve the English market.[31]

But it was the effect of food prices on the production costs of British industry that lay at the heart of both the theoretical debate and the political controversy. Capitalists argued that repeal of the Corn Laws would lower food prices because grain could be imported from Europe more cheaply than it could be grown at home. In turn, that meant that wages in British industry could be lowered—without diminishing the standard of living of workers. Finally, this would permit British manufacturers to be competitive with foreign firms because the wage savings could be passed on to consumers. At the same time, of course, lower food prices meant that consumers would have more money to spend on the manufactured goods being produced by British industry. Capitalists thus expected to sell more products at home as well as abroad after the repeal of the Corn Laws.

The most obvious opposition to the Anti–Corn Law League, the landed gentry who benefited directly from agricultural protection, were unmoved by the liberal arguments. Whatever the gains from trade might be, they certainly would not accrue to landowners, who would unequivocally lose in a free competition with cheaper grain producers in North America and Europe. Thus, the chief political battleground concerned two groups of workers with seemingly different interests: urban workers apparently tied to the health of the manufacturing sector and the peasantry, presumably tied to the sectoral interests of agriculture.

It is the latter group whose concerns were addressed most directly by Ricardian arguments, because the unique contribution of liberal theory lay in its response to the protectionists' contention that free trade would injure workers in this previously protected sector of the economy. The liberal position, illustrated by the Ricardian example of wine and cloth, offered a rebuttal to concern for the fate of agricultural laborers if repeal of the Corn Laws brought about the expected demise of grain production in England. Although Ricardo granted that employment in the production of wine might indeed decline or even disappear altogether in Britain, he maintained that there was really nothing to fear, even for workers in the wine industry because the decline in wine production would be accompanied by a compensating expansion of cloth production so that total employment would remain the same.

Following Ricardo, liberals argued that the repeal of the Corn Laws would not decrease employment but only shift it from the inefficient agricultural sector to the manufacturing sector, in which England had a comparative advantage. Liberal theory insists that it is far better to tolerate these short-term dislocations—these transition costs—than to protect an inefficient industry, because total national consumption will increase with a more efficient allocation of resources. The liberal argument for the North American Free Trade Agreement was identical: American workers losing their jobs to Mexican imports were expected to find employment in industries that export to Mexico.[32]

How is this key argument received? Those likely to immediately gain from free trade—the British cloth industry in the Ricardian example and the manufacturing sector in the case of the Corn Laws—can be expected to grant the logic of the free trade argument. After all, those in the most competitive sector have much to gain *personally* and nothing to lose, even if the liberal contention about *national* welfare should turn out to be wrong. They will typically urge those who will immediately lose—agricultural workers or wine producers—to patiently wait for growing employment opportunities in the most competitive sector to trickle down to them.

But those who will immediately suffer the dislocation are more concerned with the distributional effects of free trade than with its aggregate effects. They are likely to be more skeptical of liberal theory simply because for them the stakes are so much greater. And they will be as attentive to the short term as to the long term, worrying about how long and painful the transition may be even if the future is fully as bright as liberal theory promises. After all, it is far easier for a theorist to move a column of figures from "wine" to "cloth" than it is for a worker who has devoted his life to farming to pack up and move to a strange town in the hopes that he might find a job in an unfamiliar industry that requires skills he does not possess. He would not be persuaded by the liberal theorist's contention that his loss of income was temporary or that his loss of security and way of life was illusory because it could not be measured in terms of the aggregate consumption that defines "gains from trade."

In the case of the Corn Laws, the natural opposition of agricultural workers to a removal of protection for their sector seems to have been overcome by three factors. First, they were cross-pressured by their dual roles as both workers and consumers; in the latter capacity they appeared to benefit from lower grain prices. Second, they were not convinced that the benefits of agricultural protection had been passed down from landowners to agricultural workers. The Anti–Corn Law League was especially effective in persuading much of the peasantry that higher grain prices enriched only landowners because it enabled them to increase the land rents paid by peasants. Third, they were reasonably optimistic that job opportunities existed in the industrial sector for workers displaced from agriculture. Because British industry was by far the most productive in the world during this period, and its output was increasing rapidly, industrial employment opportunities were growing. It was possible for peasants to envision a relatively brief transition with a relatively small risk. Confidence in the future of the dominant economy and the dominant industries in the world made the Ricardian arguments seem plausible.

The industrial working class was ambivalent. On the one hand, it had little use for the landowners and the fall in food prices expected from free trade would be very welcome. However, it trusted neither of the two principal protagonists in the debate; the motivations of the Anti–Corn Law League in seeking lower food prices attracted particular suspicion. Supporters of the Corn Laws cited the "iron law of wages"—the contention that desperate unemployed workers always compete for scarce jobs by offering to work for lower wages until eventually wage rates fall to the subsistence level (that is, just high enough to keep them alive). Thus, any decline in food prices brought about by repeal of the Corn Laws would lower the wages necessary to provide subsistence, but that would not benefit workers because wage rates would be driven quickly to that new, lower level.

A placard posted in Manchester conveyed the essence of a position that would be at home in the debate over NAFTA: "Why do these liberal manufacturers bawl so lustily for the repeal of the corn laws?—because with the reduced price of corn they will be enabled to reduce the wages of working men so that they may compete with foreigners who live upon potatoes."[33] Because industrialists did portray lower prices as necessary to meet the competition of producers abroad, the motivation implied by the placard seems well founded. Certainly the sentiment it expresses has been widely shared by workers in more advanced countries: fear that their living standards will suffer when forced to compete with foreign workers whose wages seem to them indecently low. Indeed, after the repeal of the Corn Laws, identical reasoning underlay the rallying cry of protectionist forces in the United States: "Protection against the pauper labor of Europe."[34] Many even doubted that lower wages would be passed along in the form of lower, more internationally competitive prices for final goods; instead, they believed that lower wages would mean only greater profits for capitalists.

The capitalist leaders who led the drive for free trade were not viewed as friends of the working classes because of their strident opposition to acts such as a child-labor law, poor laws to provide relief to the unemployed, regulations to limit the workday, and the legalization of collective bargaining for wages. Particularly during the 1840s when the Anti–Corn Law League directly confronted the Chartists, a working-class organization that favored full manhood suffrage, worker antipathies to capitalists were somewhat greater than toward landowners. However, it appears that mass opinion marginally favored repeal of the Corn Laws by 1846.

It is by no means clear that the position of the working class was decisive, though it unquestionably had some impact even in the absence of democratic representation.[35] Nor had the capitalist class displaced the gentry in parliamentary membership.[36] However, even landed members of Parliament (MPs) had to respond to constituents whose interests were increasingly concentrated in industry and commerce, not agriculture. Agriculture lost its political clout because with the expansion of the manufacturing sector and the growth of towns, it ceased to be the driving force of the economy and the principal source of government revenue.

Still, the final repeal of the Corn Laws owes much to the power of the arguments themselves. In particular, opponents of the Corn Laws were able to counter two claims of fairness raised by protectionists in all debates over free trade, including those of the present era. The first questions the value of free trade policy in one nation when other nations do not reciprocate. The second challenges the validity of eliminating protection for some while retaining it for others.

Protectionists used the reciprocity argument to question the real benefits of **unilateral** free trade. Liberals assumed that repeal of the Corn Laws would bring an increase in both imports of grain and exports of manufactured goods, but Sir Henry Parnell's speech in the House of Commons in support of the 1815 bill noted that neither linkage would occur unless Britain's trade partners would reciprocate by emulating the free trade stance. Parnell thus argued for free trade only on the "supposition that all the nations of Europe should adopt the same common policy."[37]

This reciprocity objection is a common feature of all debates over free trade, but liberal economists are unanimous in finding it to be totally without merit because protection always hurts consumers by increasing the prices of imports. Thus, although Smith acknowledges that "revenge naturally dictates retaliation," he finds the policy unwise: "It seems a bad method of compensating the injury done to certain classes of our people

---

Explanations for Early Trade Policies

Early Mercantilism	*Nineteenth-Century Liberalism*
1. State of theory	
Religious and communitarian ethical theory assumed that to achieve the public interest in just prices required state interference in markets.	Materialist, individualist, and utilitarian ethical theory; empirical theory emphasizes that comparative advantage enables free trade to increase the consumption of all nations.
2. State of markets	
Thin markets made prices volatile; unstable political relations made trade uncertain; and English producers feared foreign competition.	Lower transportation costs and reduced political risks make potential gains from trade large; technological improvements made English industry dominant over foreign competition.
3. Political power balances	
Parliament was dominated by the Crown, the church, and especially landowners.	Parliament increasingly influenced by industrial and urban interests.

---

to do another injury ourselves, not only to those classes, but to almost all the other classes."[38]

The sole exception to the principle that retaliation is self-defeating is the allowance that temporary measures designed to induce others to eliminate the objectionable barriers may be justified. On how far in this direction it may be safe to go, sage judgment cannot be found in the analytical ability of the economist, says Smith, but in "the skill of that insidious and crafty animal, vulgarly called a statesman or politician."[39]

The second fairness contention challenges the validity of eliminating protection for some sectors while retaining it for others. Observing that the very manufacturing interests that led the opposition to agricultural protection were very heavily protected by tariffs themselves, Parnell challenged them directly: "If all those who are concerned in manufactures and commerce will consent to adopt the system of a perfect free trade, those who are now advocates for restraints on the importation of corn will willingly abandon on their part all claim to any such protection."[40] This point had a powerful internal logic and a compelling appeal to fairness. In 1815, it carried the day: Because manufacturing interests were unwilling to give up the protection afforded by tariffs on industrial imports, agricultural interests refused to abandon agricultural tariffs.

The first step in breaking this deadlock was taken in the Petition of the Merchants of London, drafted by Thomas Tooke and presented to the House of Commons in 1820 by Alexander Baring. It called for an end to all protectionist measures (allowing, however, for customs duties necessary for government revenue), citing precisely the inevitability of the line of reasoning used by Parnell. Indeed, it went farther, noting that if British producers could be protected from foreign ones, the same argument could be made for each county and that free trade even within Britain would cease. Further, it observed that British protectionist measures were used as an example by other nations; until Britain embraced free trade, neither would others. Thus, Tooke's analysis engaged both of Parnell's objections and paved the way for the gradual dismantling of the protectionist structure of British commercial policy that occurred over the following three decades.

CONCLUSION: THE TRIUMPH OF FREE TRADE

Modest movement toward free trade in industry was launched by the commercial treaty with France of 1786—which eliminated many prohibitions and prohibitory duties—but it accelerated dramatically after 1820. In 1824, the export of native wool was permitted after centuries of prohibition designed to protect the domestic textile industries. In 1825, the duty on foreign cloth was reduced from 50 percent to 15 percent. In 1842, all complete prohibitions were removed and duties on raw materials were reduced to 5 percent, on partially manufactured articles to 12 percent, and on fully manufactured goods to 20 percent. In 1846, the latter was lowered to 10 percent and the textile industries (except silk) ceased to be protected at all. During the same period, the Navigation Acts, which protected British shipping, were weakened in 1815, 1822, and 1825 before being finally eliminated in 1849. Agricultural protection in Britain ended in 1846 with the repeal of the Corn Laws.

THREE

□ □ □

The Politics of Protectionism

The repeal of the Corn Laws in 1846 symbolized the abandonment of mercantilism and the advent of the golden age of British free trade. Although by no means constituting complete free trade, British trade policy became the closest approximation to it that the world had yet seen.[1] The British example also contributed to a general decline of protectionism that occurred throughout Europe during the middle of the nineteenth century.[2] But from our historical vantage point, we can see that this change was neither complete nor permanent; instead, it was only one phase of the continuous cycle in which trade policy oscillates between relatively free and relatively protectionist.

CYCLES OF GLOBAL MERCANTILISM AND LIBERALISM

By the last quarter of the nineteenth century, the pendulum was already moving the other way, and during the 1930s, Britain was carried with the rest of the globe into a frenzy of protectionism that reduced global trade by two-thirds with average tariff rates reaching 45 percent, not far from their peak prior to 1820. The cycle began again after World War II with a global movement back toward free trade led by the United States, but by the late 1980s it appeared that the cycle of liberalism had crested and mercantilism was again gaining strength.

In this chapter, I seek to explain this cyclical pattern by returning to the central analytic question of why nations select the foreign economic policies they do. The case of the decline of British liberalism in the late nineteenth and early twentieth century is an especially intriguing one because, for the most part, nineteenth-century free trade delivered on the promises of liberal theory. With barriers to trade rapidly declining, trade volume increased and total economic output grew with it. Despite the dire predictions of landowners during the Corn Laws debate, even English agriculture thrived until the 1880s. In part, this was a tribute to the magic of the market celebrated by liberal theory: English agriculture, facing foreign competition, became more efficient, especially through the application of agricultural science and mechanization.[3] But eventually the expected flood of imports did undermine English agriculture. By 1892, British importation of wheat and flour had grown to nearly ten times its volume in 1846, constituting nearly three-quarters of domestic consumption.[4] As grain prices fell, English landowners shifted land out of agricultural production and the volume of English arable land diminished by almost half.

Thus, exactly as predicted by liberal theory, free trade brought about an economic restructuring based on comparative advantage. Britain ceased to be self-sufficient in food as the comparative advantage of American farmers derived from superior factor endowments (richer farmland) dictated the shift of English production away from agriculture. Meanwhile, Britain experienced a rise in the production and export of the manufactured goods in which it had a comparative advantage by virtue of its abundant capital endowment and its technical superiority over foreign manufacturers.

But if the claims of liberal theory were validated by the growth of the British economy, the doubts of protectionists persisted and, indeed, eventually emerged triumphant again. The tensions between mercantilism and liberalism cannot be resolved by the temporary victory of one over the other because neither can satisfy the objections implicit in the dilemmas of trade. In fact, the cyclical character of these alterations are rooted in the excesses of each approach: As policy moves toward the pure form of either mercantilism or liberalism, trade dilemmas become more starkly perceived and inevitably draw a reaction that reverses the sweep of the pendulum.

At the core of these policy reversals are changes in economic conditions, political forces, and social ideas, all of which influence how the dilemmas of trade are perceived by different groups and different nations. In the following sections, the retreat from pure liberalism in Britain is explained in terms that provide the lessons needed to understand contemporary instances of the competition between free trade and protectionism. First, the triumph of laissez-faire ideas brought a theoretical and political reaction that sharpened the confrontation between the alternative values underlying mercantilism and liberalism. Second, the very economic development engendered in part by liberalism transformed the political landscape of Britain by reconstituting its class composition and governmental structure. The resulting political economy contains the basic political forces that compete for control over trade policy in the advanced industrial democracies of our own era. Third, the rapidly growing global economy altered the power balance among nations, thus changing attitudes toward trade in ways remarkably similar to the shifts we see at the end of the twentieth century.

THE REACTION TO LAISSEZ-FAIRE

Even while free trade emerged in the middle of the nineteenth century, key parts of the edifice that supported it were already crumbling. In particular, the leading theoretical challengers to the doctrine of economic liberalism were being born at almost the same instant that the repeal of the Corn Laws in 1846 signaled its highest triumph. The greatest of the neomercantilist works, *The National System of Political Economy*, was written in 1841 by Friedrich List (1789–1846). Karl Marx's (1818–1883) influential critique of liberal capitalism, which first appeared in *The Communist Manifesto* in 1848, was the forerunner of modern socialism.[5] Both reflected the reemergence of skepticism about the distributional consequences and the ethical basis of markets.[6]

The triumph of free trade in the nineteenth century followed from social and economic theories claiming that markets produced economically efficient and ethically acceptable outcomes. However, by the twentieth century, the limitation of markets and the ethical, social, and political dilemmas they produced were coming into even sharper focus. At the forefront was the continuing development of the factory system that emerged from the Industrial Revolution.

Early in its evolution, there was little regulation of the industrial production process, especially with regard to the treatment of labor. It became apparent, however, that total reliance upon the market and total absence of governmental regulation had severe social ramifications. An excess supply of labor, signaled by high unemployment rates, drove wages near or beneath subsistence levels in conformity with the theoretical **iron law of wages**. Even factory laborers who worked twelve- to sixteen-hour days in miserable working conditions frequently lived in poverty. The market forces that held down wage rates were given free rein by labor laws highly favorable to capitalists, especially the notorious Combination Acts of 1799. These laws made it illegal for workers to act together in pursuit of economic interests: Trade unions were banned, strikes were outlawed, even holding meetings among workers was prohibited.

In this atmosphere, supply and demand for labor yielded abhorrent outcomes that undermined the legitimacy of the market. The exploitation of labor, including children, was rampant. Unregulated until 1819, the child-labor practices of that era were widely condemned, though they are a more grievous affront to modern sensibilities than to the standards of that age. The child-labor law of 1819, which was strongly opposed by capitalist interests, prohibited children eight and under from employment in cotton mills and limited those between nine and sixteen to twelve-hour days. Even after these prohibitions, children thirteen and under represented about 15 percent of the workforce in cotton and wool mills and nearly 30 percent in silk mills. In unregulated industries (that is, all but textiles), children as young as five or six years of age were frequently employed, sometimes as many as sixteen hours a day.[7] Women were not restricted to a twelve-hour day until 1844, and working hours for adult men were not regulated until 1908.[8]

These were the conditions that bred attempts to formulate an alternative ethic to that of the unbridled market. With the eclipse of an ethical theory rooted in medieval religious thought, workers sought an alternative source of protection from the vagaries of labor markets and the avarice of capitalists. They found it in the form of government regulation driven by increasing political power for the working class and informed by an economic and social theory—socialism—whose vision of economic life directly opposed that of economic liberalism.

Socialist ideas ranged from those of Robert Owen and Karl Marx to more moderate attempts to find a balance between the state and the market. The latter find expression in the British Labour Party and the various social democratic parties of Western Europe, which ushered in the mixed economy familiar to the twentieth century. Perhaps Joseph Chamberlain, a turn-of-the-century British cabinet member, put best the evolving understanding of the role of government and its place in regulating the market: "Government is the only organization of the whole people for the benefit of all its members; and the community may and ought to provide for all its members benefits which it is impossible for individuals to provide by their solitary and separate efforts."[9] It is no coincidence that Chamberlain was a leading figure in the movement to abandon free trade: Doubts about the legitimacy and efficacy of markets in the domestic sphere could not help but weaken the case for reliance upon markets in the conduct of international trade.

The reaction against laissez-faire was not based solely on normative considerations, of course. The experience with unbridled capitalism, particularly during economic downturns, had also eroded faith in the efficiency of markets. Alternative economic theories, most notably the market-interventionist views of John Maynard Keynes, challenged liberalism as an article of faith. His argument on behalf of an enhanced role for government spending to restore equilibrium and full employment has been influential in many countries, including the United States, since the 1930s. He also favored tariffs, international cartels, and state trading, all anathema to liberal theory.

THE RISE OF THE WORKING CLASS AND POLITICAL DEMOCRACY

Of course, social and economic ideas attain practical importance only when tied to political forces that can bring them into play. In the case of the reaction against markets in general and free international trade in particular, the catalyst was a growing, partially organized working class within the context of an evolving democratic political system.

An important consequence of the Industrial Revolution was the creation of a new and self-conscious social class, that of industrial labor. Because the increased scale of production led to the demise of the artisan and apprenticeship system and because the decline of agriculture limited employment possibilities in the rural sector, workers became completely reliant upon the market for industrial labor. The political arrangements of the period were such that the labor market was rigged in favor of business: Owners were permitted to collude in order to hold wages down, but workers could not organize to push them up. Together with the poor working conditions and generally low wages, this led workers to a feeling of alienation from capitalists and solidarity with labor. Further, it led to a growing trade union movement that eventually was to transform the political structure of society. The act of 1825, which legalized trade unions solely for the purpose of regulating hours and wages, was the beginning of a steady advance in the power of organized labor and a broadening of the political role of trade unions.

These developments occurred within the context of a political system that was slowly moving toward modern democracy through the expansion of the franchise. Controversies over the right to vote extend back at least to the Reform Bill of 1832, which broadened suffrage somewhat to encompass much of the growing capitalist middle class.[10] Nonetheless, working-class support was critical to passage of the reform bill, as workers became persuaded that parliamentary reform would weaken the legislative stranglehold of the wealthy minority of landed interests. As anticipated, this reform did eventually aid the repeal of the Corn Laws. Many had also hoped that the reform bill would be a stepping-stone to their own enfranchisement. Although progress was slow, the working class did eventually achieve the franchise, with the first step being the doubling of the electorate from about 1 million to 2 million via the Reform Bill of 1867, sponsored by Benjamin Disraeli, head of the landed-gentry wing of the Conservative Party. In 1884, rural workers were added to the electorate, again doubling its size. In 1918, universal suffrage was finally granted to males over the age of twenty-one and females over the age of thirty. In 1928, that age gap was removed.

By the early twentieth century, these twin developments—the emergence of political democracy and the growth of labor unions—had come together to institutionalize political representation for the working class. The Labour Party was formed in 1900 by representatives of labor unions in concert with a group of intellectuals known as Fabian socialists. The latter included the noted writers George Bernard Shaw and H. G. Wells. By 1906, Labour had won fifty seats in Parliament and was well on its way to becoming one of two dominant political parties. Together with the declining political importance of landowners that resulted from the declining economic importance of agriculture, this development marked the beginning of a new era in British politics. The sectoral cleavage between industry and agriculture receded in importance, and the British political system came to be defined by the cleavage that is the mark of all modern political economies: a party of the right self-defined as pro-business and a party of the left self-defined as pro-labor.[11] It is tempting to define the resulting right to left continuum on politico-economic issues as lying between the extremes of complete trust in the market and complete trust in the state. Although this perspective contains some truth, it is a dangerous oversimplification, particularly concerning trade policy, because labor has sometimes been committed to free trade and business has sometimes preferred protectionism.[12] However, the growth of democracy and increasing power for the working classes certainly ensured that national policies would respond more vigorously to the perspectives of labor— especially the primacy of unemployment as an economic problem—than they had a century earlier. In any case, from this time forward, distributional issues centering on class were as prominent in trade policy debates as those centering on economic sectors or geographic regions.

This is not to say that capitalists and workers were always in disagreement over trade policy. To the contrary, it is precisely their broad agreement in Britain until World War I that sustained free trade. The relative political power of these two groups determines the shape of trade policy only when conditions in international markets cast them into opposition to one another. Then their mutual opposition stems from the different stake that capital and labor have in trade. These distributional effects of trade can be seen with clarity only in the context of modern international trade theory, a topic to which I now turn.

MODERN ELABORATIONS OF LIBERAL TRADE THEORY

Since Smith and Ricardo, liberal trade theory has consistently advocated free trade, but its foundation has been elaborated and strengthened by subsequent theorists, especially Eli Heckscher and Bertil Ohlin, two Swedish economists of the 1930s. The Heckscher-Ohlin theory, abbreviated H-O or sometimes H-O-S to acknowledge the role of the American Nobel Prize–winning economist Paul Samuelson in advancing it, is important to us for two reasons. First, it reinforces free trade doctrine by specifying the precise economic conditions that constitute the sources of comparative advantage. In so doing, H-O clearly accepts the liberal tenet that governmental intervention is not required to lead the market to the gains from trade. Second, and more immediately, H-O leads directly to the Stolper-Samuelson theorem (explained further on), which exposes the class basis of the distributional effects of free trade. These distributional effects help to explain why contemporary controversies over trade policy, such as NAFTA, tend to follow a characteristic pattern in which some classes and sectors prefer free trade while others prefer protectionism.

Ohlin's classic work *Interregional and International Trade* remained squarely in the liberal tradition, but it advanced Ricardo's analysis by specifying in greater detail the sources of national comparative advantage. In the context of a simple economy, the early formulations of Smith and Ricardo were understandably rudimentary: They emphasized natural advantages such as climate or soil quality and acquired advantages such as specialized skills in weaving or metalworking. Ohlin went beyond these simple ideas to argue that a nation's comparative advantage lies in the relative abundance of some **factors of production** and the relative scarcity of others.

To reach this conclusion, he began by improving upon the simple labor theory of value that Ricardo used to demonstrate the gains from trade. Whereas Ricardo described the differences in the productive efficiency of a nation's industry solely in terms of the amount of labor required to produce any given level of output, Ohlin noted that production actually requires at least three factors of production: land, labor, and capital. All products require some quantity of each factor, but the proportion of each varies widely depending on the nature of the product and the processes used to produce it. For example, agricultural goods require large amounts of land (thus, they are dubbed land-intensive); heavy manufactures such as autos are considered capital-intensive because they require such large quantities of expensive plant and equipment; and light manufactures involving simple assembly or processing are labor-intensive because they rely on large numbers of unskilled workers. Ohlin claimed that differences in the factor intensity of various products would determine where they could be produced most efficiently.

Just as products differed in their factor intensities, Ohlin also observed that different nations possessed vastly different factor endowments. In the modern era, for example, capital is relatively abundant in the developed countries (such as the United States, Japan, and Western Europe), land is abundant in countries such as Canada and Australia, and unskilled labor is abundant in countries such as Mexico and the poorer nations of East Asia. Ohlin further reasoned that production of goods that used intensively any particular factor would naturally be more efficient in nations that possessed a relative abundance of that factor. Thus, land-abundant nations, for example, will have a comparative advantage in land-intensive products and capital-abundant nations will have a comparative advantage in capital-intensive products.

This theory of factor proportions and factor intensity perfectly explained Ricardo's classic example of British specialization in manufactured goods and Portuguese specialization in wine. Britain, with abundant supplies of capital, had a comparative advantage in the production of capital-intensive products, and Portugal, with its abundance of good land for the growing of grapes, had a comparative advantage in wine. Moreover, Ohlin's theory had broader application because it could be used to identify which nations would have a comparative advantage in which products: *Each nation has a comparative advantage in the production of those goods that use intensively the factor they possess in relative abundance.* It also was in accord with simple observations of the trade patterns among nations: Developed countries tend to export capital-intensive products while they import food from land-abundant countries and simple manufactures from labor-abundant countries.[13]

At the heart of this theory is the interaction between markets for final goods and the markets for the factors required for their production (land, labor, and capital). For example, in nations where labor is relatively abundant and land relatively scarce, the surplus supply of labor will cause wage rates to be relatively low, and the short supply of land will cause land rents to be relatively high. That is precisely why labor-intensive products are cheapest to produce in nations with an abundance of labor.

For our purposes, the consequences of trade are as important as its causes, and in this respect the contribution of H-O to understanding the interaction between goods and factor markets also is significant. That is because the distributional effects of international trade depend directly on how trade affects the supply and demand for the various factors of production.

THE CLASS DISTRIBUTIONAL IMPACT OF TRADE

To see how factor markets shape the distributional effects of trade, let us return to Britain at the time of the Corn Laws and stipulate that it is relatively abundant in capital and relatively scarce in land. That would imply that capital should be relatively cheap and easy to acquire in Britain and that land would be relatively expensive. If that is so, Ohlin would expect that Britain would be a relatively efficient producer of capital-intensive products such as manufactures but a relatively inefficient producer of land-intensive products such as grain. That seems to accord with the historical record of what happened when Britain adopted free trade: It became an importer of (land-intensive) grain and an exporter of (capital-intensive) manufactured products. Britain's food imports came largely from the United States, Canada, and Australia, all of which were abundantly endowed with land. Their manufactured exports went to nations with a relatively poor endowment of capital, including the land-abundant grain exporters.

But what were the effects of free trade on factor markets? The answer defines the distributional effects of free trade. We know that free trade led to the expansion of British manufacturing. That expansion required a considerable increase in investment in plant and equipment, which in turn increased the demand for capital. The owners of capital found that greater demand enabled them to charge a higher interest rate to manufacturers who wished to borrow capital to expand their facilities. That is, the increase in the production of capital-intensive products increased the return on capital. This result can be stated more generally as the first half of the Stolper-Samuelson theorem: *Free trade benefits the owners of the abundant factor of production.*

At the same time, the repeal of the Corn Laws caused domestic production of grains to decline in the face of foreign competition and the lower grain prices it engendered. With grain production less profitable in Britain, British landowners had to lower the rents charged to farmers to use their land; otherwise those farmers could not compete with foreign imports. British landowners, owners of the scarce factor of production, lost from free trade. Thus, the second half of the Stolper-Samuelson theorem: *Free trade harms the owners of the scarce factor of production.*

The political corollary to Stolper-Samuelson is now simply seen: Owners of the abundant factor of production will prefer free trade; owners of the scarce factor of production will oppose it. Because of this, debates over free trade frequently involve class divisions and in a political system with class-based parties—that is, all modern advanced industrial democracies—trade policy frequently becomes a highly partisan issue.

THE DISTRIBUTIONAL POLITICS OF TRADE POLICY

We can now state more clearly the distributional dilemma of trade and the resulting political patterns that emerge in the debate over trade policy. These distributional effects—that some groups gain from free trade while others lose—can be described along three lines: economic sectors, socioeconomic classes, and producers versus consumers.[14]

Those sectors of the economy that rely upon exports will ordinarily favor free trade, especially if the firms involved are relatively efficient by international standards. Those sectors of the economy that compete against foreign imports will ordinarily favor protectionism, especially if the domestic firms are relatively inefficient. Sectors of the economy that utilize imports or import substitutes will, like any ordinary consumer, favor free trade because it is likely to lower their costs.

How individuals will react to these sectoral effects can be difficult to predict. Liberals urge most workers to ignore these considerations because they contend that any factor of production—including labor—that can no longer find productive employment in a sector damaged by free trade can simply shift to a sector that benefits from it. Protectionist sentiments arise from concerns about the costs and uncertainties involved in these sectoral transitions. For some, the transition costs are exorbitant because their highly specialized skills are adapted to a particular sector. Few middle-aged steelworkers are also skilled computer programmers, for example. Others find that personal circumstances such as the employment of a spouse or reliance upon family reduces geographic mobility. Nearly all will face temporary unemployment. Many may be averse to the risk that is inherent in predicting the uncertain future course of comparative advantage. For example, at one time England was a low-cost producer of grains, though by the time of the last Corn Law its comparative advantage had shifted elsewhere. An alert worker, observing this shift, might well question where and when the next change might take place. Indeed, by the middle of the nineteenth century, the comparative advantage in textile production, the earliest and largest of the English manufacturing industries, was also beginning to shift away from England. Thus, protectionism can be comforting to workers who, though currently employed in a competitive industry, fear that they may be next to be displaced. This risk element helps explain why protectionism can be sustained politically even when it appears to benefit so few and harm so many. This argument carries even more weight in the modern era of more rapidly changing comparative advantage.

However, Stolper-Samuelson suggests that both these liberal and protectionist views will remain incomplete so long as they focus on the sectoral composition of the economy. Instead, a class perspective may be more appropriate because trade policy affects the owners of different factors of production very differently: Free trade benefits owners of the abundant resource and harms owners of the scarce resource. For example, since the United States is capital-abundant and labor-scarce relative to the rest of the world, Stolper-Samuelson predicts that wage rates for unskilled labor will decline under free trade just as the profit rates for capital will increase.

Predicting the responses of individuals is further complicated because workers are also consumers—and their interests in these roles are often contradictory. Liberal trade theory emphasizes that consumers benefit from free trade because they can purchase goods more cheaply from those countries that have a comparative advantage than from inefficient domestic producers. From this vantage point, one would expect that consumers would be a major actor in the distributional politics of trade policy; indeed, they should be the strongest advocates of free trade. In fact, they usually are not.

There are several reasons consumers are seldom effective advocates of free trade. First, the costs of protectionism are ordinarily difficult for consumers to see because the trade barriers that affect the prices of foreign goods are not easily visible. Readers are invited to test this proposition for themselves: Can you identify the tariff rate presently imposed on *any* product by the United States?

Second, even if tariff costs were precisely known, they are seldom large enough to motivate any single consumer. For example, trade barriers in the textile and clothing industries are among the highest in any sector of the U.S. economy, yet they probably increase the price of clothing in the United States by under $100 per person per year.[15] Is this impact on your personal budget enough to persuade you to hire a Washington lobbyist to overturn the Multi-Fiber Agreement, which sustains these trade barriers?

Third, because those hurt by protection are geographically diffused and only marginally affected by trade legislation, they are unlikely to organize very effectively to press for free trade. By contrast, because those who benefit from protection tend to be geographically concentrated and intensely affected by trade legislation, they are much more likely to organize effectively and use their political influence to achieve protection. For example, the Multi-Fiber Agreement provides $22 billion in benefits to U.S. domestic firms that employ more than 2 million American workers. Those firms and their employees have far greater motivation and opportunity to lobby in favor of protectionist trade policies than consumers have to oppose them.

All of these factors are commonly present in debates over trade policy, and they help explain why consumers were not in the forefront of the drive for repeal of the Corn Laws. However, for several reasons, consumers were actually a stronger force in opposition to the Corn Laws than is common in trade policy controversies, a fact that helps explain both why free trade achieved a rare triumph in 1846 in Britain and why it later faded.

Because the free trade issue was fought out over food, the welfare effects of the Corn Laws were much more visible than is usual for protectionist legislation. Since food occupied the largest share of the budget in most households and since imports constituted a significant share of food consumption, citizens were unusually attentive to the factors that influenced the price of imports. Thus one key to the emergence of free trade in England at this time is the unusually visible effect of the Corn Laws on an unusually large share of the population. Because the stakes were so large, so immediate, and relevant to so many, political action was easy to organize.

By the twentieth century, trade policy debates in Britain ceased to revolve around food prices, so consumers ceased to be a major factor in them. In most modern developed democracies, class-based political parties have been the major protagonists in the battle between free trade and protectionism. In most of those battles, the outcome is driven by the condition of markets, especially the relative efficiency of domestic and foreign producers.

THE EFFECTS OF MARKET DOMINANCE AND DECLINE

When an industry is confident that it is able to compete effectively against foreign manufacturers, it typically advocates free trade. An industry in doubt about its competitiveness seeks protection or subsidy. Workers ordinarily follow the lead of the industry in which they are employed; other citizens usually follow the industry dominant in their region. Thus it is for nations in aggregate: Liberal policies will suffice when a favorable balance of trade can be maintained without actions that encourage exports and discourage imports. Protection is the preferred policy when balance-of-trade difficulties signal declining competitiveness. That pattern was perfectly manifested in the period we have been considering.

Until the middle of the eighteenth century, the productive efficiency of British industry was not superior to that of its continental competitors. Indeed, in some important areas it lagged behind such early leaders as the Dutch. As we have seen, the government responded as early as the sixteenth century by encouraging the growth of key industries with a variety of subsidies, legal monopolies, and trade restrictions. Moreover, English manufacturers who lacked economic advantages over foreign competitors generally supported the measures that gave them political advantages: the colonial system, the Navigation Acts, and the great trading companies that monopolized trade with the colonies; the tariff and prohibition barriers that enabled them to develop infant industries; and the restrictions on exports of raw materials, technology, and skills designed to retard the development of competitors abroad.

However, the technological advances of the Industrial Revolution came a generation earlier to England (circa 1760) than to its continental competitors, giving British producers a natural competitive edge against others by the early nineteenth century. When English manufacturers became confident of their ability to compete successfully with foreigners on economic terms alone, they gave up their own tariff protection in exchange for the repeal of the Corn Laws.

Thus, it is no surprise that free trade was adopted more completely and for a longer period in Britain, the dominant economic power, than in any other nation: Competitive industries do not need protection, so the governments that represent them oppose it. Still, even Britain encountered protectionist movements during economic downturns, first the Fair Trade movement of the 1870s and then the Tariff Reform crusade of 1903, but unlike the less competitive nations of Europe, it retained its free trade orientation. The Great Depression of 1873–1896 produced increasing protectionism throughout Europe as nations sought to defend employment and profits, especially against the competition of the British. Thus in the 1920s, Britain still maintained among the lowest tariff barriers in the world. By the end of the 1930s, however, when the end of Britain's economic dominance left it unable to resist the global move toward protectionism, Britain had become as protectionist as any.

In the twentieth century this pattern remains clearly visible: The economically dominant nation advocates free trade, but challengers opt for mercantilism. Immediately after World War II, the United States, by then the most productive and cost-efficient economy in the world, took up from the British the mantle of the leading champion of free trade. Both Japan and most of Europe, recovering from the war, adopted a sharply mercantilist stance.

By the 1990s, the positions had changed again. The policy of the United States, whose share of world exports declined from 45 percent in 1950 to under 20 percent in 1990, has become increasingly protectionist (though its rhetoric remains mostly liberal). Moreover, the United States assumes very different stances with respect to different sectors of the economy. It is protectionist in declining heavy industries such as steel and automobiles in which it no longer enjoys a comparative advantage but adopts a very liberal position in those areas in which America still dominates, such as technology, services, and intellectual property.

Theorists have long contended that a policy of free trade may be beneficial for dominant nations but harmful for others. For example, List countered free trade doctrine on the grounds known to posterity as the infant-industry argument. It states that an industry in its early stages requires protection against its better-established foreign competitors.

Only after it has benefited from a protected domestic market can it achieve the maturity, efficiency, and **economies of scale** necessary to withstand foreign competition. Premature free trade will doom an economy to specializing only in those products the dominant power may choose to ignore, presumably because they offer little profit or limited growth opportunity.

List urged France to avoid free trade and the specialization in wine that would result from it. Because he doubted that wine production could fuel broad and diversified economic development, he instead advocated the creation of new French industries even though they would require tariff protection against established British firms until they matured. He noted that centuries earlier Elizabethan England had similarly emphasized developing infant industries in order to augment its agriculture and had similarly protected them. From our vantage point in the late twentieth century, we can add to the list of nations opting for this approach. A nearly identical choice faced the Japanese in the American-dominated post–World War II period. They too rejected free trade—and the specialization in textiles, their comparative advantage at the time, that it would have implied. Instead, Japan elected the mercantilist path of protecting the fledgling firms in its electronics and automobile industries.

Indeed, this gap between the rhetoric of the dominant nation and the self-interest of its challengers has produced more than a little bitterness. For example, in this passage, List wrote powerfully in defense of the proposition that free trade is the policy of the dominant power and protection is the policy of the challenger:[16]

> It is a vulgar rule of prudence for him who has reached the pinnacle of power to cast down the ladder by which he mounted that others may not follow. In this lies the secret of Adam Smith's theory, . . . as well as all of his successors in the government of Great Britain. A nation which by protective duties and maritime restrictions has built up a manufacturing industry and a merchant marine to such a point of strength and power as not to fear the competition of any other, can pursue no safer policy than to thrust aside the means of elevation, to preach to other nations the advantages of free trade, and to utter loud expressions of repentance for having walked hitherto in the way of error, and for having come so lately to the knowledge of the truth.

Although considerations of relative efficiency suggest that nations will choose quite different trade policies, specific historical events will often cause nations to respond more similarly. Indeed, both the dramatic collapse of trade in the 1930s and the rise of liberal trade in the 1940s were global phenomena.

TRADE AND THE GREAT DEPRESSION

The collapse of the global economy during the 1930s affirmed an important lesson: Liberal theorists advocate free trade even if a nation must adopt it unilaterally, but its greatest benefits can occur only if liberalism is practiced by all nations. The experience of the Great Depression reveals both an economic and a political reason for this.

The economic reason stems from the simple fact that one nation's exports must constitute another nation's imports. Since no nation can export unless another imports, free trade cannot be fully effective unless all nations approximate this ideal at the same time.

Parnell's role in the Corn Law debates also suggests a political reason that unilateral free trade policies are very difficult to enact: They impose painful adjustments that will be strongly resisted without assurance that other nations are experiencing similar disruptions. This demand for reciprocity is partly a natural psychological reaction against free riders who enjoy the open markets of others but refuse to open their own. After all, no nation wants to be taken advantage of any more than individuals do. Moreover, the cost of adjusting to free trade will exceed the benefits unless a substantial expansion of trade results, which cannot occur unless other nations reciprocate.

As a result, both free trade and protectionism usually occur as global processes. One dominant nation that champions free trade can sometimes induce others to follow suit, as happened under the leadership of Britain in the middle of the nineteenth century and again under the leadership of the United States after World War II. But when one nation moves sharply toward protectionism, others also tend to follow—sometimes with disastrous consequences. That is exactly what happened during a sequence of events that led to the collapse of world trade during the Great Depression of the 1930s. And that is why, in the mid-1990s, some fear a trade war between the United States and Japan.

Though protectionist sentiment had familiar domestic roots, international politics fanned its flames after World War I. British protectionism focused on accusations that Germany was undermining its rivals by dumping iron and steel. Coming soon after the war and in an industry critical to war planning, these claims received greater credence than now appears to be justified by the facts.[17] British tariffs were also motivated by the need to grant imperial preferences to members of the British Empire, which presupposes tariffs from which the empire would be exempted. In all countries, tariffs were said to be useful in strengthening the nation's bargaining position in dealing with other nations who practiced—or threatened—protectionism.[18]

These national security and reciprocity concerns produced a spiral of protectionism with competitiveness issues at its base. Initially, severe unemployment triggered political pressures in several countries to save jobs, but the extreme protectionism that resulted had two dire consequences. First, it exacerbated the economic downturn itself by sharply reducing the gains from trade. Second, it goaded nations to increase their own protectionist policies in retaliation. European protectionism against the onslaught of competitive American firms had been building for years; the Smoot-Hawley Tariff, enacted by the United States in 1930, overwhelmed the last supporters of liberalism even in Britain.

After Smoot-Hawley, more than sixty nations retaliated directly against the United States.[19] The resulting global trade war produced a spiral of retaliation that cut trade further, and the political relations between nations continued to deteriorate. In 1930, 85 percent of goods had entered Britain free of duty, but by April 1932 only about 30 percent did so. Meanwhile, the average tariff level had reached 45 percent in the United States, 41 percent in Germany, 38 percent in France, and up to 70 percent elsewhere in Europe.[20] By 1935, 70 percent of global trade also was subject to nontariff barriers, mostly quotas.[21] In just three years global trade plummeted by 70 percent. The Great Depression and the global trade war fed on one another to produce the most devastating economic chaos of modern times.

Unemployment reached 22 percent in Britain and more than 30 percent elsewhere in Europe, America, and Asia. However, the consequences were not just economic. Unemployment exceeding 40 percent in Germany fueled the growth of Nazism, which in turn led to the outbreak of World War II.[22] Diminishing trade prospects strengthened militarism in Japan, which was already building toward a second locus of the coming global war. As economies nosedived, more than half of the republics of South America experienced revolts in 1930 or 1931. When

---

Why Liberalism Was Overturned by the 1930s

1. State of theory
Government intervention was justified by socialist theory (because markets produce unethical outcomes) and Keynesian theory (to relieve unemployment).

2. State of markets
Even English producers feared foreign competition; market intervention by other governments brought retaliation.

3. Political power balances
Domestically, organized labor achieved power through democracy; globally, there was no dominant nation to lead.

unemployment in the United States grew from around 5 percent to more than 36 percent between 1928 and 1932, the popular vote for the Communist and Socialist Parties tripled. With unemployment constantly over 25 percent for nearly a decade—before the advent of unemployment insurance and other welfare programs to ease the burden—both the marriage rate and the birth rate declined by 25 percent in the United States.[23]

It must be emphasized that the Great Depression was not caused by protectionism: Many forces conspired to make the global economy of the 1920s vulnerable to a serious contraction.[24] Neither did global protectionism begin in the late 1920s: In fact, it had been on the rise for half a century. But protectionism did reach a frenzied peak at the onset of the 1930s, and the Great Depression was certainly deepened by the protection-inspired trade wars that followed.[25] Moreover, these events—the Great Depression, World War II, and the collapse of global trade—became so indelibly linked in the minds of policymakers in the 1940s that they created the Bretton Woods system, discussed in Chapter 4, in order to prevent a recurrence.[26] Their recent experience with depression and war made economic prosperity and international peace more compelling than alternative values such as national autonomy, employment security, and distributional considerations, which in other times had inclined nations toward mercantilism. Furthermore, ascendant liberal theory suggested that these values would be best achieved by practicing liberalism. As a result, they were frightened into constructing an international trade system built more upon multilateral liberalism than unilateral mercantilism.

CONCLUSION: THE SOURCES OF POLICY CYCLES

Classical mercantile trade policy evolved in response to existing conditions in the economy and foreign affairs, in tune with prevailing currents of social and economic theory, and in recognition of the realities of the distribution of power. By the middle of the nineteenth century, these foundations had crumbled—and liberalism was erected on the ruins. The process was repeated a century later when the chaotic protectionism of the 1930s yielded to the American-led liberal system of the 1940s and beyond.

It is striking that the two great liberal movements in modern times were both a response to the worst excesses of protectionism. It was the extreme and irresponsible Corn Law of 1815 that spawned a liberal reaction against the agricultural protection that had been sustained for centuries. Similarly, Bretton Woods was the product of **beggar-thy-neighbor** protectionism enacted in the 1930s as a mad drive to retain employment in desperate circumstances. It is doubtful whether a less radical protectionism could have so thoroughly discredited mercantilism, which in its sober, classical form had been well rooted in established values and consistent practice. Nor would a less severe implosion of the global system have generated the same enthusiasm for the supranational solution created at Bretton Woods.

Of course, liberalism was no more immune from changes in prevailing theories and values, conditions in markets, and domestic and international power balances than was classical mercantilism. It was swept away in the 1930s only to reemerge in altered form in the post–World War II period.

FOUR

□ □ □

The International Politics of Trade

The discussion thus far has emphasized the domestic factors that influence national trade policy. However, because trade policy is also foreign policy, it is greatly influenced by interactions with other nations. Moreover, those interactions occur in the context of international institutions that themselves constrain policies. In fact, most contemporary trade issues revolve around these international institutions and the foreign policy considerations they raise.

THE ORIGINS OF BRETTON WOODS

The institutional foundation of the postwar international economic system was laid in July 1944 at a meeting of Allied ministers in Bretton Woods, New Hampshire. The institutions created there remain at the core of the global economy today: the International Monetary Fund, the **International Bank for Reconstruction and Development** (IBRD, but known as the **World Bank**), and the General Agreement on Tariffs and Trade. They are collectively known as the Bretton Woods institutions even though the GATT was actually created two years later to replace the abortive **International Trade Organization** (ITO), which was originally designed as the third leg of the liberal order.

The Bretton Woods system, particularly the GATT, provides the legal context for current trade debates and the mechanisms through which trade controversies between nations are resolved. To appreciate the role that these institutions play today, we must return to their founding to discover the principles that motivated their architects. We will see that the foundations of Bretton Woods were laid directly over the fault lines

71

between liberalism and mercantilism—and between the interests of different nations. What we see today as trade policy disputes are the surface rumblings of these older seismic forces.

The Great Depression and World War II shaped Bretton Woods by profoundly affecting the forces that created it: the prevailing state of theory and values, the condition of markets, and the balance of power among actors. These events made economic growth and global peace the twin values sought most ardently by policymakers. By discrediting mercantilism, they also strengthened liberal theory as a model of how to structure economic relations in order to achieve these values. The disastrous state of the global economy—especially the collapse of trade markets—contributed to the belief that the international system required greater management along liberal lines. It also convinced policymakers everywhere that a prosperous national economy was impossible without a well-designed international system. Finally, World War II left the United States as the dominant global power, capable of mobilizing other nations to create such a global system and willing to provide the leadership required to make it a success. The result is Bretton Woods, the most liberal global trading order the world has yet seen, created in the wake of the most protectionist period in the modern era.

Efforts to return the global economy to free trade began with bilateral approaches in both Britain and the United States. However, because of protectionist pressures on national governments, it was widely acknowledged that free trade required powerful international institutions to ensure global cooperation and sustain stable financial arrangements. It was equally obvious that such a system would require leadership that could be provided only by a single dominant nation, called a **hegemon**. **Hegemonic stability theory** posited as the requisites of a world leader attributes possessed only by the United States: economic size, military might, political power, ascribed status, and political will.

HEGEMONIC STABILITY THEORY AND AMERICAN GLOBAL LEADERSHIP

The central tenet of hegemonic stability theory is that cycles of global liberalism and protectionism coincide with cycles of hegemonic leadership and decline.[1] As a hegemonic power is in its ascendancy, it pushes the system toward greater liberalism, but as it declines the system tends to revert to regionalism and protection.

Indeed, nineteenth-century free trade was initiated by the championing of liberal principles by Great Britain, tentatively in the 1820s and decisively with the repeal of the Corn Laws in the 1840s. Britain's leadership, which rested on its increasingly dominant economic and military power, contributed to global liberalization in several ways. British diplomacy induced movements toward liberalism in Europe through a series of bilateral agreements, beginning with the Cobden-Chevalier Treaty of 1860, which freed trade between Britain and France. Britain encouraged nations to emulate its successes with an open economy by serving as a market for their goods, especially continental grains. Finally, Britain provided the financing that would facilitate trade: Sterling became an accepted medium of exchange and the City of London offered extensive credit.

By the early twentieth century, however, the relative decline of British power eliminated the hegemon that enforced the rules of global liberalism. The theory of hegemonic stability predicted the result: The system slipped slowly into protection and regionalism, then rapidly and violently into instability, depression, chaos, and war. A liberal system could not reemerge until championed by another ascending hegemon, a role played by the United States in fashioning the Bretton Woods system after World War II.[2] By that time the United States was three times larger than its nearest rival in total production, with twice the per capita income and trade volume of the next nation and seven times greater foreign investment flows than its nearest rival.[3] In conformity with the central tenet of hegemonic stability theory, the United States assumed the mantle of global leadership, championing Bretton Woods in the 1940s and sustaining liberalism through the 1960s. Since the early 1970s, however, American dominance has declined, and as predicted by the theory, both mercantilism and regionalism have reemerged to challenge the expansion of global liberalism.

A global liberal regime backed by hegemonic leadership is needed to overcome the natural inclination of most nations to retain their own trade barriers while inducing other countries to lower theirs. Such a **free rider** can take advantage of open markets elsewhere to expand exports but avoid the painful (if ultimately beneficial) adjustment to import competition. Even though all nations would benefit from global free trade, very few will adopt it unilaterally without assurance of reciprocity. To break this logjam requires a hegemon to take the lead and induce other nations to follow. The hegemonic nation will usually have to subsidize the organizational costs and also offer recalcitrant nations a more favorable deal than strict reciprocity would require. In fact, a hegemon frequently offers side benefits in exchange for cooperation in creating an international regime, such as the massive infusion of foreign aid provided to Europe by the United States under the **Marshall Plan** in the late 1940s.

American hegemonic leadership was especially critical in this period because conditions were not favorable for free trade in most major trading nations. In particular, depression-depleted and war-ravaged Europe could not be optimistic about its competitiveness, especially vis-à-vis the

United States. Nor were the free trade tenets of liberalism unchallenged. One dissent emerged from within liberal theory itself. Known today as the **optimum tariff** argument, it shows that a tariff can sometimes improve national income by forcing foreign producers to lower their export prices.[4] However, this benefit, which comes at the expense of trading partners, accrues only to countries whose large market gives them leverage on total global demand. Following Keynes's influential analysis, many also contended that protectionism could "export unemployment," contrary to the assumption of full employment used by Ricardo to generate the gains from comparative advantage. Together these arguments refuted the free traders' contention that the gains from protectionism were illusory, a position strengthened by recent analyses suggesting that British protectionism actually benefited the British economy.[5] Moreover, government control over trade was a logical corollary to then-prevailing sentiment in Europe, which favored government supervision of the domestic economy, especially during its transition from a wartime orientation to a peacetime equilibrium.

Furthermore, although prosperity and peace were dominant values in the postdepression, postwar world, two devastating wars within twenty-five years also inspired a desire for national security and autonomy. Europe feared economic dependence on the United States, particularly because of the widely held view that the Great Depression had been caused by poor management of the American economy. Since another U.S. recession would also spill over into other economies, Europeans insisted that the ITO include a full-employment mandate to prevent the contractionary policies to which the United States seemed prone. Thus, together with the ever present distributional implications of trade policies, these dilemmas ensured that global liberalism would face opposition.

However, several factors unique to the era made it easier for the United States to foster agreement. Most significantly, Europe was unusually susceptible to the side benefits that a global hegemon could offer. It badly needed the American market for its exports, American capital to rebuild its infrastructure, American dollars to finance trade and investment, and American military protection in the chaotic world of the 1940s. The presence of the Soviet Union as a military threat and global communism as an ideological threat reinforced the common interests of Western nations. Not only would Bretton Woods strengthen Western forces against the Soviet Union by promoting rapid recovery and cementing closer ties, it would also reduce the appeal of communism at the same time that it highlighted the attraction of democracy, capitalism, and alliance with the United States. A final factor was especially conducive to founding a liberal regime—the conviction that **multilateral liberalism** and the resulting interdependence would lead to peace.

LIBERAL INTERDEPENDENCE AND PEACE

Policymakers saw several ways that an institutionalized liberal trading system could promote peace among nations. The growth of global institutions could weaken the hold of nationalism and mediate conflict between nations. Trade-induced contact could break down nationalistic hostility among societies. **Multilateralism** (nondiscrimination) would tend to prevent grievances from developing among states. Interdependence could constrain armed conflict and foster stability. The economic growth generated by trade could remove the desperation that leads nations to aggression.

Despite previous American indifference to international economic cooperation, this promise of peace inspired the United States to assume economic leadership and motivated Europe to follow it.[6] President Franklin Roosevelt's secretary of state, Cordell Hull, held an extraordinary belief in the efficacy of free trade as a guarantor of peace, largely because he ascribed to trade disputes a major role in promoting conflict. This view has been neatly summarized by the slogan "If goods can't cross borders, soldiers will."[7] As early as 1916, Hull even went so far as to contend that bitter trade rivalries were the chief cause of World War I. Though few historians would accord them such importance, economic tensions were certainly present: Between 1890 and 1914, tariff wars erupted between Switzerland and France, between Italy and France, between Germany and Spain, between Germany and Canada, between Germany and Russia, and between Russia and the United States.

Each was precipitated by discriminatory trade policies in which different quotas or duties were imposed on the products of different nations. Trade barriers became tools of foreign policy rather than economic policy. Preferences offered to one nation but not to others (i.e., positive discrimination) were used to create spheres of influence, as Germany did before World War I; to build empires, as Japan and Italy did in the 1930s; and to reinforce existing colonial ties, as Britain and France had done for years. Negative discrimination directed against particular nations was useful as an element of statecraft, but it created commercial rivalries and exacerbated national tensions. Such politicized trade could lead to tariff wars, but Hull believed that free multilateral trade would build bridges rather than create chasms between peoples and nations. As Harry Hawkins, Hull's deputy, said in 1944, "Nations which are economic enemies are not likely to be political friends for long."[8]

Indeed, even as late as 1938 Hull apparently believed that war could be prevented by negotiating a trade agreement with Nazi Germany. The Axis powers contended that discriminatory trading arrangements restricted their ability to export on equal terms, and because they were therefore unable to earn the **foreign exchange** necessary to purchase raw materials, they were forced to go to war to secure access to them. Thus, Hull championed the nondiscrimination principle, which had also been contained in the third of President Wilson's Fourteen Points for promoting peace at the end of World War I. In fact, because Hull's vision of the postwar order emphasized nondiscrimination in trading arrangements even more than expansion of trade volumes, multilateralism became the cornerstone of the GATT.

By contrast, the British valued free trade more than nondiscrimination, arguing that tariff reduction produced economic growth and that prosperity encouraged peace. Certainly interwar Europe illustrated that mercantilism could lead to economic failure, which in turn could generate dangerous levels of domestic instability. Such instability could foster antidemocratic and anticapitalist forces, as witnessed by the rapid rise of one-party governments throughout Europe in the early 1930s. Some of these were committed to economic and political programs—Nazism in Germany, fascism in Italy—that were bound to threaten international peace.

Liberals also borrowed an argument that had been developed a century earlier by Ricardo: that extensive trade among nations created a powerful incentive to avoid war that would disrupt it. Proponents of the Corn Laws had cautioned that to rely upon others for key commodities would compromise the autonomy of the nation's foreign policy, especially because one could not threaten war against nations that supplied essential food. Ricardo noted, however, that if free trade created a permanent need for England to import grain, then other nations would permanently arrange to produce a surplus to meet that demand. Eventually, England's reliance upon trade for consumption would be balanced by the other nation's dependence upon trade for export revenues, jobs, and profits. Therefore, domestic interests would exert enormous pressure on both governments to maintain friendly relations. Since then, interdependence theorists have used this argument to claim that free trade contributes as much to national security as self-sufficiency does.

For a combination of these reasons, policymakers in many nations came to share the view, expressed by President Roosevelt in a 1945 address to Congress, that an open trading system was necessary to make "the economic foundations of peace . . . as secure as the political foundations."

THE IDEALS AND INSTITUTIONS OF THE BRETTON WOODS SYSTEM

Specific historical factors sharpened the appeal of liberalism by accentuating the values of economic growth and international peace that liberalism emphasizes. Because the primary threats to those values—instability, protectionism, and discrimination—emanated from uncoordinated national policies, the Bretton Woods institutions were created to impose on national governments a liberal discipline they were incapable of achieving on their own. Each institution was designed to prevent one of the three forms of beggar-thy-neighbor policies that abounded in the 1930s: tariff barriers (GATT), competitive exchange-rate devaluations (IMF), and capital controls (IBRD). Although a liberal trading order was the paramount objective of Bretton Woods, mercantilist concerns never disappeared, and as a result, the tensions and discontinuities embodied in these two visions became imbedded in the system itself.

THE PRINCIPLES OF GATT

The Bretton Woods conference envisioned an International Trade Organization that would facilitate negotiations to reduce trade barriers, govern trade between negotiating sessions, and resolve other trade disputes. However, its aggressive quest for trade expansion, which went well beyond dismantling direct trade barriers such as tariffs and quotas, brought it into conflict with other national goals.[9] For example, recognizing that trade levels were determined not only by explicit barriers but also by general macroeconomic conditions, the ITO charter called on nations to maintain full employment policies. But powerful opposition, especially in the United States, viewed this provision as a violation of national sovereignty, arguing that each nation should be free to choose its own domestic economic policy. In America, this issue aroused great passion, in part because opponents were convinced that the full employment policies urged by Britain were a product of European beliefs influenced by socialist values. Thus, though the ITO charter was adopted at the United Nations Conference on Trade and Employment in Havana in 1948, it was never ratified in either the United States or Britain, the two chief negotiators.

Because the ITO was never created, the GATT, originally set up as a temporary vehicle to facilitate global tariff-reduction negotiations, has assumed a somewhat larger role.[10] Still, its principal activity has been the facilitation and supervision of a series of "rounds" of multilateral negotiations to reduce trade barriers, beginning with the 1947 Geneva negotiations involving twenty-three countries. By 1949, the GATT had thirty-three signatories and governed four-fifths of global trade. By the end of the Uruguay Round in 1994, ninety-six nations had become contracting parties to the GATT and twenty-eight others were in the process of negotiating accession, or entry, into the agreement.

The ultimate goals of GATT are classically liberal—the expansion of trade and the maintenance of a trading system free of political conflict—but the means used to accomplish them reveals an underlying philosophy that contains both liberal and mercantilist assumptions. After all, if nations accepted the liberal proposition that unilateral reduction of trade barriers is beneficial regardless of the policies of trading partners, negotiations would hardly be necessary. In fact, in contrast to the nineteenth-century British stance, the Bretton Woods philosophy assumes that beggar-thy-neighbor trade barriers can sometimes benefit a nation more than unilateral free trade, especially by exporting unemployment. This possibility was especially significant because the high unemployment experienced by all nations in the 1930s left policymakers wary of the simple Ricardian models that assumed full employment. It also left them unwilling to adopt free trade without some assurance that the expansion of exports would boost their employment as much as the growth of imports would erode it. Indeed, policymakers have come to think of employment growth as a more significant embodiment of the gains from trade expected of liberalism than lower import prices.[11]

Thus, under the GATT, any nation that lowers an import barrier is deemed to have made a "concession," because reduced protection risks the loss of jobs and profits in that sector. That concession produces a benefit to other nations that can seize this export opportunity to expand production. Negotiations are necessary to induce one nation to grant concessions to others. The actual negotiating procedures were not laid out in the initial agreements and have varied considerably in the various rounds of negotiations.[12] However achieved, the negotiations must meet two basic principles of GATT—**nondiscrimination** and **reciprocity**—while allowing exceptions for the third basic principle, the freedom to retain certain **national safeguards**.[13]

In theory, reciprocity is exceedingly simple: Each nation is expected to offer concessions equivalent to the benefits it derives from the concessions of others. For example, each nation's tariff reductions are expected to generate the same export revenue for other nations as the first will enjoy from the tariff reductions of others.[14] There are at least two major drawbacks to bilateral bargaining under the reciprocity principle, however.

First, it would not permit tariff reductions when trade patterns were "triangular." Suppose, for example, that Barbados exported sugar to the United States but not to Britain (because of shipping costs), that the United States exported computers to Britain but not to Barbados (because the demand was small), and that Britain exported autos to Barbados but not to the United States (because the steering wheel is on the "wrong" side). In such a circumstance, bilateral bargaining would fail because although the United States would be willing to lower its tariff against sugar from Barbados, Barbados would have nothing to offer to the United States in return. Likewise, Britain would be willing to increase its imports of American computers in return for equivalent concessions by the United States, but in this example, it sells nothing in the United States.

Second, bilateral bargaining would lead to as many tariff schedules for each product as there were trading partners. The United States would charge one duty for Haitian sugar, another for Jamaican sugar, and a third for sugar from Barbados—with the rate calibrated to the concessions offered by each. This complex system would invite deception by misrepresenting a product's origin or even by transshipping it through a third party to secure the lowest possible duty. Moreover, it would violate the liberal precept that a product should be exported by the most efficient producer—not the best negotiator.

Still, if the only goal had been to increase trade, such a system would have been workable. However, there was a more fundamental objection to it: Charging different duties to different nations constitutes discrimination—and that would inevitably politicize trade. Recall that the nondiscrimination principle was key to Hull's vision of a trading order that engendered peaceful political relations as well as efficient economic relations. Indeed, the importance of this principle may be gleaned from its location at the very beginning of the GATT, where it is embodied in Article 1's most-favored-nation (MFN) clause: "Any advantage, favor, privilege or immunity granted by any contracting party to any product originating in or destined for any other country shall be accorded immediately and unconditionally to the like product originating or destined for the territory of all other contracting parties." In other words, each signatory nation of GATT is prohibited from discriminating against any other signatory—either positively or negatively—by maintaining different trade barriers for different countries.[15] Similar provisions had been contained in all American treaties negotiated bilaterally since 1934 and most treaties negotiated by European nations since 1860.[16]

This system has undeniable appeal, but it considerably complicates the negotiation process. If a single tariff schedule applied to all trading partners, strictly bilateral negotiations could not be very effective because any concession granted to one nation would automatically be enjoyed by all the others as well. In effect, a nation would have an incentive to free ride by refusing to offer concessions that would meet its reciprocity obligations because under the nondiscrimination principle, it would still be able to benefit from the concessions granted by others. By contrast, without the nondiscrimination principle, reciprocity would be self-enforcing in the sense that nations unwilling to offer concessions would find themselves unable to achieve access to the markets of other nations. Though this free-rider problem never completely disappears, the unconditional MFN principle has been retained, in part because a certain degree of free riding has been considered preferable to enduring the economic costs and political consequences of discrimination. Since the hegemon is usually the principal victim of free riding, it can exercise either its tolerance or its power to mitigate the problem. Furthermore, various negotiating arrangements have been found to reduce the severity of free riding.

In the first five GATT rounds (Geneva, 1947; Annecy, 1949; Torquay, 1950–1951; Geneva, 1955–1956; and the Dillon Round in Geneva, 1960–1961), bargaining began with a series of bilateral negotiations using the principal-supplier rule to identify the parties to a negotiation. That is, each pair of nations would exchange requests for item-by-item tariff reductions on those products for which each was a principal supplier of the other. Each pair would then negotiate an agreement that achieved bilateral reciprocity by granting equivalent concessions to each side. Of course, because these tariff reductions would become available to all nations under the MFN clause, no nation could accurately assess the balance of concessions and benefits until all the preliminary agreements involving all pairs of nations had been concluded. At that point, the preliminary agreements would be amended through multilateral negotiations to take account of the indirect benefits received by each nation from the generalization of the bilateral agreements reached by other parties. This approach was adequate for the initial round in 1947, which achieved large nominal cuts (about 20 percent, covering about 78 percent of total imports), because many 1930s-era tariffs were too high to serve any real protectionist purpose and nations were thus willing to give them up easily.[17] However, the next four rounds produced very small gains (2–3 percent each, covering products that made up only about 10 percent of global trade) because the item-by-item approach permitted domestic interests to rally support for protection. The principal-supplier method resulted in a relatively low incidence of free riding, however. A nation that attempted to free ride usually found that tariffs on its leading exports remained high because other nations were not willing to offer concessions in exchange for benefits that they would share with a free rider. The last three rounds (the Kennedy Round, 1962–1967; the Tokyo Round, 1973–1979; and the Uruguay Round, 1986–1994) used a formula approach that began with an across-the-board cut followed by negotiations of item-by-item exceptions. This method produced a 35 percent cut in the Kennedy Round and another 30 percent cut in the Tokyo Round.

However, Bretton Woods is far from a pure free trade system. Old tariff barriers remain because complex negotiations to remove them take time, and new nontariff barriers have arisen in recent years. Moreover, significant antiliberal features—exceptions to the nondiscrimination and reciprocity principles—were built in to Bretton Woods from the outset.[18]

In fact, the GATT contains so many of these escape clauses that they may be said to collectively constitute a safeguard principle, which acknowledges that certain national interests are so essential that no international agreement could—or should—prevent nations from defending them. Thus, GATT accommodated these deviations from liberal principles because few nations could have accepted the agreement without such assurances. Three of these provisions are especially striking—though none has much import today—because they permit behavior that was central to classical British mercantilism. Under the grandfather clause of Article 1, paragraph 2, the British were permitted to retain the imperial preferences of the old British Empire. In extreme **balance of payments** deficit situations, Article 14 allows nontariff barriers (which otherwise would violate Article 11's prohibition of import quotas), even discriminatory ones (which would otherwise violate the MFN clause).[19] Under Article 21, a nation may take any action it "considers necessary for the protection of its essential security interests . . . in time of war or other emergency in international relations."

A more important exception to the non-discrimination provision is found in Article 24, which permits regional tariff preference areas such as the European Union and the North American Free Trade Agreement. A member of such a regional organization may apply a tariff schedule more favorable than the most-favored-nation rate to other member countries, but these discriminatory arrangements must meet three conditions to be considered GATT-legal. First, they must lower barriers inside the region rather than raise the others. Second, they must be completed over a "reasonable amount of time." Third, they must cover "substantially all" products. Although no regional arrangement has ever fully met these standards, all have been tacitly permitted.

Other escape clauses include Article 19, which permits nations to "suspend the obligation [of the GATT] in whole or in part"—that is, they may reduce or delay tariff reductions—if imports threaten domestic industries with "serious injury." Nations invoking this clause must offer equivalent compensation to affected parties, who are free to take retaliatory measures if they do not. Under Article 35, a member need not recognize GATT obligations toward new contracting parties, a provision originally included at India's request in anticipation of South African entry but used by fifteen nations upon the accession of Japan in 1955. Finally, Article 25 authorizes the contracting parties, on a two-thirds vote, to grant waivers of GATT obligations "in exceptional circumstances not elsewhere provided."

The sum of these exceptions compose a significant mercantilist element within a structure that is ostensibly liberal. Indeed, business interests in the United States opposed the Havana Charter in part because they felt that these provisions would have made the agreement "a step away from, not toward, the goal of multilateral trade."[20]

THE FINANCIAL INSTITUTIONS OF THE BRETTON WOODS SYSTEM

The financial institutions of Bretton Woods—the IMF and IBRD—were designed to facilitate this new trading order. To do so, they had to resolve the problems that led to a disintegration of the international monetary order of the interwar years, which was fully as damaging as the collapse of the global trading system. In fact, problems in each realm contributed to the demise of the other. For our purposes, the most significant difficulty concerned the inability of nations to finance trade through the easy conversion of their currencies into acceptable media of exchange.[21]

Conventionally, economists divide the challenge of maintaining an adequate international financial system into three interrelated problems: **liquidity**, adjustment, and confidence. In order to finance trade, the international financial system must provide a medium of exchange, that is, some "liquid" asset that traders will accept as money. Without such liquidity, private actors could exchange goods only through barter. National currencies do not provide a complete solution, since firms resist accepting payments in a foreign currency unless assured that it can be easily converted into the currency in which they conduct most of their business.

Ordinarily, the central banks of individual nations provide this assurance—and thus facilitate trade—by exchanging national currencies for one another. However, they are willing to perform this exchange function only if they have enough confidence in the values of these currencies to hold sufficient stocks of them. Just like private firms, central banks are reluctant to accumulate foreign exchange unless they are assured that it is liquid, that is, that it can be easily exchanged at a reliable and predictable price. Unless the system provides some basis for this confidence, banks will not maintain a large enough inventory of currencies to provide the liquidity necessary to accommodate a large volume of trade.

From 1870 to 1914, the mechanism that solved these two problems was the **gold standard**; central banks accepted gold as the ultimate liquid asset and individual national governments guaranteed a fixed conversion rate between gold and their national currency. Since each nation maintained a reserve of gold to back its currency—each nation's central bank agreed to exchange its currency for gold at a fixed price—the system worked well to facilitate trade and investment transactions. In fact, so long as the supply of gold was adequate and confidence was high that national monetary authorities would redeem currency for gold as promised, it was possible for nations to allow temporary imbalances in their accounts to accumulate. Any successful system must tolerate such temporary disequilibrium because it is inevitable that levels of imports and exports will fluctuate in the short term as prices and other economic conditions change.

Of course, there are limits to the confidence one can have in national monetary authorities and thus limits to the tolerance for disequilibrium. These limits are a function of the size of the deficits that are accumulating, the size of the gold reserves nations maintain to settle those deficits, and the ability of national governments to adjust their economies in the event that it becomes evident that those deficits result from long-term rather than short-term factors. For example, if a nation's exports continually lag behind its imports—presumably because its production is not competitive with firms in other countries—it has available three methods of adjustment. First, it may lower the price at which it agrees to exchange its currency for gold. This devaluation of the exchange rate makes it more expensive to purchase foreign currency and therefore foreign products, so imports should decline. Devaluation also makes a nation's own currency cheaper for others to purchase, so its exports will grow. Second, a nation may erect barriers to inflows of goods (imports) and outflows of capital (foreign investment). Third, it may contract the domestic economy so that citizens have less money to spend and consequently purchase fewer imports. In all three cases, a new equilibrium should be reached in which imports and exports once again balance each other. Confidence in the system is better maintained if trade stability causes disequilibria to be temporary and small, if liquidity is high enough to make adjustment relatively rare, and if a hegemonic actor can force countries to adjust responsibly when adjustment becomes necessary. During the period of British hegemony, the latter role was played effectively by a combination of the political power of the British government and the economic power of the City of London, whose banks controlled a large portion of the world's gold supply and influenced a still larger portion of the capital available for investment and loans.

Responsible adjustment is important to the system because any form of adjustment by one nation is inevitably disruptive to all others. Rapid or massive exchange-rate adjustments undermine the predictability of transactions and discourage trade. Devaluations especially arouse the ire of foreigners who are holding a currency when its value declines—and makes them wary of holding it in the future. Other nations are also resentful of any form of adjustment that shifts competitiveness more than required to reestablish equilibrium. Of course, they are particularly opposed to forms of adjustment, such as import barriers and capital controls, that restrict their ability to trade.

The gold standard worked efficiently so long as the gold supply was adequate to the routine liquidity needs of the system, so long as confidence in the pound sterling was sufficient to augment that liquidity in an emergency, so long as confidence in the hegemony of Britain to manage the system was unquestioned, and so long as the imbalances to be financed were small enough in relation to gold reserves that adjustments were modest and infrequent. After World War I, none of these conditions held. Severe inflation eroded the purchasing power of gold so that it no longer provided enough liquidity to facilitate trade, let alone the enormous amount required for payment of huge German war reparations owed to European nations and massive war debts incurred by European nations to the United States. Aided by the dislocations of a global economic downturn and considerable speculation in currency markets, rapidly shifting supply and demand for currencies left nations unable to maintain exchange-rate stability. The gold standard was abandoned, leading to a period of sharp volatility in the relative prices of currencies that discouraged trade.

Britain's ability to manage the system waned because its economic power declined. Further, international norms broke down as an increasing variety of national political systems arose—from the New Deal in the United States to fascism in Europe—each dominated by different values and committed to different economic theories. Nations selected adjustment policies in keeping with their own perspectives, seemingly indifferent to the disruptions these adjustments caused abroad.

Specifically, nations adopted protectionist trade policies and beggar-thy-neighbor exchange-rate policies in which they devalued their currencies in order to encourage exports and discourage imports. These competitive exchange-rate devaluations, like the tariff increases and export subsidies that they mimicked, elicited retaliatory responses from other nations that soon degenerated into a spiral of chaotic rate fluctuations. The resulting instability in exchange rates increased the uncertainty and risk of trade, which in turn inevitably led to falling trade levels. Nations also restricted the external flow of capital both to better control their exchange rates and to keep investment at home, where it was needed to rebuild the economy. Just as trade declined enormously, so did financial flows. Hence, the Great Depression had roots in monetary chaos as well as the collapse of trade. Further, national hostilities generated by beggar-thy-neighbor monetary policies exacerbated those stemming from trade disputes.

Thus, a new international financial system had to be created that would solve the problems of liquidity, confidence, and adjustment against the backdrop of new political and economic realities. Some of these economic realities—such as the increase in liquidity required by the meteoric rise in trade, investment, and loan levels—posed greater challenges, but the political reality of a powerful United States committed to hegemonic leadership offered a greatly enhanced capacity to meet them. The method chosen was the Bretton Woods system, centered around the dollar-gold standard, an IMF-enforced system of fixed exchange rates, and massive capital flows provided by the World Bank and the United States.

Liquidity was provided by a combination of gold and the U.S. dollar, which were linked by the U.S. Federal Reserve's commitment to freely exchange gold and dollars at the rate of $35 per ounce. Given the gold shortage, nations held most of their international reserves in the form of U.S. dollars, the system's reserve currency. This meant that the liquidity of the dollar-gold standard rested on huge U.S. gold stockpiles and the willingness of the United States to export enough dollars—through balance-of-trade deficits, investment flows, loans, and Marshall Plan aid—to maintain reserve assets and facilitate trade. Confidence in this system also rested on trust in the United States because the dollar could be debased at any time through irresponsible action by U.S. monetary authorities or miscalculation of the system's liquidity needs. Hegemonic stability theorists correctly note that only the U.S. dollar commanded sufficient respect to guarantee the confidence of most observers and that only the United States had sufficient political and economic power to silence those that did not share it.

It was still necessary, however, to restrict the ability of nations to choose adjustment policies that harmed others, especially the trade barriers, capital controls, and competitive exchange-rate devaluations that had contributed to the collapse of the 1930s. In particular, the International Monetary Fund was created to supervise a new system under which the **par value** of each currency was defined in relation to the U.S. dollar. Each nation was required to use its reserves in order to maintain this par value by buying or selling dollars in exchange for its own currency until supply and demand once again balanced at the agreed upon rate. Furthermore, governments were prevented from undertaking a unilateral change in this exchange rate without IMF approval, which was considered a means of last resort to resolve persistent balance-of-trade deficits. Neither could nations "adopt any monetary or general price measure or policy" that would threaten the balance-of-payments equilibrium of other nations without a four-fifths vote of IMF member states. Thus, in the hope of preventing the wild currency speculation, capital flows, and bank failures that were common during the Great Depression, the IMF was empowered to constrain extreme and illiberal macroeconomic policies of governments. But the cost—in terms of sacrificing national sovereignty—was high.

In practice, these restrictions encouraged adjustment to trade deficits by contractionary domestic policies, including high interest rates and either high taxes or low government expenditures. Although these policies would slow the economy enough to restrain imports and would restore equilibrium with minimal impact on others, they were also likely to promote domestic unemployment. Since the pressures on national governments to maintain full employment were well understood, the system also provided means by which major adjustments could be delayed as long as possible in the hope that the disequilibrium would prove to be temporary or that minor adjustments would work given enough time.

Those means involved short-term loans from the IMF itself and long-term loans for war-recovery purposes from the IBRD. The latter provided a financing facility to repay war debts, provide for reconstruction, and aid balance-of-payments difficulties. The motivation for the World Bank was not only to provide an option for nations tempted to control trade and investment; it was also predicated on the assumption that the loan-induced prosperity of Europe would contribute to trade that could raise the prosperity of all the nations of the globe together. The same logic later applied to the Third World, where the bulk of IBRD loans have been directed since the 1950s.

Thus, the Bretton Woods system was an attempt to encourage nations to maintain liberal trade policies while allowing some measure of national autonomy. For many years it worked; global trade increased at an unprecedented historical rate and the global economy expanded rapidly. Since its founding, however, the Bretton Woods system has undergone major changes, especially with respect to finance. Confidence in the dollar eroded as persistent American balance-of-payments deficits dumped more dollars onto international currency markets than could be redeemed by U.S. gold stocks, eventually forcing the United States to abandon the commitment. With the link between gold and the dollar broken in the early 1970s, most developed nations ceased to peg their currencies to either gold or the dollar. In fact, because the huge increase in private capital flows has overwhelmed the ability of nations to control currency values, since the 1970s most major currencies "float," that is, their exchange rates are determined by supply and demand in global currency markets. Consequently, the surveillance of member's foreign-exchange policies is no longer the prime function of the IMF, which now plays a much more important role in Third World development.

Of course, all of the Bretton Woods institutions have adapted to changing circumstances, though not as dramatically as in monetary arrangements. Changes in the trade dimension of Bretton Woods can be seen in the most recent incarnation of GATT, the just-concluded Uruguay Round of trade negotiations.

THE URUGUAY ROUND OF GATT

The eighth round of GATT negotiations, the so-called Uruguay Round, was launched in September 1986 with the Punta del Este Declaration. After the longest and most difficult bargaining in GATT history, the 22,000-page Marrakech protocol was signed in April 1994 by 123 nations. The agreement entered into force in January 1995 after protracted ratification fights in several nations, especially the United States.

The difficulties and delays were due in part to a continuing deterioration in three conditions that had once been helpful in achieving trade agreements. First, the interests of the various parties to GATT agreements have diverged. The major trading nations are now trade competitors rather than allies in either hot or cold wars. Further, they no longer share the values and theories that once underpinned both national policies and the multilateral system. Second, the distribution of power among nations has fragmented. The erosion of American preeminence has left the system without hegemonic leadership, and the ascendance of Third World nations to positions of greater competitive danger in markets has increased their influence. Negotiations have become much more complicated as membership has expanded from 23 to 123. Third, global growth has slowed and the political pressure on national governments to improve economic performance—especially when threatened from abroad—has correspondingly risen. As a result, the agenda of trade negotiations must now reflect many more perspectives.

At the same time, the issues discussed produce greater rancor, especially because they touch the fundamental dilemmas of trade more deeply. In this, the GATT suffers from the legacy of its own success: Because the first seven rounds of negotiations had already accomplished the easiest tasks, the remaining ones represented challenges to the global trading system that were both profoundly different and substantially more difficult than those surmounted previously.

For example, the across-the-board tariff cuts that had formed the centerpiece of previous rounds did not occupy the core of the Uruguay Round negotiations. After previous GATT rounds had lowered tariff rates to about a 4 percent average on most industrial products, they were no longer a significant barrier in most products and in most markets. However, the tariffs that remain, which are concentrated in a few "peaks" surrounded by virtually zero rates on most products, are very resistant to further reduction. Because decades of negotiations have rooted out most tariffs, the remaining ones are invariably those that pose the most serious dilemmas and thus command the strongest political support. Thus, across-the-board tariff reductions were a high priority only in relation to a handful of newly industrializing countries (NICs), especially South Korea and Brazil, whose protectionist policies are no longer tolerated now that they compete effectively with more developed nations. Still, further progress was made with average tariff reductions of 36 percent (including at least 15 percent in all categories) phased in over six years.

However, the Uruguay Round negotiations were dominated by two other agenda items. First, GATT principles and procedures were extended into sectors not previously covered, especially agriculture and services. Second, the rules of trade were clarified and the procedures to deal with disputes that arise under them were institutionalized by creating the World Trade Organization (WTO).

The extension of the GATT into new sectors reflects both changes in the nature of modern economies and shifts in the power balances among nations. For example, the inclusion of textiles and tropical products reflects the growing importance of less developed countries (LDCs), but U.S. bargaining power minimized the changes they sought. While the highly protectionist Multi-Fiber Agreement is being phased out, the United States will lower its textile tariffs by an average of only 12 percent, phased in over ten years, not the 50 percent cut demanded by the EU. Even so, U.S. Senate ratification of GATT was delayed by Senator Ernest "Fritz" Hollings of South Carolina, a powerful committee chairman who claimed that 40,000 jobs in his home state would be endangered by even these modest reductions.

At the insistence of the United States, the service sector, which now accounts for about two-thirds of the American economy, was incorporated into GATT for the first time. Several areas were liberalized, especially accounting, advertising, computer services, and engineering; negotiations continued in telecommunications and several other areas that were not completed in time for the Marrakech protocol. The United States achieved some successes in trade-related aspects of intellectual property (so-called TRIPs) but failed in others. Because pirating currently costs Americans between $40 and $60 billion annually, the United States sought to guarantee that other nations would honor patents, copyrights, trademarks, and designs, especially in the software, chips, biotechnology, and entertainment sectors. For example, computer programs are now treated as literary works that require copyright fees. However, barriers to trade in services remain, such as French restrictions on the percentage of radio and television content that originates abroad or in languages other than French, restrictions that were challenged by Hollywood and by American rock musicians. The United States also pressed trade-related investment measures (TRIMs), contending that regulating foreign investment by multinational corporations unfairly restricts access to markets.

The most challenging new sector to be addressed in the Uruguay Round was agriculture. On the one hand, liberal theory makes an especially compelling case for free trade in agriculture: Agricultural policies in industrial countries cost consumers between $200 and $300 billion per year.[22] However, trade dilemmas have also enlisted the support of an unusually formidable collection of political forces. Indeed, many countries wanted agricultural trade on the agenda, but only a small group of highly efficient exporters (headed by Canada's and Australia's grain-exporting interests) unequivocally supported free trade in agriculture. Most of the rest, including the United States, wanted liberalization only in their main export crops. As a result, agriculture produced the most difficult bargaining of the Uruguay Round, resulting in so many delays and missed schedules that many doubted that an agreement could ever be reached.

Agriculture presented a unique challenge because its special role in most political economies ensures that any liberalization in this sector will induce extensive distributional consequences and uncomfortable trade-offs with other values. Nearly all nations are committed to sustaining a healthy agricultural sector because a relatively large, geographically concentrated and occupationally inflexible population is dependent upon it. Many cultural and political issues also swirl beneath the surface, exemplified by the Japanese symbolic commitment to self-sufficiency in rice production. Moreover, because agricultural policy in most nations is a complex combination of various subsidies and nontariff barriers (NTBs), it is difficult to compute its actual protective effect. As a result, the agreement requires that all nations replace NTBs with equivalent (or lower) "bound" tariffs. This "tariffication" simplifies negotiations because it allows a better comparison of the protectionist effects of different national policies.

Tariff rates were reduced in all products, guaranteeing at least minimal access to even previously closed markets such as Japanese and Korean rice. Among developed countries, the rates on each product must be reduced by at least 15 percent, with an average reduction across all products of 35 percent after a phase-in period of six years. LDCs are permitted ten years to phase in reductions of at least 10 percent, with an average of 24 percent. Markets receiving $8 billion in U.S. agricultural exports were affected by the elimination of NTBs.

The principal protagonists in the dispute over agriculture—the United States and the EU—clashed with particular ferocity over subsidies. The United States, which itself subsidizes farmers in a variety of ways, nonetheless took a hard line because about 60 percent of U.S. agricultural exports face subsidized export competition. The EU, whose Common Agricultural Policy (CAP) has been described as "the acknowledged paragon of farm-trade lunacy," resisted strongly, not least because the diversity of interests among its twelve member nations made any agreement, even among themselves, exceedingly delicate.[23] Before the agreement, the United States spent about $1 in subsidy for every $100 in agricultural exports, and the EU spent about $25. The agreement requires at least a 21 percent reduction in volume of each subsidized agricultural export as well as a 36 percent reduction in budgetary outlays overall, to be phased in over six years. As a result, the EU would cut subsidies by $5–$7 billion, the United States about $500 million. LDCs are permitted ten years to phase in minimum reductions of 14 percent by volume and 24 percent in total cost.

The agreement also attacks government support for agriculture other than explicit export subsidies. Some of these programs are exempted, for example, research, pest and disease control, extension services, and crop insurance, but the remainder must be cut by 20 percent from the 1986–1988 base period over six years (LDCs have ten years to cut 13 percent). This modest reduction has already been achieved by recent changes in both the EU and the United States.

Perhaps the most visible accomplishment of the Uruguay Round is the creation of a permanent trade institution, the **World Trade Organization**, nearly fifty years after the proposed ITO was abandoned. The WTO will supervise trade rules that have been clarified and tightened. For example, distinctions are drawn more clearly between export subsidies (which are prohibited) and subsidies to meet goals such as regional development, environmental protection, and improved industrial research (which are not). The use of "health measures" as protectionist devices will be disciplined by requiring scientific evidence to support the need for an import restriction. Similarly, technical barriers to trade—the use of testing, certification, and other procedures as a protectionist measure—are now restricted. Finally, there are more precise rules for countervailing duties.

The WTO's dispute-resolution mechanism has been the most controversial issue during the ratification debate in the United States. Under the old GATT procedure, disputes were investigated by a special panel, but because its rulings were subject to a consensus among all the GATT members, every nation had a veto over any adverse judgment. By contrast, the decision of the WTO's dispute-resolution panel would stand unless reversed by a consensus on appeal. These panels are also given a more explicit standard of review that will increase the predictability of action, and investigating authorities are now required to provide public notice and written explanations of their actions. These improvements are long overdue because some enforcement mechanism is necessary if GATT is to be effective. Further, trade disputes, which so often reflect technically complex and politically difficult trade dilemmas, have become more heated since the early 1980s. Indeed, the United States argued most strongly for the new rules because of frustration over the ineffectiveness of the old GATT mechanism, which it used more than any other nation.

However, a surprising variety of American groups have opposed the WTO as a violation of national sovereignty. Environmental groups such as Friends of the Earth, Greenpeace, and the Sierra Club have been joined by consumer advocates such as Ralph Nader but, surprisingly, also by conservatives such as Ross Perot, Pat Buchanan, Jesse Helms, and Howard Phillips of the Conservative Caucus. They fear that a WTO panel could rule that various U.S. government policies constitute unfair trade practices. Already, a GATT panel has ruled that the Marine Mammal

Protection Act is an unfair trade restriction because it prohibits the importation of tuna caught by nets that also kill dolphins. EU automakers have also challenged the U.S. law that establishes standards for auto emissions and fuel economy. Buchanan says, "WTO means putting America's trade under foreign bureaucrats who will meet in secret to demand changes in U.S. laws. . . . WTO tramples all over American sovereignty and states' rights."[24] Because the WTO could not force a change in American law, GATT director general Peter Sutherland called this position "errant nonsense," but the WTO could impose sanctions or authorize an offended nation to withdraw trade concessions as compensation for the injury.[25] Thus, in July 1994, attorneys general from forty-two states wrote President Clinton saying the agreement could jeopardize state sovereignty. A survey conducted by the U.S. Chamber of Commerce in June 1994 found that 67 of the 170 House members who responded and that 13 of the 44 Senators listed the WTO-sovereignty issue as among their principal areas of concern.

CONCLUSION: TRADE DILEMMAS AND INTERNATIONAL INSTITUTIONS

The controversies surrounding contemporary international institutions are replete with trade dilemmas. The familiar liberal benefits claimed for GATT are too huge to be dismissed even if U.S. trade representative Mickey Kantor's prediction of $1 trillion in gains over ten years is disputed by the much smaller estimates of the World Bank, the Organization for Cooperation and Development (OECD), the Institute for International Economics, and the Economic Policy Institute. These benefits must be balanced, however, against other considerations.

Liberalizing trade produces winners and losers. The World Bank predicts that Africa will be a net loser of the Uruguay Round because its costs for food imports will rise and the prices of commodities exported by African nations, such as tea, coffee, and cocoa, will fall. In the United States, the distributional dilemma of trade has been raised by industry groups ranging from corn growers to textile producers.

If the present conception of the WTO is controversial, it would become more so under a **social clause** considered by the preparatory committee for the WTO. Various proposals under this clause would exempt from GATT benefits any exports produced by slave labor, child labor, workers prohibited from organizing and bargaining collectively through labor unions, or those denied a minimum wage or health and safety protection. Such proposals are unlikely to be accepted, however, because they seek agreement where none is possible: Not all nations share the values implied by the willingness to sacrifice commerce for other ends.

Neither has time diminished the dilemmas concerning the effect of trade on the state. Instead, many contemporary issues revisit enduring problems of national sovereignty, such as the various safeguard measures employed by nations pursuant to Article 19. The very mercantilist exceptions that made the liberalism of Bretton Woods acceptable to nations have come under attack, revealing the inherent inconsistencies of the system. Indeed, the international trading order struggles with the coexistence of systemic institutions more liberal than mercantilist and national policies inclined to be more mercantilist than liberal.

FIVE

□ □ □

Neomercantilism and Bilateral Trade Issues

The Bretton Woods system achieved its goals of material prosperity and international peace, but these successes were neither complete nor permanent. International institutions can constrain—but ultimately cannot prevent—the adoption of national policies that disrupt market-based trade or create foreign policy friction. Nowhere is this more evident than in the conflict-ridden trade relations between the United States and Japan, the focus of this chapter.

U.S.-JAPANESE TRADE TENSIONS

The signs of trade-induced strain between the United States and Japan are evident in both formal diplomatic relations and in public opinion, with so-called Japan-bashing often heard on street corners and in Congress. Polls show that Americans now have a less favorable opinion of Japan than of longtime enemy Russia.[1] U.S. complaints center on the bilateral trade deficit with Japan, which has hovered around $50 billion annually since 1985 and which exceeded $65 billion in 1994.[2] Japan rejects culpability for the deficit: A 1993 poll revealed that 85 percent of Japanese felt that America unfairly blames Japan. Furthermore, Japan complains that American efforts to reduce the trade deficit violate principles that are both imbedded in international law and regularly professed by American trade officials. As a result, a recent poll found that only 45 percent of the Japanese now regard America as trustworthy.[3] Diplomatic relations reached a low point in summer 1995 with the parties exchanging threats of trade sanctions amid heated bilateral negotiations that did more to aggravate tensions than to resolve issues.

93

Friendly partners? Danziger—©*The Christian Science Monitor*

It is difficult to overstate the significance of this trade conflict between the globe's two largest national economies, which together account for about one-third of total world production. It jeopardizes their bilateral trade, which at more than $150 billion per year in the early 1990s exceeded that of any other pair of nations except the United States and Canada. Japan depends on U.S. markets to accept 30 percent of its exports and on American products, which constitute 25 percent of its imports.[4] The fallout from the trade dispute could also endanger other facets of the economic relationship. For example, the United States relies on Japanese capital to supply needed investment funds—Japanese investors hold more than $100 billion in foreign direct investment in the United States and a similar amount in U.S. Treasury bonds—and Japanese investors depend upon the health of the American economy to generate returns on that investment.[5] Furthermore, the credibility—perhaps even the survival—of the newly created WTO, the centerpiece of the new world trade order, may hang in the balance. In June 1995, the United States, which had been the chief sponsor of the WTO when created only six months previously, threatened sanctions against Japan that, if imposed, would have violated WTO rules.

At the heart of the dispute are complaints by American business that Japan exports too much and imports too little. Accusations of unfair trading practices have been accompanied by calls for the management of trade by the United States in order to ensure a level playing field. In fact, the phrase "fair trade" is now more often articulated as a goal than "free trade." U.S. labor has reacted stridently to the influx of Japanese products in the United States, arguing that imports steal American jobs. The bitterness is reflected in heated rhetoric, such as U.S. Representative John Dingell of Michigan's declaration that "there's only one reason our automobile industry is hurting—those little yellow people."[6] The view from the other side of the Pacific is different: Yoshio Sakurauchi, the speaker of Japan's lower house, opined that America can't compete because "U.S. workers are too lazy" and that "about 30 percent" of American workers "cannot even read."[7] It is difficult to avoid the conclusion that racism plays a role in the perceptions by each nation of the other, but real economic differences lie beneath the bombast.

The case for attributing the bilateral trade imbalance to unfair Japanese practices receives support from the observation that Japan has maintained a trade surplus with the rest of the world—not just with the United States. In fact, other nations have also denounced Japan's trade surplus, which exceeded $100 billion per year from 1992 to 1994 and now stands at about 3 percent of its **gross domestic product** (GDP). Indeed, Japan has had difficult economic relations for some time: Fourteen nations invoked Article 35 of the GATT in refusing to accord MFN status to Japan when it became a contracting party in 1955. In the 1980s, Japan was warned by the German economics minister that "trade should not be a one-way street" and by the British prime minister that the trade imbalance "cannot continue without threatening the breakdown of the free trading system."[8]

This antagonism is magnified because Japan runs large trade deficits with countries that supply raw materials and large surpluses with most developed nations.[9] In the latter countries, such as the United States, sectors that compete with Japanese imports constitute a strong domestic political constituency that is hostile toward Japanese trade. Ordinarily, protectionist pressures emanating from import-competing sectors are counterbalanced by liberal lobbying from the export sector, but the bilateral trade deficits that most advanced countries run with Japan translate into a deficit of political action in favor of liberalism. As a result, Japan has been forced to reach agreements with European governments similar to those negotiated with the United States, such as export restraints on automobiles.

Nevertheless, with a **current account** surplus during the 1980s of about $700 billion, Japan has become the largest creditor in global history. Japanese ownership of foreign assets exceeded $2 trillion early in the 1990s and continues to grow at more than $100 billion per year, a pattern bound to alarm those who see trade as a zero-sum game in which one nation can gain power at the expense of others. In short, the U.S.-Japanese trade gap reflects forces at work in Japan's relations with other nations as well.

At the same time, however, Japan uses a similar logic in locating the source of the bilateral imbalance in U.S. economic policy, noting that the American trade deficit is not unique to its links with Japan. Indeed, the United States has become the world's largest debtor after a decade of current-account deficits amounting to about $1 trillion. Because the gap with Japan accounts for only about 40 percent of that, many feel that Japan is being used as a scapegoat for a broader American problem. They argue that the bilateral trade imbalance with Japan—and the related decrease in the value of the dollar from over 300 yen in the 1960s to under 100 yen in the 1990s—may be a symbol of American decline but not its cause. As one commentator put it, "To blame Japan for U.S. trade deficits is a lot like blaming your banker because you are in debt."[10]

Indeed, American fixation on the trade deficit with Japan is partly a reflection of anxiety about the loss of American hegemony. Although still the world's largest economy and exporter, the United States is no longer as far ahead of its competitors as it once was. In the early 1950s the United States accounted for about 45 percent of total global production (including 80 percent of the world's cars), held 43 percent of international reserves, and furnished about 20 percent of global exports. By the beginning of the 1990s, U.S. production and exports had grown significantly, but because that growth was not nearly as rapid as that in the rest of the world, U.S. production had slipped to about 25 percent of total output, international reserves were down to 6 percent of the global total, and U.S. exports made up less than 12 percent of international trade. American firms no longer produced 80 percent of the autos driven in the United States, let alone in the entire world.[11] Meanwhile, Japan's exports had grown from 2 percent to 10 percent of the global total.[12]

Americans, having gotten used to global dominance, naturally assumed that something had gone frightfully wrong when it began to diminish. Realistically, however, it is the 1950s that should be considered exceptional—U.S. dominance in the immediate postwar period represented the greatest concentration of economic power by any one nation in history. The global depression of the 1920s and 1930s, a massively devastating war fought on the territory of the other leading economic powers in the 1940s, and the unusually prominent role of the United States in Europe in the immediate aftermath of that war all helped to propel the United States to a position of dominance that could not possibly be sustained after the recovery that eventually ensued.

Still, it cannot be surprising that such a steep relative decline would be psychologically disturbing to Americans. Furthermore, hegemonic stability theory reminds us that bilateral conflicts, along with the rising tide of regionalism and mercantilism that helps spawn them, are characteristic of any period of declining hegemony. Thus, because the 1990s mark the culmination of two decades of relative decline by the United States and five decades of remarkable growth in Japan, the contemporary strain in bilateral relations between these two powers should not be too surprising. Also, these conditions merely bring to the fore a conflict that is always latent among trading nations because it stems from a fundamental dilemma built into the way that international trade affects the state.[13]

THE EFFECTS OF INTERNATIONAL TRADE ON THE STATE

Despite liberal insistence that trade produces peace, the historical record shows that trade-related conflict is far from unique to the American-Japanese case. Theorists such as Harold Laski and E. H. Carr argue that the expansion of trade frequently creates competitive struggles for markets, raw materials, and investment outlets. The hostilities that led to World War I have been attributed to national rivalries sharpened by a drive for colonies motivated by this competition. Both Japanese and German justifications for World War II cited similar goals in the drive for spheres of influence that ultimately became campaigns of conquest.

Common to these cases is a structural reality emphasized by mercantilists: States cooperate for economic gain; they also use trade to compete for political power. It is ironic that this dualistic facet of international relations is portrayed most vividly by the liberal theorist Adam Smith:

> Being neighbors, [England and France] are necessarily enemies, and the wealth and power of each becomes, upon that account more formidable to the other; and what would increase the advantage of national friendship serves only to inflame the violence of national animosity.[14]

Thus, the attitude of a nation toward the economic success of a trade partner is torn between these two visions.

> The wealth of a neighboring nation, however, though dangerous in war and politics, is certainly advantageous in trade. In a state of hostility it may enable our enemies to maintain fleets and armies superior to our own; but in a state of peace and commerce it must likewise enable them to exchange with us to a greater value, and to afford a better market...for the produce of our own industry.[15]

A market perspective sees neighboring nations as potential customers, but the state must also see them as potential enemies. Which resolution of this dilemma will dominate policy depends upon circumstances. If conflict seems likely—or even possible—the state must consider not only the absolute gains from trade but also its relative gains. Following Smith's famous observation that "defence is more important than opulence," it may then be necessary for a state to refrain from trade that would be more advantageous to its potential enemies than to itself. As a result, conflict becomes most likely when changes in respective power levels become visible, because that is when a nation becomes less concerned with its own absolute gain than with the relative gain of a rival.

Whereas few analysts expect the American-Japanese economic rivalry to erupt into war, many do suggest that the United States should seek to strike a balance between these two considerations. That is, in recognition of the dilemma, the United States should manage trade so as to minimize the long-term threat to national interests that the rapid ascendance of a rival may represent. In practice, that means insisting upon reciprocity in trade relations so that neither party gains more than the other even if it requires limiting trade and sacrificing some of its benefits. It also means emphasizing trade with partners who are more likely to be allies than enemies, because trade may cement a friendly relationship while intensifying the conflict in an antagonistic one. Such a policy is a dangerous tightrope, however, because, as liberals note, interference with trade, especially in a discriminatory way, has often triggered major conflicts. Nonetheless, critics of American trade policy point to the persistence of the trade deficit as evidence that the United States has been less attentive than Japan to the long-term implications of trade for these power-related dimensions of the national interest.

Trade may also generate dilemmas for the state by conveying macroeconomic conditions such as inflation, employment levels, and interest rates from one nation to its trading partners. For example, during the 1930s, the American depression spread worldwide, in part because the decline of American imports meant unemployment for the export sectors of other nations. The consequences of this interdependence will be relatively benign if trade partners have similar macroeconomic goals, but if they do not, trade may be disruptive enough to produce foreign policy tensions.

Unfortunately, the United States and Japan pursue quite different values, and the resulting divergence in economic policy brings injury to both. For example, the two countries display very different attitudes toward the value trade-off represented by the choice of consuming today versus saving for tomorrow. Japanese economic policy strongly encourages savings and discourages consumption, thereby reinforcing a preference that appears to be prevalent among Japanese households anyway. Restraining consumption carries the side effect of limiting Japanese imports, which constrains the exports and slows the growth of other economies, especially the United States. In response, other nations have pressured Japan to stimulate its economy through increased government spending in the hope that the resulting rise in Japanese imports would also stimulate their economies.[16] By contrast, the United States maintains an unusually low national savings rate.[17] As a result, high levels of individual, corporate, and government debt require foreign borrowing that limits the supply of investment funds available elsewhere in the world. Consequently, other nations—especially Japan—have urged the U.S. government to cut its budget deficit, which would lower imports (by limiting American consumption) and stem the disruptive flow of capital out of their economies.[18]

The tensions created by such disruptive interdependence can be minimized if the injured party accepts a charitable interpretation of the motivations of the other, but this is likely only when nations are already inclined toward friendship. For example, during the Cold War, the presence of the Soviet Union as a common enemy unified American and Japanese foreign policy interests and soothed economic tensions. Now, however, differences in culture and ethnicity reinforce lingering wariness from World War II, all of which inflame and complicate a conflict that remains rooted in a $50 billion per year bilateral trade imbalance.

Of course, Senator John Danforth has said that "the issue is not the size of the trade deficit; the issue is to make sure that both sides play by the same rules."[19] But that is precisely the problem: It is difficult to agree upon rules when judgments of what is fair are so deeply imbedded in such very different cultural and theoretical systems. Because the issues touch upon dilemmas of trade that are evaluated very differently on opposite sides of the Pacific, each party finds it easier to see the other as a competitor and an enemy than as a partner and an ally.

DIFFERENCES IN TRADE POLICIES

Simply put, major differences in the economic policies of the United States and Japan make a collision between them inevitable. In particular, American and Japanese trade policies have moved in opposite directions since the end of World War II, just as predicted by List when he observed that dominant nations are typically free traders and trailing nations usually adopt a protectionist stance. Japan, which had lagged behind Europe and North America in productivity even before the war devastation, adopted a mercantilist trade policy that emphasized promotion of exports and protection from imports. Since about 1975, however, when Japan became fully competitive in global markets, its trade policy has moved away from mercantilist extremes.[20] Indeed, by the mid–1980s Japanese tariffs were comparable to those of the United States and the EU, though the actual level of imports remains lower in Japan than in other developed nations.

Meanwhile, as American economic and political dominance declined after the early 1970s, U.S. policy slowly drifted away from the liberalism it had embraced as a hegemonic leader. Though the United States remains committed to a liberal international system, American policy has become more aggressive in tone, more unilateral in spirit, and more mercantilist in substance. Its trade policy now emphasizes a range of defensive tools that, though meant to support its liberal rhetoric, are increasingly seen as protectionist by others and as the *source* of trade tensions rather than an antidote to them. In short, most commentators still see American trade policy as predominantly liberal and Japanese trade policy as predominantly mercantilist, but the differences between them have dramatically narrowed in recent years.

Still, the differences between the trade policies of the United States and Japan are much greater than can be explained by the competitiveness of their firms in international markets. In fact, they lie in prevailing theories and values, the state of markets, and the balance of power among key domestic and international actors. Each of these factors helps to explain why the two nations have judged the dilemmas of trade so differently and adopted divergent policies that reflect their respective judgments.

JAPANESE TRADE POLICY

Though Japanese trade policy includes some components of classical mercantilism that were shared by American commercial policy for most of the republic's history, fundamental structural disparities in the American and Japanese political economies reflect the great variations in historical forces that have shaped modern life in the two countries. The most striking differences stem from the divergent paths they followed in the immediate postwar period. One compelling characterization of their respective goals is that Japan sought to create a production machine, whereas as America emphasized a consumer society. In particular, Japanese economic policy since World War II has been shaped by an unusual commitment to rapid growth fueled by an export sector geared to the global market. It has also been fostered by an unusually dominant role for the state in mobilizing the energies of the private sector to fulfill that philosophy.

In one sense, this strategy needs no special explanation because less competitive nations are almost always mercantilist. But the ferocity of Japan's commitment to a trade policy that emphasizes national power over individual welfare and future growth over current consumption is explained by that country's unique position and history. The experience of World War II and the postwar American occupation illustrated graphically how much Japan lagged behind the rest of the developed world and how significantly that gap could affect Japanese life. The result was a national commitment to recover from the humiliation of this period and restore national pride. At the same time, because Japan was very poorly endowed in key natural resources, it had to maintain a significant level of imports. The need to sell exports to pay for them thus ruled out any form of autarchic development. Finally, unlike European nations, it was located in a region consisting of very poor economies that offered few marketing opportunities, so it had to orient its trade relationships to global rather than regional markets. Thus, it was imperative that Japanese firms be able to compete successfully in export markets against companies from far more developed nations that had a considerable head start.

Consequently, trade became the focal point of a far-reaching industrial policy through which the state shaped Japan's postwar economy. Policy makers sought to develop globally competitive firms in a few well-chosen sectors that promised long-term growth. The methods combined initial import protection—motivated by infant-industry arguments that date to at least Elizabethan England—with vigorous export-promotion programs centered around credit provided at very favorable terms by the state-run Japan Development Bank. Achieving rapid export growth required a complex set of policies that controlled credit and imports, permitted mo-nopoly situations unthinkable in the American context, and deprived cer-tain sectors (and consumers in general) to advance others. Direct subsidies, tax relief, and public support of research and development con-sortia, in addition to easy credit, fueled a huge expansion of investment.[21]

These efforts were coordinated by Japan's Ministry of Finance (MOF) and **Ministry of International Trade and Industry** (MITI). The unusu-ally close connection between the government and private industry and the unusually prominent position of MOF and MITI within the govern-ment gave rise to the term **Japan, Inc.** to describe the total social mobi-lization undertaken in support of these fledgling export industries. This could occur only because of the unique communitarian values, the rare national consensus, and the unusual structure of Japanese government. Bureaucrats attained high social prestige during the Tokugawa (feudal) period (1603–1867) and retained it as they led the modernization process under Emperor Meiji (1867–1912). In the mid-1990s, MITI and MOF offi-cials, who are mostly graduates of Tokyo University, Japan's most presti-gious, remain a business elite. Usually career bureaucrats, they achieve considerable power to influence the behavior of private firms through "administrative guidance." When they eventually retire from govern-ment service to the private sector, they are said to "descend from heaven." The less lofty prestige of government officials in the United States is reflected in the comparable American colloquialism that they enter a "revolving door."[22] As a result, government efforts to steer the Japanese economy encounter little of the resistance from the private sector that is such a distinguishing feature of the American political system, especially during the current era dominated by antigovernment sentiments.

The propensity of government policy to intervene in markets is so central to its system that Japanese scholars have suggested that the Japanese political economy represents a structurally distinctive system. In fact, Japan has been called a "non-capitalist market economy" by one and an example of "network capitalism" (distinguished from American market capitalism) by another.[23] Indeed, interference with the market mechanism is a core feature of the Japanese political economy and is by no means restricted to government intervention.

The so-called *keiretsu*, a network of firms linked through product markets, labor markets, and financial markets, exemplifies the prominent role played by nonmarket forces in the Japanese economy. These business empires had their origins in the family-controlled holding companies called *zaibatsu*, which prospered prior to the imposition of antitrust policy by American occupying forces immediately after World War II. The four largest of them accounted for about one-quarter of all capital in Japan in 1946 and controlled half of the financial markets and a third of heavy industry.[24] When holding companies were outlawed, many zaibatsu reformed under a similar structure of cross-shareholding called keiretsu, centered around banks.

For example, the Mitsui keiretsu consists of twenty four major companies linked together by stock in each firm that is owned by the others. In fact, more than 50 percent of the shares of these firms is held within the group. The companies also buy and sell from one another as well as share market information, provide credit, and cooperate in various other ways. Mitsui includes two banks, two insurance companies, a real estate firm, a shipper, a warehouse, an engineering company, a retailer, and producers of textiles, chemicals, mining products, and petroleum, as well as world famous firms that produce electronics (Toshiba) and automobiles (Toyota). The six largest keiretsu now account for about 16 percent of capital and profits in the Japanese economy and hold about 25 percent of the outstanding shares on the Tokyo and Osaka stock exchanges.[25]

Naturally, these industrial structures shape the behavior of firms. Japanese companies are likely to respond to a variety of stakeholders—especially affiliated firms—whereas U.S. corporations are more single-minded in producing profit for shareholders. As a result, the planning perspective of Japanese companies is long-term and broad in scope; indeed, they may not even be profit maximizers in the same way that American firms are. For example, a company may pass up the lowest-cost supplier in order to buy from another member of its keiretsu, since as a shareholder in the latter it would earn part of the profit. Further, these large keiretsu often cooperate with one another to form an oligopoly, which, like monopoly control over a market, raises prices for consumers and increases profits for business.

Moreover, oligopolies are much more common in Japan than in the United States because antitrust policies, though by statute similar to American ones, have been weakened by amendment and are underenforced. For example, antitrust exemptions allow legalized cartels in declining industries (to cooperate in reducing excess capacity), among small- and medium-sized enterprises (to achieve economies of scale), and for "rationalization" (to improve an industry's overall performance), as well as to facilitate exports and limit imports. All these cartels operate under the principle that "excessive competition" can be injurious to a firm and an industry, thus undermining its competitiveness against foreign firms. By the 1960s more than 1,000 cartels had been explicitly exempted from the antimonopoly law by the Fair Trade Commission. Even when the Fair Trade Commission has attempted to discourage collusion and centralization, it has often been pitted against the more politically powerful Ministry of Trade and Industry, which helped to create and sustain many of these very same cartels. Further, no plaintiff has ever won a private antitrust suit in Japan.

State-based export-promotion policies have also been integrated with private efforts. Large general trading companies (*sogo shosha*) have formed to facilitate the entry of smaller firms into foreign markets by providing marketing expertise, transport facilities, and credit. The nine largest, each associated with a particular keiretsu, handle 47 percent of Japanese exports, 65 percent of imports, and 18 percent of domestic wholesale sales.[26] Aided by the government-run Japanese External Trade Organization, which maintains offices in more than fifty foreign countries, Japanese firms find it relatively easy to monitor foreign markets so as to compete more effectively. By contrast, U.S. firms lack such extensive help in marketing in Japan and often bear the further burden of ignorance of Japanese language, customs, and business practices. Every anecdote about Japanese government interference with trade— from minor annoyance to outright ban—can be matched with another tale of the difficulty of doing business in Japan without appreciating that the rules of business interaction in Japan are as different as the rules of social interaction.

It is not hard to see why these arrangements have aroused the ire of other nations, especially the United States. They diminish the role of purely market-based competition that is open to all in favor of cooperative networks of elites that tend to be closed to outsiders, especially foreigners. Not only do they encourage exports and discourage imports, they do so through nongovernmental processes that cannot be easily identified or targeted as outright violations of GATT.

For example, Japan's notoriously inefficient retailing system suppresses imports. Most retailers are small shopkeepers who must rely upon an extensive network of wholesalers to supply the goods they sell. However, these wholesalers are usually affiliated with manufacturers, who can legally prohibit retailers from selling the products of competitors. Furthermore, because retailing licenses are required and existing merchants can block the granting of new ones, it is difficult to establish large chain stores that would be less reliant upon existing wholesalers and more price competitive. All of these arrangements make it difficult for new producers or foreign firms to get their products onto store shelves, the central allegation made by Kodak against Fuji in a 1995 dispute over color film that brought the two nations near a trade war. Of course, by severely restricting competition this system also drives up consumer prices.

At the same time that these structural features of the Japanese political economy discourage imports, others tend to increase exports. For example, in keeping with the Japanese tradition of lifelong employment, companies do not usually lay off workers even when sales decline. This constraint shapes labor-management relations, transforms the trade-offs involved in pricing and production decisions by firms, and changes the nature of political pressures on government macroeconomic policy. It is especially prominent in motivating corporate behavior that is otherwise inexplicable; for example, American competitors contend that Japanese firms engage in "dumping," selling products in the American market at a price that does not earn a profit. Since workers will be paid anyway, Japanese firms have an incentive to continue production under market conditions that would make an American firm discontinue operations.[27]

Thus, under the influence of both overt mercantilist policies and more subtle influences built into the fabric of economic structure, the Japanese economy in general—and several specific export industries in particular—achieved great technical sophistication and market success. Specifically, Japanese firms achieved global dominance in textiles in the 1950s, electronics in the 1960s, and autos in the 1970s and 1980s.

As the conditions that sustain this policy have changed, Japanese policy has moved in a markedly more liberal direction since the late 1970s. Industrial policy is now much less aggressive, allowing market forces to assume a considerably greater role. Further, import protection has assumed the pattern more common in other developed market democracies, emphasizing the support of declining industries rather than the expansion of those with growth potential. Though tariffs and most non-tariff barriers have visibly declined, critics contend that protectionism has not diminished so much as the predominant methods of import control have shifted. They now include arrangements that are difficult to document, such as administrative guidance on the part of government officials designed to intimidate importers, incomplete enforcement of intellectual property rights, government procurement policies biased against imports, and technical barriers to trade such as misuse of customs procedures and product standards.[28] On the evidence of actual import levels, which are much lower in most industrial sectors than in other countries, various structural impediments remain, especially involving restrictions on distribution channels for imports.[29] For example, only 3 percent of autos in Japan are imported, but in most developed nations the proportion is between one-third and one-half.[30]

American attempts to assess Japanese economic policy typically stumble over two major puzzles. How can such antiliberal policies succeed? Why have they been tolerated? Both questions arise because liberal theory contends that all of these structures that supplant the private market—keiretsu, cartels, vertically integrated retailing, import barriers, export subsidies, and other government intervention—sacrifice consumer welfare. It is certainly surprising that policies that harm consumers could persist so long within a democracy. The key to understanding the differences between Japanese and American trade policy lies in the recognition

---

Japanese and American Responses to Trade Dilemmas

Japan	United States
1. Value trade-offs	
Trade should be regulated to achieve social justice, domestic stability, and future national power and prosperity.	Trade should be free to maximize individual consumption, global efficiency, and stable world order.
2. Distributional outcomes	
Trade should be regulated to protect workers, benefit desirable sectors, and shift welfare into the future.	Trade should be free to maximize current consumer welfare and encourage efficient sectors.
3. Effects on the state	
Trade should be regulated to enhance national power and autonomy.	Trade should be free to achieve interdependence and peace.

that they pursue different goals, each representing a distinctive response to the trade dilemmas that all nations must resolve.

Although a full explanation of these choices would carry us too far afield, it is essential to realize that foreign trade permits these apparent sacrifices of consumer welfare to be interpreted in ways that strengthen their appeal. Most important, trade provides a means to exchange some loss of current consumption for alternative values such as full employment (to minimize instability and inequality), Japanese national power, and future consumer welfare. Moreover, Japanese economic policy—in both its domestic and international dimensions—rests on economic theory that directly challenges key assumptions of liberalism.

STRATEGIC TRADE THEORY AND POLICY

Like early English mercantilism, postwar Japanese trade policy was not erected on an edifice of formal economic theory. Whereas liberalism contains an integrated body of precise premises, refined logical arguments, and universalistic policy conclusions, **neomercantilism** has always consisted of fragmented practical wisdom derived from an eclectic mix of past policy successes, tactical judgments, and a smattering of theoretical ideas. However, economic theorists have always followed in the wake of successful practice, so in recent years a body of thought now called **strategic trade theory** has arisen to explain the most novel aspects of the Japanese neomercantilist approach.

Of course, many elements of Japanese policy reflect age-old motivations and well-known policy initiatives. The distinctiveness of the Japanese experience lies in its artful integration of domestic industrial policy with promotion of the export sector and protection against imports. Indeed, the administration of these policies has been so artful that many commentators—especially liberal theorists—doubt that such an approach can be made to work outside the special circumstances of postwar Japan. Few governments inherit the structural conditions and public consensus necessary to implement an approach that depends so centrally on trust in governmental institutions and sacrifice of current welfare for the promise of future payoffs. Indeed, Japanese policy has moderated somewhat since the 1970s as these requisite conditions have eroded—and a major transformation may be on the horizon for the late 1990s.

Nonetheless, recent theoretical advances—stimulated in part by the Japanese model—make a compelling case for export promotion and industrial policies. Strategic trade theory, which breaks with liberal theory in several important ways, is a refinement of older economy-of-scale ideas. Most important, it provides a defense for two propositions that are antithetical to liberal and free trade canon, though they have been accepted by countless governments for centuries. First, comparative advantage is not discovered by the savvy investor but actually created by a powerful state. Second, export promotion may be as essential to some infant industries as import protection because in some sectors a firm cannot be sustained by the market of a single country. For both reasons, government intervention is sometimes necessary to trade successfully. To see how this alternative explanation for trade suggests a greater role for the state, we must review the liberal premises that strategic trade theory challenges.

The liberal counsel that the state should avoid intervention in trade flows naturally from the Heckscher-Ohlin assumption that the sole basis for comparative advantage lies in national endowments of land, labor, and capital—which governments can do very little to affect. However, these endowments may play a smaller role in determining relative production costs of modern high-technology products than they did with respect to the simpler products considered by Smith and Ricardo. Further, factors of production are no longer immobile across national boundaries. For example, American capital is readily available to Mexican firms if they have the other attributes needed to be competitive, such as technology, consumer brand-name loyalty, marketing expertise, product innovations, and, most important for our purposes, favorable government policy (especially subsidies). Of course, government subsidies have always been capable of affording competitive advantage to firms over those of other countries, but such a policy was regarded as self-defeating for the economy as a whole because subsidies require tax revenue to fund them.

However, government intervention would be appropriate if comparative advantage rested on some factor that could be provided at no net cost only by the state. Strategic trade theory suggests at least three such candidates: very large scale capital, coordination among competing firms, and a credible commitment to aggressive export-promotion policies. To be successful, though, all require the existence of economies of scale; that is, the unit cost of production must decline as the volume of production increases. Of course, to some extent all products benefit from economies of scale. After all, it is hard to name a product that cannot be mass produced more cheaply than made one at a time. But most products reach a point where higher production volumes carry no further cost advantage because a very large organization becomes increasingly inefficient.

Economies of scale sometimes persist even at a volume that saturates the market, however, especially when the variable costs of production are low in relation to the fixed costs. For example, the major cost for WordPerfect Corporation in producing its computer software—paying programmers for the creative process of writing it—is fixed regardless of how many copies are sold. Its variable costs—buying blank disks to distribute the software—are very small. Consequently, once WordPerfect has sold enough copies to recoup its fixed costs, it can sell additional copies profitably at a price that cannot possibly be met by a new firm that produces a competing product in much smaller volumes.[31] Because comparative advantage in such industries resides wherever large-scale production is initiated, an industrial policy that subsidizes start-up may be beneficial to firms breaking ground in new technologies. Of course, subsidies will be absolutely essential to start-up firms in such sectors if foreign firms are already established.[32] Subsidies need not cause a loss of consumer welfare but only a postponement of it, because the mature firm should eventually generate employment, profits, and tax revenue that repay the state for its initial support. If so, a mercantilist industrial policy may itself be a source of comparative advantage and a major national asset.

Critics of industrial policy correctly observe that the state is not the only source of venture capital to initiate such industries and that private entrepreneurs may be better at picking winners and losers than government bureaucrats. Nonetheless, when very large scale capital is required for a risky venture, the state may be the only realistic source. That is especially true when economies of scale accrue outside the firm itself but inside the nation in which it is located. For example, the concentration of chipmakers and computer industries in the Silicon Valley of California makes it profitable for similar firms to locate in the same area, taking advantage of the skilled technicians and the research expertise of those already employed there. Because the original companies produce advantages enjoyed by new companies—pioneers such as IBM and Apple paved the way for WordPerfect—it may not pay private investors to initiate a dynamic industry even though it would benefit the economy of the nation. In cases of market failure like this—that is, when the private market fails to provide adequate capital because of externalities—the state can play a pivotal role.

Furthermore, a state with an activist industrial policy can bestow sources of comparative advantage that no private market can provide, such as subsidies for pure research or relief from onerous laws and regulations (e.g., antitrust). But the most formidable weapon of strategic trade policy is the reputation of the state itself for aggressively supporting an industry and ruthlessly competing with rivals. The promise to subsidize firms (or benefit them in other ways) well beyond the capacity of an unsubsidized firm to respond can intimidate potential competitors in other countries. Indeed, if the intimidation is great enough, neither the initial advantage nor the economies of scale need be especially large. Certainly the reputation of Japan, Inc. discouraged some American firms from competing in consumer electronics because they were convinced that the

Japanese government commitment to capturing the American market would make their efforts futile and costly.

Thus, where economies-of-scale considerations loom large, government interference with the private market yields benefits not recognized by free trade theory. But why has Japan been so much more aggressive than the United States in exploiting these possibilities? Why has Japanese trade policy been predominantly mercantilist and American policy more liberal?

THE DIFFERENT ROOTS OF AMERICAN AND JAPANESE TRADE POLICY

It is useful to recall the lesson contained in our analysis of early England: An intimate connection always exists between a nation's trade policy and the remainder of its political economy. The same forces that shape a nation's response to trade dilemmas—various strands of social and economic theory, the state of markets, and prevailing power balances among key actors—also influence the evolution of the domestic economy.

The liberalism of American trade policy reflects a domestic economic policy that also avoids state intervention in the market. For example, Japan (and most European nations) adopted an industrial policy that confers government benefits to selected sectors in order to build globally competitive industries; in contrast, the United States has emphasized a competition

---

Explanations for Postwar Trade Policy

Japan	United States
1. State of theory	
Communitarian ethical theory; neo-mercantilist and state-directed theory of trade and industrial policy.	Materialist and individualist ethical theory; liberal macro-economic and trade theory.
2. State of market	
Dependent on global markets, but inefficient.	Industry dominant over foreign competition.
3. Political power balances	
Dominance by state personnel, keiretsu, and rural sector.	Private sector dominant.

policy that emphasizes antitrust actions to prevent monopolies or oligopolies.[33] In particular, the Federal Trade Commission prevents market dominance by blocking mergers or acquisitions that would lower the number of competitors beyond a critical threshold. This strategy exemplifies the liberal conviction that efficiency is best promoted by competition among multiple firms and that government need only prevent business collusion that would lead to stagnation in productivity enhancement, product innovation, and consumer welfare.[34] By contrast, the Japanese approach deemphasizes antitrust, instead relying on foreign competition to fill whatever gaps are left by the absence of domestic competitors. Japanese leaders recognize that concentration of market power, control over prices, and sharing of effort is necessary to compete against foreign firms, especially those not restricted by antitrust laws in their own countries.

The difference can be explained simply: Japanese policy evolved in response to foreign competition, and American policy has its roots in an era in which foreign competition was insignificant in the United States. During its formative period, the United States enjoyed relative autonomy from international forces. Because of the sheer size of the American market and a plentiful endowment of natural resources, the country could produce most of what it needed and could sell within its own borders most that it could produce. This made it feasible for the United States to limit trade to a degree utterly impossible for Japan, whose dearth of resources and smaller market prevented self-sufficiency. At first because of the protection offered by tariffs and by high transportation costs resulting from physical isolation from trade competitors, the U.S. economy evolved an internal orientation almost without precedent. Even the post–World War II liberalization did not threaten most American firms, which had become competitive abroad and so dominant at home that as late as 1960 imports made up less than 5 percent of U.S. GNP. In the face of these market conditions, it is hardly surprising that industrial policy did not arise but antitrust policy did: Industrial policy is motivated by the presence of foreign competition, whereas antitrust policy is imperative in its absence.

Even though persistent U.S. balance-of-trade deficits demonstrate that foreign competiton became much more formidable after the mid-1970s, an American industrial policy still has not emerged. The U.S. government lacks the ability to engage in successful industrial policy because it has no counterpart to Japan's MITI, whose expertise in coordinating import protection, credit subsidies, research and development consortia, cartel formation, marketing schemes, and export promotion are indispensable tools. Strategic trade policy also requires a level of trust between government and business that exists in Japan but not in the United States, where the relationship between the public sector and private business is more adversarial.

This strategy is especially well suited to the Japanese business environment because it rewards firms that pursue market share rather than immediate profit. By underpricing the competition, a firm can acquire a dominant position in a foreign market, which provides the leverage to raise prices in the future when the competition has been weakened or driven out of business altogether. Achieving market share is a goal consistent with the long-term view characteristic of Japanese firms but is not common in the United States.

Moreover, these strategies require that consumers sacrifice immediate welfare, which is more compatible with Japanese values than American ones. The Japanese willingness to defer consumption is symbolized by both a high savings rate and a trade surplus; the American budget deficit, trade deficit, and consumer debt levels are all testimony to the propensity of Americans to demand gratification sooner rather than later.

In fact, cultural differences between the two countries extend to a broad range of ethical theories and value judgments that are reflected in divergent economic structures and policies. The more communitarian tradition of Japanese culture finds expression in a variety of economic forms: reliance on personal networks rather than impersonal markets, lifelong employment practices, and consumption decisions that give preference to Japanese products, among others. This tradition also helped Japan achieve a national consensus after World War II in favor of a comprehensive industrial policy designed to use trade to achieve national goals and shift welfare from the present to the future. The U.S. political economy—and the trade policy that follows from it—has far different roots. It is built upon a structure formed by liberal theory and the individualistic and materialistic values that sustain it, much like the liberal period in nineteenth-century Britain. Thus, liberal theory has become an article of faith in America but not in Japan, which embraces the precept that too much competition can be as injurious as too little.

At the same time, the political power of key actors in both countries has played a major role in policy choice. For example, Japan's political structure allows the farm vote—the single strongest source of support for import protection—to elect something approaching 25 percent of the Diet, the Japanese parliament. Further, so many individuals benefit from each of the exclusionary arrangements—keiretsu, import restrictions, retailing networks, lifelong employment—that a substantial constituency exists for the system as a whole. Finally, the political culture does not encourage the challenges to community consensus or government policy that are more common in the United States. As a result, the Liberal Democratic Party, which created and sustained Japanese trade policy, enjoyed a near monopoly of political power for most of the postwar period.

In the United States, some critics have suggested an emulation of Japanese or European industrial policy, observing that a liberal approach leaves American workers vulnerable to foreign competition, which is particularly alarming because welfare provisions in the event of unemployment are much less generous in the United States than in Europe. However, because the United States lacks the leftist parties centered around a strong trade union movement, which marks the European social democracies, this argument has not been championed by an effective political power base. For a number of reasons, political power in the United States has been decentralized, and a sharp class-based cleavage has not appeared. As a result, the American state was smaller and less active in promoting welfare benefits than the typical European state, and less powerful and interventionist in shaping the economy than the typical Asian state.

Because Americans have such strong faith in the market—U.S. producers were among the most competitive in the world in all the leading sectors—and so little affection for government, it cannot be a surprise that American trade policy after World War II took on the same liberal orientation found in its domestic economic policy. Indeed, the United States sought to remake the global political economy in its own liberal image, confident that the burdens imposed on the country by the Bretton Woods commitments could be easily borne.

CONTEMPORARY AMERICAN TRADE POLICY

By the middle of the 1970s, however, this optimism had faded; several key American industries, especially steel and autos, had lost their global dominance and a substantial share of their home market. Not surprisingly, these industries began to take a sharply protectionist view and an especially hawkish attitude toward trade policy with Japan. As theoretical conviction gave way to material interests, American policy slowly drifted in a more mercantilist direction, partly driven by the mercantilism of others.

American protectionism took several forms, some of which were fully in accord with GATT rules (and even consistent with liberal principles); others exploited gray areas in the agreement. GATT rules allowed nations to respond to sudden changes in imports that diminished the income of any economic sector even if they arose naturally from market forces and were desirable for long-term aggregate welfare.[35] In the United States, Section 201 of the Trade Reform Act of 1974 implemented GATT's Article 19 escape clause. It charged the U.S. International Trade Commission with investigating petitions for import relief and recommending action to the president. Between 1974 and 1986, fifty five cases were investigated under Section 201 and relief was provided in eighteen of them.

GATT's Article 6, which permits "counter-vailing duties" to offset foreign subsidies, was implemented by Section 301, which authorizes retaliation against any foreign manufacturer found to be engaging in "unjustifiable, unreasonable or discriminatory" trading practices. Countervailing duties are used by the United States primarily to protect American industry from injury caused by the dumping of foreign manufacturers, which consists of either selling a product abroad for below its cost of production or below the price for which it is sold in the home market. Antidumping charges were first filed by American television manufacturers against Japanese electronics firms in 1968, with the U.S. Customs Service finding that Japanese-made televisions were sold in the United States for as little as half their price in Japan. Since the late 1980s, antidumping actions have been frequent: GATT reports that between 1988 and 1990, the U.S. Department of Commerce investigated seventy-one cases and found dumping to have occurred in sixty-eight of them. Subsequently, the U.S. International Trade Commission found that this dumping produced "injury" to American manufacturers in two-thirds of those cases, thus authorizing countervailing duties.[36] Japan has been the most frequent target, but actions against India and Brazil in 1989 also attracted considerable attention.

The Super 301 provision of the 1988 Trade Act places pressure on the president to undertake these actions by designating "priority foreign countries" who maintain "unfair" trading practices and by setting a deadline for progress in correcting them. The major target was clearly Japan, but both 301 and Super 301 have been broadly used in recent years. Moreover, all such actions produce "procedural protection" by serving as an example to other foreign producers who will avoid even the appearance of dumping so as to avoid the rigors of the U.S. legal process and possible retaliation. They also provide the teeth that encourage nations to seek bilateral negotiations with the United States over trade disputes.

In fact, it has become common for nations—especially the United States—to require competitors to "voluntarily" reduce exports through bilateral voluntary restraint agreements (VRAs). Of course, when the United States asks another nation to restrict its exports and threatens retaliation if it does not agree, the agreement is voluntary in exactly the same sense that one hands over one's wallet to a gun-toting mugger voluntarily.[37] The first voluntary export restriction, in cotton textiles, was adopted by Japan in 1955 and replaced in 1957 by a more formal bilateral agreement. Negotiations produced a series of bilateral and multilateral arrangements restricting trade in televisions through the 1970s. Accusations of dumping against the Japanese steel industry also brought voluntary export restraints in the 1970s and other agreements have covered machine tools, steel, and apparel.

The most notable of the VERs, however, arose from a conflict over automobiles that began in the 1970s and culminated in the early 1980s. In June 1980, the U.S. Senate adopted—by a vote of 90 to 4—a resolution calling on the Carter administration to send a signal to Japan by reviewing American import policies. However, significant American opposition to import controls came from consumer groups who valued the energy-efficient imports during a time of high gasoline prices and resented the lackadaisical approach of Detroit automakers to foreign competition from Japanese cars that were widely perceived to provide higher quality and lower prices. Heated public debate in the United States was mirrored by heated negotiations at the industry and governmental levels. The Reagan administration, committed to free trade but alarmed by the decline of the American auto industry, sought a voluntary export restraint by Japanese automakers that would achieve the desired end—a limit to foreign imports—while saving face for both sides. The United States did not wish to impose limitations that violated free market principles and the Japanese wanted to avoid action that would imply wrongdoing on their part. Eventually in 1981, a VER was negotiated that limited sales to 1.68 million units per year with subsequent renewals occurring at higher volumes. However, the ceiling, at 2.3 million units per year, has not been reached since 1987, largely because Japanese manufacturers have shifted production to the United States, thus avoiding the limit.

Though narrowly successful in achieving their limited aims, these sector-specific talks have pleased no one. Liberals in both countries assail them for violating free trade and legitimating other nontariff barriers that interfere with market efficiency and lower global welfare. Consumers complain that U.S. NTBs, which were estimated to reduce American manufactured imports by about $50 billion in 1983 (around a quarter of actual imports), raise prices while protecting inefficient industries.[38] Japanese exporters contend that they are being punished for their own efficiency; the American firms they compete against feel that the protection offered is inadequate.

Critics fear that these gray-area measures undermine international institutions, observing that GATT cannot adequately police—or even document—agreements that are informal, unwritten, and, technically speaking, voluntary. A recent GATT review identified forty-seven such arrangements, but the United States denies that many of these exist. Efforts to achieve a standstill of further policies that contravened the letter or spirit of GATT or rollbacks of existing violations were centered on the United States (which accounted for about half of the protests lodged). These developments have been especially distressing because as national policies have skirted the international institutions that constrain protectionism, nontariff barriers have mushroomed. Already more than a quarter of the imports of industrial countries are covered by NTBs, including 36.1 percent of agricultural goods and 16.1 percent of manufactures.[39] The result must be lower levels of trade and reduced consumer welfare.

Moreover, these arrangements dangerously politicize trade. This not only favors nations with greater bargaining power rather than those with superior legal arguments, but it also invariably engenders tensions among trading partners, none more prominent than those between the United States and Japan. Still, so long as the two nations cannot agree on either the general principles of what constitutes fair trading practice or the specific facts of the individual cases, no better means of resolving conflicts is evident.

RECENT TRADE DISPUTES

In the 1990s, the central issues in American-Japanese trade disputes have centered around the claims of each nation that the other denies it market access. The United States contends that its import barriers, described earlier, are necessary to counteract the unfair trading practices imbedded in Japan's systematic mercantilism. Japan denies that the failure of U.S. products to penetrate Japanese markets is caused by Japanese government policy and accuses the United States of preferring liberalism only in sectors it dominates while adopting ad hoc mercantilism whenever that would suit its interests.

The most heated trade tensions have revolved around American complaints about access to Japanese markets, even though liberal theory suggests that the main losers from Japanese import restrictions are Japanese consumers. For example, Japan's rice market is very heavily protected by quotas, and the United States is the second largest rice exporter in the world. In 1985, Japan produced and consumed about 15 million metric tons of rice at a total cost of about $21 billion. That same volume was worth less than $3 billion at prices prevailing in the United States and other global markets. Thus if free trade would drive rice prices in Japan to global levels, the increased sales of rice exporters (in the United States and elsewhere) might benefit them by $3 billion but would benefit Japanese consumers by closer to $18 billion.[40] In manufacturing, where NTBs on U.S. products are estimated to be equivalent to a tariff rate of about 25 percent, complete trade liberalization might increase Japanese imports of U.S. products by $10–$15 billion annually, but these estimates are quite speculative.[41]

As we have seen, however, these seeming losses are balanced by other benefits from the standpoint of the Japanese consumer. Thus, contrary to liberal theory, the loser in American-Japanese trade has been seen as the American worker, not the Japanese consumer. As a result, foreign pressure has played an unusually large role in shaping Japanese trade policy, with dispute resolution attempted at the unilateral, bilateral, and global levels. Unilateral efforts include Japanese initiatives in 1985 to designate October as import-promotion month, MITI's adoption of the motto

"Spread friendship worldwide by promoting imports," and Prime Minister Yasuhiro Nakasone's urging each citizen to buy $100 worth of U.S. products.

At the global level, periodic attempts have been made to coordinate economic policies that produce trade disequilibrium, especially by the **Group of Seven** to stabilize the yen-dollar exchange rate. However, the GATT, which has been the most effective agency for dealing with other trade disputes, has been unable to deal with American complaints that Japanese markets have been effectively closed. In particular, GATT rules do not prescribe a remedy for the chief American complaints. Although GATT permits tariffs to protect domestic producers against imports that benefit from export subsidies by foreign governments, nations cannot use export subsidies to countervail foreign subsidies to import-competing industries. Thus, the United States could obtain no relief if American firms are prevented from exporting to Japan by subsidies to Japanese domestic firms. Nor could direct action be taken when export subsidies affect competitiveness in some third market. In both cases, the injured party could seek relief by appeal to the GATT Subsidies Committee, but in practice bilateral negotiations usually occurred instead. The new WTO was intended to correct these deficiencies, but recent American actions to bypass its procedures suggest that even its chief sponsor doubts the effectiveness of dispute resolution by global institutions.

Indeed, most efforts to resolve trade conflicts between the United States and Japan have involved bilateral negotiations, mostly because they can more easily deal with the specific issues of market access that American trade officials attribute to Japan's unique economic structure and unusual consumer behavior. GATT was designed principally to reduce the overt barriers to trade commonly erected by all governments, but formal trade barriers like tariffs or quotas have ceased to play the major role in limiting American exports to Japan. Even direct government subsidies and technical barriers, which the WTO can address, have receded in recent years. Instead, American trade officials now focus their complaints on the private behavior of private actors and on the so-called structural impediments to trade that help shape that behavior. In doing so, they encounter more than the routine differences of opinion between nations that can usually be bridged by compromise—they confront a chasm formed by different philosophical positions concerning the fundamental dilemmas of trade.

Simply put, Japanese consumers and businesses appear to prefer domestic to foreign products. Japanese negotiators point out that the government is powerless to force consumers to demand imports, since consumer tastes cannot—and should not—be controlled by legislation. After all, they note that consumer freedom is an essential cornerstone of capitalism because it motivates the business competition that makes market-based allocation efficient and guarantees that citizen welfare will be maximized. They insist that the responsibility to reduce the bilateral trade imbalance resides in the private sector, principally with American businesses, which must either improve their products, tailor them more effectively to Japanese tastes, or market them more skillfully. Free trade, they contend, already exists.

This stance frustrates Americans, who insist that a refusal to buy foreign products cannot be considered fair trade whether or not it conforms to classical definitions of free trade. Moreover, American negotiators point to a number of structural impediments that prevent Japanese consumers from realistically comparing domestic to foreign products. For example, the inherently exclusionary keiretsu arrangements act as formidable barriers to the entry of foreign firms, and the notoriously inefficient structure of Japanese retailing makes it difficult for foreign products to compete. One study estimates that for various reasons, the prices of selected U.S.-made products are about 70 percent higher in Japan than in the United States.[42] Thus it is hard not only to generate the kind of free trade that the United States seeks but even to establish whether free trade exists when the very meaning of the term is contested.

These structural impediments to trade produce a conundrum in American efforts to open the Japanese market to U.S. firms. Eliminating formal trade barriers is an inadequate negotiating goal because it will leave intact those structural features of the Japanese political economy that tend to diminish imports. Standard approaches are no solution when a nation impedes trade through a societal rather than a state-based policy apparatus. However, any effort to attack these structural impediments forces a stark confrontation with trade dilemmas involving national autonomy and the preservation of alternative values. After all, asking for fundamental reform of the Japanese retailing system is equivalent to asking Americans to eliminate shopping malls.

As a result, negotiators have struggled with a variety of approaches to these inherently tendentious issues with very limited success. The most farreaching negotiations were the structural-impediment-initiative (SII) talks, initiated in 1989. In attacking the structural arrangements that affect trade, these talks laid bare the dilemmas that arise whenever trade is linked to other aspects of national life. For example, the U.S. list of structural impediments to trade included Japanese savings and investment patterns, land policy, the distribution system, exclusionary business practices, keiretsu relationships, and pricing mechanisms. It was even suggested that because narrow Japanese roads discriminated against large American cars, they should be considered an unfair barrier to trade. The Japanese identified the chief impediments to imports of American products as the lack of U.S. investment in quality production methods, deficient worker training, and the poor American educational system. With an agenda like this, it is not surprising that the negotiations were acrimonious and unproductive.

Progress has been somewhat better when negotiations have focused on specific sectors of interest to potential American exporters, most notably telecommunications and electronics, forest products, medical equipment, pharmaceuticals, and, most recently, auto parts, air transport, and photographic supplies. For example, the United States has asked Japan to bring its requirements on electrical appliances into line with international ones. Meanwhile, the EU has asked Japan to abolish the restrictions on the sale of beer by supermarkets. In June 1994, the Japanese government issued a list of 279 deregulation promises.

In a series of so-called framework talks that covered automobiles, insurance, medical technology, and telecommunications, the United States sought to shift the focus away from formal trade barriers (because they are not the principal problem) and away from particular structural impediments (because they are difficult to measure or even identify with clarity). Instead, the United States has placed pressure on Japan to set numerical targets for imports by establishing "temporary quantitative indicators," a prediction of "what would happen in a particular sector if Japanese businesses and consumers made purchase decisions on the sole basis of commercial considerations."[43] The United States could then leave it to the Japanese government to find a way to import that quantity of American goods, thus shifting the pressure to identify and eliminate the unofficial import barriers to the Japanese government.

Japan has resisted, seeing this approach as a thinly disguised quota that smacks of managed trade—a direct conflict with America's professed commitment to free trade. The difficulty of papering over huge philosophical differences through such a voluntary import expansion (VIE) is exemplified by the semiconductor arrangement in which the Japanese government publicly stated that it "expected" that 20 percent of the semiconductors used in its computer industry would be imported from foreign firms (mostly the United States). However, the United States contended that this agreement should be considered a guarantee, and Japan rejected that interpretation of this "expectation." Thus, this approach, while sidestepping the most dramatic national sovereignty issues, invites misunderstanding and violates liberal precepts.

The two sides have been somewhat more successful in agreeing on quantitative measures of some structural impediments to trade. For example, in the auto area, the United States wants to count the number of Japanese auto showrooms displaying American cars; Japan wants to count the number of American companies teaching the Japanese language to sales personnel or conducting seminars on how to do business in Japan.

The slow pace of U.S.-Japanese trade talks. Danziger—©*The Christian Science Monitor*

However, U.S.–Japanese relations reached a new low in 1995, when the parties could not agree on provisions to increase Japanese purchases of American car parts. At this time the auto sector accounted for more than half of an escalating bilateral trade deficit. In frustration at the slow pace of negotiations, the United States announced plans to impose a 100 percent tariff on all Japanese cars priced above $30,000, which accounted for about $6 billion in sales in 1994. Japan, supported by the EU and most private economists in the United States, appealed to the WTO, claiming the retaliatory action brazenly violated the fundamental principles and specific rules of the WTO, which the United States had itself ratified several months earlier.[44] Although American actions were consistent with U.S. law, they clearly violated the obligation to use the WTO's dispute-resolution mechanism, designed for exactly this purpose. The stakes were high. As an American professor of international law put it, "America is flouting the core and central obligation since the beginning of GATT. This is just about the worst possible way to launch the WTO."[45] Indeed, continued American defiance would squander the hard-won benefits of the decade-long negotiations over the Uruguay Round, which created the WTO, and if the United States refused to accept the WTO's judgment, surely other nations would cease to be bound by it. Furthermore, as the deadline for the imposition of these sanctions approached in June 1995, many cross-cutting retaliations in other sectors, especially air transport, were announced by both parties. A full-blown trade war, complete with a collapse in the legitimacy of the international institution that might otherwise contain it, could not be ruled out. At the last minute, a settlement was arranged, but it was more a public relations achievement to allow both parties to save face than a compromise that actually settled any issues. Moreover, less than a week after this potential disaster was averted, a public brawl over color print film was instigated by the American firm Kodak and championed by the Clinton administration. The chief evidence for the existence of unfair practices was the claim that Fuji controlled more than three-quarters of the market in Japan, yet Kodak outsold them dramatically in every other national market in which they competed.

CONCLUSION: THE FUTURE OF AMERICAN-JAPANESE RELATIONS

Fortunately, despite the dire short-term outlook, there is some evidence that the problems in American-Japanese relations may be self-limiting. The Japanese priority on exports has diminished, and they now constitute a smaller share of GDP than in the United States. Japanese export performance has grown only at about the pace of its overall macroeconomic growth, which has been slowing, since the late 1970s.

Moreover, most analysts see a convergence in the two systems as the inherent limitations of the Japanese system generate both internal and external pressure to harmonize Japanese practice with that in the rest of the developed world. Japanese citizens who work longer hours and face higher prices than workers and consumers elsewhere are tiring of the sacrifices. Japan has discovered that production cannot grow indefinitely without a greater increase in consumption. At the same time, the United States has discovered that consumption cannot grow unabated without more energy directed toward production. In some areas American firms are moving toward the Japanese: in worker empowerment, just-in-time inventory practices, total-quality management, and greater integration and partnership among firms.

However, trade issues remain especially difficult for Japan because they dramatically expose the dilemmas involving distributional issues, effects on the state, and the trade-off between alternative values. Liberalization in general has been a divisive force in Japan, increasing the role of foreigners in a traditionally xenophobic society, diminishing the role of the bureaucracy, eroding the communitarian vision of the economy, and bringing into the open the conflicts among the interests of firms, consumers, and the government, between economic and political considerations, and between domestic and international goals. As a result, the consensus among policymakers responsible for the coherence of policy during the era of Japan, Inc. has dissolved in recent years with some agencies, such as MITI, favoring liberalization and others, such as MOF, more often opposing it.[46]

Still, convergence may be the ultimate answer to defusing trade tensions that originate in different economic policies, which in turn result from different values and economic theories, different conditions in markets, and different balances of political power in the two countries. The alternative, discussed in Chapter 6, is to use regional arrangements like the EU or NAFTA to encourage trade between similar nations and discourage trade among dissimilar ones.

SIX

□ □ □

Regional Integration

In response to the dilemmas of trade, most nations have fashioned some amalgam of mercantilist and liberal policies, seeking to capture the benefits of each approach without surrendering to the liabilities of either. One increasingly popular strategy is **regional integration**, which creates free trade within a group of nations but practices mercantilism toward nations outside that group.[1]

In this chapter I examine two variants of regional integration at very different stages of evolution: the European Union (EU) and the North American Free Trade Agreement (NAFTA). The NAFTA and the EU represent economic experiments that may foreshadow future changes in the global political economy. If they are successful, similar trading blocs could arise elsewhere, signaling an end to the open structure that has defined international economic affairs since the end of World War II.

THE EVOLUTION OF THE EUROPEAN UNION

The European Union was created in 1993 as the most recent of a progression of institutions that embody a vision of regional integration laid out in a 1946 speech by Winston Churchill: "I see no reason why, under the leadership of the world organization, there should not ultimately arise the United States of Europe, both those of the East and those of the West, which will unify this Continent in a manner never known since the fall of the Roman Empire, and within which all its peoples may dwell together in prosperity, in justice, and in peace."[2]

For nearly fifty years this image has guided a regional integration effort that has widened from six to twelve nations and deepened from a narrow

123

technical focus to an ambitious social, political, and economic agenda. The Treaty of Paris, signed in 1951 by France, Germany, Italy, Belgium, the Netherlands, and Luxembourg, founded the European Coal and Steel Community (ECSC).[3] The treaty not only pooled and centralized the production of coal and steel, it also introduced the High Authority, the Council of Ministers, the Court of Justice, and the Parliamentary Assembly, all of which remain part of the institutional framework of the much broader EU, which has subsequently evolved.

The Treaty of Rome, signed in 1957 by the same six nations, established the European Atomic Energy Community (EURATOM) and the European Economic Community (EEC), which greatly expanded the scope of the ECSC treaty by calling for the dissolution of barriers dividing Europe, the improvement and equalization of living and working standards, the abolition of restrictions on international trade, the removal of obstacles to concerted action among governments, and the enhancement of peace and liberty through closer relations among states. In 1969, the European Community (EC) was created by merging the ECSC, EEC, and EURATOM and establishing the European Social Fund (ESF) and the European Investment Bank (EIB). Britain, Ireland, and Denmark became members of the European Community in 1973; Greece in 1980; and Portugal and Spain in 1986. The European Monetary System (EMS) and the European currency unit (ECU) were launched in 1978 and 1979.

The Single European Act, which went into effect in 1987, was designed to create the "single European market" that had been envisioned in the Treaty of Rome but had not been realized. However, many of the steps scheduled for the christening of the EU in 1993 remain unfulfilled—and some appear unlikely to be achieved anytime soon. Indeed, the future of the EU itself is presently uncertain, since considerable opposition has arisen in many member countries. A long-standing objection of critics is that European integration implies a substantial abdication of national sovereignty because it requires that national law be brought into accordance with EU law.[4] More recently, the treaty on political and economic union signed at the Maastricht summit in December 1991 was rejected by a national referendum in one member country and survived very close votes in others. Its most controversial elements were the call for a common defense policy and a monetary union with a single currency.

INTEGRATION: LIBERAL ON THE INSIDE AND MERCANTILIST ON THE OUTSIDE

Regional integration is best thought of as trade policy that is liberal on the inside and mercantilist on the outside. Within the community, free trade is encouraged by the elimination of trade barriers and the harmonization of economic policies. Trade barriers remain against the outside world, however, and the community achieves mercantilist goals of self-sufficiency and enhanced power that would be impossible for the constituent nations individually.[5]

Though liberals argue that both peace and prosperity could be achieved more fully through *global* free trade, regional integration may deal more effectively with trade dilemmas. First, regionalism assuages mercantilist worries about sacrificing national self-sufficiency. Regional interdependence is less risky than surrendering control of the economy to the vicissitudes of global markets and the economic policies of 150 other nations, especially because regional nations are likely to share basic values and economic structures. Second, regional integration creates a level of governance above the nation that can mitigate the dislocations and resolve the disputes that inevitably arise from trade.

It is not wholly clear whether regional strategies like NAFTA and the EU are ultimately compatible with the ideal of global liberalism. The bicycle theory of trade policy argues that the two approaches are mutually supporting because as long as free trade moves forward it stays upright, but it inevitably falls if it slows down or stops. Any movement toward free trade (even if regional) keeps the forward momentum going, thus resisting the natural drift toward protectionism that occurs whenever trade policy becomes strictly a national matter.

However, even though free trade areas are GATT-legal under Article 24, they contravene the liberal spirit of the nondiscrimination principle embodied in the MFN clause.[6] In fact, the term "most favored nation" has become a misnomer: The EU, for example, applies the MFN rate to only seven nations—the United States, Japan, Canada, Australia, New Zealand, South Africa, and Taiwan. Nearly all others are charged a *more* favorable rate. Free trade or preferential tariff rates apply not only to the twelve EU members but to most other European nations (partners in the European Economic Space), twelve Mediterranean nations (EU associates), sixty-nine African, Caribbean, and Pacific countries (under terms of the Lomé convention), and all other developing countries (under the Generalized System of Preferences). As these arrangements multiply—by the 1980s almost half of all global trade flows were conducted under preferential agreements—the liberal foundations of the global order suffer severe erosion.[7]

The mix of liberal and mercantilist motivations for regional integration is most easily illustrated in connection with customs-union theory, which adapts Ricardian ideas concerning global free trade to the special case of regional trade preferences. Canadian economist Jacob Viner's classic 1950 book *The Customs Union Issue* identifies two effects of initiating free trade among members of a regional organization while continuing protection against the outside world.[8]

Trade creation occurs when a customs union allows goods once produced domestically to be imported from a more efficient producer in a
member country. The result is the familiar Ricardian gains from trade, in
which both countries are better off and the rest of the world is not ad-
versely affected. However, a second pattern, which Viner calls trade diversion, may arise if the establishment of a customs union shifts
production from an efficient outside producer to a less efficient inside
one. For example, suppose that Germany initially imports a good from its
most efficient global producer, a firm in the United States. After the creation of a customs union between France and Germany, Germany would
impose a higher tariff on the American product than on the comparable
French one. As a result, French imports could replace American imports.
This trade diversion modifies the positive liberal assessment of a customs
union because it shifts production from a more efficient to a less efficient
producer. Whereas trade creation benefits member states without affecting others, the benefits of trade diversion come to member nations at the
expense of outside nations.

THE MERCANTILIST ROOTS OF THE EU

The presence of trade diversion makes it clear why outside nations
typically see the mercantilist face of regional integration rather than its
liberal face, which is turned inward. From their standpoint, regionalism
not only furthers the classical mercantilist goal of protecting domestic industry, it does so through a classical mercantilist melding of foreign policy concerns with economic aims. Rather than erect trade barriers against
all foreign competitors equally, the EU discriminates against nations outside the region, often because they are seen as a threat.

Indeed, from its beginnings, European unification has accelerated
whenever threats from outside have been perceived. The early EC was
designed to protect Europe against the Soviet military threat posed by a
large army and aggressive doctrine as well as the American economic
threat posed by large productive capacity and expansionist marketing
plans. The Single Market initiative culminating in 1992—Carlo
DiBenedetti called it "a deadline not to be dead"[9]—was energized by the
economic threat of rapidly growing productivity in Asia and the resulting
"Euro-pessimism."[10] Again we see that nations turn in a mercantilist direction when their industries fear more competitive firms abroad and
when their states fear the rising power of rivals. The EU's goals are no different than those of Queen Elizabeth's sixteenth-century industrial development or Japan's postwar export promotion: its uniqueness lies in the
regional emphasis of its mercantilism, which can be seen most clearly by
contrasting liberal and mercantilist viewpoints on trade diversion.

Whereas liberal theory disapproves of trade diversion because it compromises efficiency, mercantilism finds it perfectly acceptable if it helps to

achieve other national goals. Since many values and goals conflict with efficiency, nations may prefer to trade with one country rather than another for several reasons. First, a nation may divert trade in order to benefit an economy whose resulting prosperity produces greater side benefits for it. For example, for reasons of physical proximity and economic integration, Germany is much more likely to gain from the prosperity of France than it is from the prosperity of a nation—for example, Japan or the United States—that is thousands of miles away. Second, trade diversion under regional integration is reciprocated: Germany diverts its trade toward France, and in exchange, France diverts its trade toward Germany. Third, most European nations are more comfortable with depending upon other Europeans than upon Japan or even the United States. Not only do they share more security concerns with their European neighbors but they also have more common views on issues that always arise in trade matters (e.g., dilemmas involving job security, welfare arrangements, and environmental protection).

THE LIBERAL ROOTS OF THE EU

Despite these undeniable mercantilist motivations, the EU is also deeply rooted in liberal ideas, especially the gains from trade promised by Ricardian theory. For example, the Cecchini report (1988) was instrumental in gathering support for the Single Market initiative by estimating trade gains resulting in a 35 percent boost in GDP.[11] However, gains from specialization and enhanced competition are not the only benefits of the EU seen by liberal theorists.

Economies of scale, which have always been a strong motivation for the smaller countries of Europe, were especially visible in the ECSC. Because steelmaking requires large-scale plants and equipment that are efficient only when producing large volumes of output, a steel industry could never emerge in a small country unless a firm could be guaranteed access to the larger European market. The ECSC provided that guarantee in the form of the pledges by European governments not to interfere with free trade in these goods.[12] The result was a key industry with production facilities scattered among different countries, each dependent on other nations to provide both demand for the final product and part of the supply capacity. A side benefit of this arrangement was the fulfillment of the liberal dream of an interdependence that would prevent war by making it suicidal.

In fact, the EU's economic institutions were constructed for a political purpose. The mission of European integration, as stated in the preamble to the ECSC treaty, is to "substitute for age-old rivalries the merger of their essential interests; to create, by establishing an economic community, the basis for a broader and deeper community among peoples long divided by bloody conflicts; and to lay the foundations for institutions which will give direction to a destiny henceforward shared."[13] Thus, the

ECSC was an innovative form of peace treaty, designed, in the words of Robert Schuman, to "make it plain that any war between France and Germany becomes, not merely unthinkable, but materially impossible."[14] In the aftermath of two devastating wars in the previous thirty years—which more conventional tools of international politics such as the European balance of power, the League of Nations, and international law could not prevent—European nations were willing to tolerate the erosion of autonomy and self-sufficiency implied by interdependence in order to weaken the nationalism that had provoked so much violence.

THE POLITICAL ROOTS OF THE EU

Throughout its history, European integration has been seen as a means of escaping the liberal and mercantilist horns of trade dilemmas by providing a regional level of governance to deal with common problems that no single nation could solve. For example, the Common Agricultural Policy (CAP), born in 1962, embraced a concern with the distributional dilemma of trade that would have been at home in parliamentary debates of the eighteenth century: Its goals included "the assurance that those working in agriculture will enjoy a standard of living comparable to that enjoyed by workers in other sectors." Because it was evident as early as 1951 that this motivation implied an ambitious institutional design, the Treaty of Paris went well beyond limited economic objectives to create the executive and legislative institutions that remain at the heart of the contemporary EU. Later, the Treaty of Rome's social and political provisions—which included the creation of the Economic and Social Committee (ESC) to provide a strong voice for workers, employers, consumers, and academics—made the EC much more than a mechanism for advancing free trade.[15]

These arrangements were a direct outgrowth of the values and theories that influenced *national* economic policies in Europe, especially where working-class political parties of the left came to power—Labour in Britain, Social Democrats in Germany and Scandinavia, and Socialists in France, Italy, and Spain. Rooted in powerful trade union movements, those parties embraced values of egalitarianism that emphasized the welfare and security of workers and shared the conviction that it was safer to entrust these goals to the state than to free markets. They erected welfare states to provide institutional protection against the vagaries of markets that were quite distinct from the more laissez-faire arrangements in the United States. For example, vacations, maternity leave, and health insurance, which are all voluntary fringe benefits in the United States, are determined by law in most EU states. Furthermore, because some constitutions list the right to work among human rights, the ability of firms to hire and fire workers is sharply constrained.[16] When European national governments spend an average of 25 percent of GDP on social protection, it is hardly a surprise that an agreement to increase trade would include a provision to compensate those who would lose in the resulting dislocations. Indeed, the Social Fund, created in 1951 to finance worker retraining and relocation necessitated by the ECSC and now charged with aiding trade-damaged geographic regions, has become the second largest expenditure in the EU budget (behind agriculture).

Economists contend that compensating losers—though second best to laissez-faire—is preferable to protecting jobs through trade barriers, which are inefficient because the price increases they induce cut consumption and reward less efficient domestic producers.[17] The second-best alternative is to augment free trade with programs that directly compensate displaced workers, such as unemployment insurance. However, because the taxes to finance such programs may be more visible to voters than trade barriers, protectionism may be politically first best though economically third best, at least where redistributive measures have limited philosophical support, such as in liberal America. The European socialist tradition makes it easier to sustain much more generous welfare provisions, but such policies are not costless. They may be responsible for unemployment levels of over 10 percent throughout Europe in the 1980s and 1990s, which would be completely unacceptable in the United States both because of the hardship on the unemployed and the tax drain of supporting them. By contrast, European polities would not tolerate the American approach, which accepted "high risk and high reward, and left its losers to be pushed far from the economic and social mainstream," resulting in a "frisky, but cruel economy."[18]

However, it is difficult to maintain social protection—which inevitably imposes costs on business—when diminishing trade barriers force firms to compete with those in other countries that do not bear such burdens. For example, French firms demand a level playing field in competing with Spanish firms whenever the French government mandates employee benefits, health and safety rules, or environmental regulations more costly than those in Spain. In fact, free trade tends to harmonize many national policies, making it especially difficult for a nation to sustain different tax policies than its neighbors. Denmark, for example, found it impossible to maintain a value-added tax (VAT, i.e., sales tax) 8 percent higher than neighboring Germany's because Danish citizens could simply evade the tax by purchasing goods in Germany and bringing them across the border duty free.[19]

Thus, some trade barriers must exist if nations wish to maintain different laws with respect to many aspects of economic, social, and political life. Of course, different nations do choose different policies because they reflect different values and theories, different economic circumstances, and different balances of political power. Different tax policies, for example, reflect fundamentally different philosophies concerning how big the state should be, what functions it ought to perform, and how progressive taxation should be. In most nations, such key issues trigger mighty partisan battles over philosophical principles and the distribution of costs and benefits. In short, trade poses fundamental dilemmas, made more troublesome when nations pressed together by trade ties view such dilemmas differently, as in the case of the United States and Japan. Indeed, regional integration is attractive to many nations precisely because it increases trade with regional neighbors—who are presumably similar in important ways—while retaining insulation from nations who are more distant not only geographically but in policy preferences.

Even in Europe, however, these dilemmas have been recognized but not resolved; instead, the battleground has shifted from national-level to regional-level politics. For example, workers fear that without regional coordination, diminishing trade barriers will tend to harmonize national policies by driving all nations to emulate those with the weakest social protection, an outcome called social dumping. Recognizing that national policies would increasingly converge, leftist parties successfully sought to foster harmonization in which the more laissez-faire countries emulate those with the most elaborate social policies. For example, the goal of the EU's Social Charter in 1989 was to promote "convergence between social protection policies to avoid . . . competition between the systems with the attendant risk of decreasing social standards." In particular, the European Parliament recognized "fundamental social rights which should not be jeopardized because of the pressure of competition or the search for increased competitiveness."[20] Of course, such a preference runs directly contrary to the values, theories, and political constituencies of more conservative parties throughout Europe, who prefer more laissez-faire arrangements.

The EU transformed this political contest between parties of the left and right into a controversy over the dilemma concerning effects of trade (and trade organizations) on the state, especially in Britain. In the 1980s, British labor unions recognized that the social legislation they preferred was more likely to be enacted by the EU than by a British government dominated by Conservatives. In effect, they preferred to have labor law written by the French Socialist Jacques Delors, president of the European Commission, rather than by Conservative British prime minister Margaret Thatcher. By allying with the Socialist Parties of Europe, the British Labour Party sought to reverse through EU legislation the conservative revolution that Thatcher had achieved through national legislation. Such calculations lead to controversies over how much national sovereignty must be sacrificed in order to achieve the gains from trade. Thatcher condemned the EU as an attempt "to suppress nationhood and concentrate powers at the centre of a European conglomerate."[21] She is certainly correct in that assessment, but one wonders whether her defense of national sovereignty would be as spirited if the majority of the EU were more inclined to support her brand of conservatism. In any case, citing national sovereignty, Britain opted out of both the Social Charter in 1989 and the social-policy annex to the Maastricht Treaty in 1992. In 1994, Conservative prime minister John Major blocked the election of the head of the European Commission because the leading candidate favored a larger role for the EU at the expense of the constituent national governments. The link between trade and other values cannot be severed.

Still, despite the loss of sovereignty implicit in economic interdependence, we can now see why regional trade liberalization generates momentum to create even closer forms of integration. In the liberal vision, every increment of liberalization hints at the greater benefits that lie ahead if integration progresses. For example, if free trade permits low-wage labor in Spain to produce products cheaply for the rest of Europe, free movement in factors of production such as capital would obviously enable Spain's comparative advantage to be exploited even more fully. In the mercantilist vision, regional integration also tends to generate momentum: Because each step increases interdependence, it is natural that each nation would welcome more intensive integration arrangements that impose greater constraints on the disruptive policies of other governments.

Thus, even though the deepening of regional integration encourages greater integrative steps, it tends to sharpen political clashes over the form that it should take, especially the role it should play with respect to trade dilemmas. Liberals emphasize the economic dimension of free trade, in part because its tendency to undermine the capacity of national governments to sustain social protection could further the laissez-faire agenda of diminished state activity and an enhanced role for private enterprise. Fearing just such an outcome, the left accepts free trade in exchange for the package of protection against the dilemmas of trade embodied in the social dimension. That is, it opts for an activist regional government to replace the increasingly impotent national governments.

However, greater levels of integration in Europe will require the precise resolution of ambiguities that, up until the early 1990s, were responsible for the acceptance of integration by groups with incompatible views. A key issue has been whether the leveling of trade barriers will arise from the opening of the most protectionist nations or the closing of the most liberal ones.[22] The 1992 Single Market initiative was valued by some for its free trade face (Germany, England, Belgium, and Luxembourg); others were attracted by its protectionist face (France, Italy, and Spain).

The assessment by nations outside the EU will also depend heavily on the balance between trade creation and trade diversion. The real danger is that the complicated games among European governments and interest groups will be resolved principally by shifting costs onto foreigners. The ambivalent U.S. attitude toward the EU has always been heavily dependent upon how protectionist it would become.[23] However, the

United States originally supported the EC as a means to European recovery at a time when Europe was seen to be more valuable as a political and military ally than it was seen to be dangerous as an economic competitor. The EC also tied West Germany to the West, discouraging a policy of neutrality or alignment with the Soviet Union in pursuit of German reunification. In the mid-1990s, however, the U.S. interest concerns the 24 percent of its exports that go to the EU. Further, because any preferential tariff area has the potential to become a heavily protectionist trade bloc, the behavior of the EU is continuously monitored by those who see it as the precursor of an international system composed of such regional arrangements.

Within Europe, however, the major controversies concern the tensions provoked by the dilemmas of trade, an enlightening example of which is the chaos surrounding the near collapse of the European Monetary System (EMS) in the aftermath of the Maastricht Treaty.

THE DILEMMAS POSED BY EXCHANGE-RATE POLICY

Since 1992, exchange-rate policy has been at the center of the trade dilemmas concerning national sovereignty, which have threatened to derail further integration. As traditional trade barriers have declined, the trade-dampening effects of a system of multiple currencies have acquired increasing visibility. The most obvious effects are the simple transaction costs associated with currency exchanges: A consumer purchasing goods made in another country must pay the costs of exchanging the currency of his or her country for that of the nation in which the good was produced. Some costs are direct and visible, as when tourists pay a fee to a foreign-exchange broker; others are born by businesses and passed along invisibly to consumers. Currency conversion alone costs European business $15 billion per year, and transaction costs associated with currency exchanges have been estimated to waste 2 percent of the value of trade.

Firms must also maintain accounting systems and bank balances in several currency units simultaneously and cope with multiple currencies in legal contracts, taxation, and strategic planning. Moreover, the values of currencies vary with supply and demand conditions, creating uncertainty concerning future currency valuations and risks for business. Long-term production and marketing plans are complicated because firms cannot predict costs and revenues that are denominated in different currencies. In particular, firms fear that an increase in the value of their nation's currency will leave them suddenly uncompetitive in a foreign market. This uncertainty discourages trade because firms prefer to plan for the relative predictability of their domestic market.

Thus, as a logical extension of the desire to increase trade, a single European currency to replace the twelve national currencies has been a long-term goal of the EU for more than a decade. However, nations have strongly resisted giving up central elements of their national sovereignty: the rights to issue currency, to profit from the creation of a monetary asset, and to manage the economy by controlling the money supply. Any state harboring even a modicum of the mercantilist inclination to influence the economy—and all states do—would find the ceding of monetary policy to a regional authority an uncomfortable prospect. Moreover, a single currency would not be feasible until the various economies converged into a single market with similar levels of growth, inflation, and interest rates.

In the meantime, a less ambitious strategy has been followed that preserves national currencies but restrains changes in their relative valuation. EU nations that joined the Exchange Rate Mechanism (ERM) pledged to maintain currency valuations within a mandated range much like a regional version of the fixed exchange-rate system created under Bretton Woods. Whenever the value of their currency drifted beyond its agreed upon bounds, they were obligated to use foreign-exchange reserves to buy or sell currency until supply and demand were once again in balance at the accepted value. When such actions were ineffective, however, governments were further bound to alter domestic interest rates or other macroeconomic policies in order to stabilize the values of their currencies. It was expected that national economic policies would eventually converge, thus minimizing exchange-rate volatility and the need for governments to take extraordinary action to maintain their treaty obligations. In fact, however, because the priorities of different governments conflict, they often adopt policies that become incompatible with their obligation to maintain stable exchange rates. Thus, because monetary integration requires that governments undertake policies that they would prefer to avoid, it poses the dilemmas of national sovereignty and value trade-offs.

These dilemmas were brought home dramatically in fall 1992 when the ERM shattered and the prospects for further European integration consequently dimmed. At the time, Germany was suffering high inflation while struggling to unify formerly communist East Germany with capitalist West Germany. To restrain further price increases, German monetary authorities maintained high interest rates to slow the economy's growth. Meanwhile, both Britain and Italy, which were suffering high unemployment, sought low interest rates in order to accelerate growth. However, high interest rates in Germany induced British and Italian investors to transfer capital into Germany. As they sold investments denominated in the lira and the pound, the decreased demand for those currencies drove down their values while the higher yielding Deutsche mark increased in value.

Under the terms of the ERM, Britain was required to sustain the pound at a value above 2.78 Deutsche marks (DM), and Italy was bound to maintain a value of 1,000 lira at DM1.30. As the German central bank refused to lower its interest rates, both the pound and lira drifted to the bottom of their legal bands and finally sank beneath them. Britain spent more than $15 billion (half its total foreign-exchange reserves) to support the pound, and the Bundesbank spent nearly $50 billion to support the lira; but those sums were not enough. Italy was forced to acknowledge that it could not meet its treaty obligation to maintain the lira's value and withdrew from the ERM. Britain raised interest rates from 10 percent to 15 percent in a last futile attempt to remain in conformity but eventually abandoned the effort and similarly withdrew from the ERM. The pound quickly fell to DM2.53 and the lira to DM1.18 per 1,000. The Spanish peseta was also devalued by 5 percent.

To maintain the stable exchange rates that sustained free trade required nations to abandon the freedom to choose policies that would satisfy other goals. Faced with this clear dilemma of national sovereignty, several governments chose policy independence over the regional arrangement to encourage trade. The ERM nearly collapsed in a hail of recriminations. In August 1993, the first attempt to rebuild it acknowledged the primacy of national sovereignty: Nations were required to maintain their currencies only within a very wide band of 15 percent on either side of their central target rather than the previous stringent requirement of 2.25 percent. Thus, trade free of monetary fluctuations was sacrificed in this interim agreement. Certainly, the future of European monetary integration rests on the ability of nations to find a way out of this fundamental dilemma of trade. That means of escape is not now visible. Further, this incident has undermined faith in the ability of the EU to simultaneously accomplish regionwide goals while respecting differences in national-level priorities.

We now turn to the case of NAFTA, in which the dilemmas of trade manifest themselves in a remarkably similar way despite a very different type of regional trade arrangement.

THE NORTH AMERICAN FREE TRADE AGREEMENT

The North American Free Trade Agreement created a preferential tariff area among the United States, Canada, and Mexico beginning on January 1, 1994. However, the drive for regional economic cooperation had begun as early as 1851 with bilateral free trade negotiations between the United States and Canada. A free trade area involving the United States and all of Latin America was advocated by U.S. secretary of state James Blaine in 1881.

The first successful effort, however, was the landmark 1965 agreement that allowed duty-free trade in automobiles and original equipment parts between the United States and Canada. The resulting explosion of trade in the auto sector—from $625 million in 1964 to over $40 billion (about a third of total U.S.-Canadian trade) by 1984—motivated the Canada–United

States Trade Agreement (CUSTA), which expanded free trade to most sectors of the economy beginning in 1989. Most of CUSTA's provisions were retained in NAFTA, which took effect in 1994 after ratification processes in all three countries revealed considerable public uneasiness over issues commonly associated with the dilemmas of trade.[24]

Although some of the motivations for NAFTA parallel those of the EU, both their provisions and the institutional structures that support them are vastly different. NAFTA is indisputably an economic agreement, lacking both the broader social and political sweep of the EU—it contains nothing resembling the EU's Social Charter, for example—and its more ambitious long-term goals for common foreign and defense policy. More narrowly yet, NAFTA is principally a trade agreement with only limited provisions concerning investment and none addressing the monetary arrangements and economic policy coordination that are such a prominent part of the EU. The core of NAFTA consists of a phased elimination of tariff and most nontariff barriers over ten years with a few sectors having a fifteen-year transition period. The remaining elements of NAFTA qualify this liberalization and provide a sparse institutional structure to implement the agreement and resolve disputes that arise under it.[25]

Predictably, liberals lament that NAFTA does not go further in promoting free economic exchange. NAFTA attacks tariffs, but it does not prevent other barriers to trade such as subsidies and the procurement practices of governments.[26] Some of these barriers pose the now familiar dilemma of competing values: Policies designed for other purposes— even Canada's government-sponsored national health insurance and America's defense-contracting practices—can be seen as trade barriers because they confer a competitive advantage on some firms. Negotiations on such matters were difficult because the structure of protection is so different across these countries, with the United States objecting principally to Canadian subsidies and Canada protesting that the United States used its trade-remedy laws to stifle legitimate competition.[27]

Liberals also complain that NAFTA does not remove the barriers to movements of capital, barriers that prevent the most efficient combination of all factors of production. For example, a government review board is still required to approve foreign investment in some sectors of the Canadian economy, and parts of the energy sector remain off limits in both Canada and Mexico.[28] NAFTA also contains no provision to control fluctuating exchange rates, which can distort trade because an undervalued currency will "tax" imports by making them more expensive (because it makes foreign exchange more expensive) and "subsidize" exports by making them cheaper. During the CUSTA negotiations, the National Association of Manufacturers and the AFL-CIO contended that the undervaluation of the Canadian dollar acted as a protectionist measure, but exchange rates for the Mexican peso, which have fluctuated wildly, are potentially even more unsettling. For example, the value of the peso declined 25 percent in relation to the dollar during one week in December 1994, wreaking havoc in accurately pricing imports and exports.

If NAFTA is flawed from the standpoint of liberals, its limitations are even more alarming to those concerned about the issues that arise from trade dilemmas. Provisions to deal with those concerns, which are prominent in the EU, are largely missing from NAFTA, in part because the motivations for regional integration were somewhat different in these two cases.

MOTIVATIONS FOR NAFTA

Like the EU, NAFTA is the product of multiple motivations, the importance of which differs across the three countries. Both Canada and Mexico are driven principally by liberal incentives. However, NAFTA promises efficiency gains associated with Ricardian comparative advantage that amount to less than 1 percent of GNP for Canada. Relatively few areas of factor endowment–based comparative advantage remain unexploited because the American and Canadian economies are structurally similar and already largely open. For example, nearly 90 percent of U.S.-Canadian trade faced tariffs of less than 5 percent even before CUSTA.[29] The liberalization that produced trade expansion among EU members began from much higher levels of protection.

However, reminiscent of the ECSC's effect on smaller European countries, NAFTA offers Canada gains from economies of scale that may reach 10 percent of GNP. Furthermore, because the agreement restrains the U.S. trade-remedy laws, which produced nearly forty cases of countervailing duties and antidumping sanctions between the United States and Canada from 1980 to 1987, Canadian firms can now exploit these economies of scale without fear that an economic downturn or a political campaign will trigger a disastrous protectionist turn in the United States. Such benefits may be even more significant for Mexico because its smaller market ($214 billion compared to Canada's $572 billion) offers fewer opportunities for large-scale production. Mexico also would seem to benefit more from Ricardian gains from trade even though before NAFTA its exports faced an effective trade-weighted tariff rate of only 3.5 percent in the United States (plus NTBs equivalent to another 1.3 percent).

Mexico's principal motivation, however, was to improve industrial productivity both by exposing Mexican business to foreign competition and by encouraging foreigners to invest in Mexico. The Mexican economy had stagnated, especially during the 1970s and early 1980s, under the Mexican Partido Revolucionario Institucional (PRI), the ruling party for more than

three-quarters of a century. The PRI's economic approach, said to constitute a third way between capitalism and socialism, had featured an activist
state, sharp restrictions on foreign investment, and extremely protectionist
trade policies. For example, in June 1985, Mexico's average tariff rate was
23.5 percent, import permits were required (and usually rejected) for products constituting 92.2 percent of tradable output, and official prices bound
18.7 percent of products. Since the mid-1980s, the PRI has undergone a
revolution in economic policy, which now emphasizes privatization (selling 1,000 of the 1,200 state-owned companies, including the national air-
lines and the telephone company); fiscal deficit reduction (from 16 percent
of GDP to under 1 percent); elimination of government price fixing; inflation reduction (from over 200 percent to under 30 percent per year); and
import liberalization (by December 1987, tariffs averaged 11.8 percent and
only 25.4 percent of goods required import permits).[30]

NAFTA became the symbol of that revolution because it lends credibility to such a marked departure from historical practice even though more
liberalization occurred before NAFTA than is expected after its implementation. In particular, NAFTA encourages foreign investors to regard
liberalization as permanent because it binds Mexico under international
law to an agreement also enforced by the power of the United States.
Otherwise, they would not risk a return to the old policies that could
make their investment unprofitable.[31] Without an influx of foreign investment, capital from domestic sources would be inadequate to fuel the
growth made possible by Mexico's cheap labor force and direct access to
the American market.

Judging American motivations is more difficult because the liberal
gains that dominated the calculus of both Canada and Mexico were expected to be much smaller for the United States. Because of its much
greater size, any gains in access to the markets of its nearest neighbors
would have a negligible effect on the American economy: In 1992, total
trade with Canada and Mexico amounted to only about 2 percent of U.S.
GDP. Obviously, the gains from economies of scale must be tiny, and reducing already low trade barriers promises little improvement in efficiently allocating resources.

These judgments are borne out by many macroeconomic models constructed to predict the effects of NAFTA on American output and employment. The gains are difficult to estimate, but even the most optimistic
assessment foresaw a positive U.S. trade balance with Mexico of only
$7–$9 billion annually with a net increase of only 170,000 U.S. jobs, a little
more than one-tenth of 1 percent of the U.S. workforce.[32] The corresponding efficiency gains would be under $2 billion annually in an economy of
more than $5,500 billion.[33] These gains are so small that in a dynamic
economy we wouldn't be able to verify them even after the fact.

Why the big push for NAFTA if the promised gains are so modest? Some of the explanation centers on the indirect benefits the United States could expect to derive from the Mexican prosperity predicted to result from its recent liberalization—if NAFTA could make it permanent. Even if NAFTA created no net trade increases but only shifted some labor-intensive American imports from Asian to Mexican sources, the trade diversion would benefit the United States, which gains more from growth in Mexico than growth elsewhere.[34] Because 70 percent of Mexico's trade is with the United States—and because Mexico seemed likely to run a trade deficit for years to come—Mexican prosperity promised to improve the U.S. balance of trade. Expansion of Mexican trade was especially welcome because about half of Mexico's export earnings since 1982 have gone to repay foreign debt, much of it to American banks. Development in Mexico might also help to stem the tide of immigration that is increasingly politically divisive, particularly in the American Southwest.[35] Mexico's success would also be welcome as a liberal model for other Latin American nations (and debtors) who have engaged in heavily protectionist import-substituting industrialization (ISI) in the past. In fact, negotiations are under way to expand NAFTA throughout the Western Hemisphere.

American motivations are also related to other strands in its trade policy. It may be no coincidence that the Uruguay Round of GATT successfully concluded only after NAFTA had been approved. Because the EU has always been able to fall back on regional free trade whenever global negotiations turned sour, the United States lacked the bargaining power to complete the deal until NAFTA demonstrated that the United States had a similar alternative. Moreover, NAFTA introduced innovations that became precedents for global agreements, including its dispute-resolution mechanism (particularly compulsory arbitration and surveillance of trade policies), its treatment of services, and its elaboration of specific rights and obligations concerning national treatment.

The United States was also interested in several specific sectors even though their aggregate effects might not be large. By opening the Canadian energy sector to American investment, for example, NAFTA enhanced U.S. energy security, demonstrating that regional integration can secure a classic mercantilist objective by expanding the borders of a self-sufficient area. Domains such as financial services and intellectual property represent growth sectors in the global economy in which the United States has a comparative advantage.

But the best explanation for American interest in NAFTA may derive from the Bush administration's desire to restructure the American political economy according to laissez-faire principles of deregulation, liberalization, and privatization. Such a liberal ideal might achieve lower taxes, weaker labor organization, and a diminished welfare state by appealing to the necessity of competing with Mexican firms in the more competitive environment created by NAFTA. To see what such a position entails, we must consider how the various trade dilemmas posed by NAFTA are viewed by political actors in all three nations.

THE DILEMMAS IN NAFTA AND THE POLITICAL RESPONSE

Public opinion concerning NAFTA divides along the familiar fault lines of nation and class, but national sentiment does not reflect analysts' expectations of relative gains. For example, most analysts believe that the United States will gain less than either Canada or Mexico—and some question whether there will be any trade expansion for the United States at all—but the objection to NAFTA on these grounds has been negligible among the American public. Apparently, asymmetrical benefits provoke little concern unless the nations involved are perceived as rivals; reciprocity is more important in dealing with Japan than with Mexico. Moreover, NAFTA may have less impact on aggregate economic outcomes than it will on the issues raised by the dilemmas of trade. Thus, in the United States, the greatest protests have emerged over NAFTA's effect on unskilled labor (in response to the distributional dilemma) and the environment (in response to the dilemma of competing values).

In Mexico, NAFTA initially escaped much of the criticism usually directed against the distributional implications of free trade policies simply because the liberalization that preceded NAFTA had already drawn most of that fire. The dislocation costs had already been borne, and most saw NAFTA as a means to capture with greater certainty and permanence the benefits that the unilateral policies of the previous five years had only promised. However, a peasant revolt that began in the southern Mexican region of Chiapas in 1993 was directed against the economic priorities of the PRI—especially a tolerance for adverse effects on the poor—which were manifested in both NAFTA and earlier liberalization policies.

NAFTA became a principal target of Mexican unrest when its first year of existence witnessed a serious economic collapse featuring a 43 percent decline in the value of the peso, a 38 percent decline in the Mexican stock market, inflation soaring toward 60 percent, a large decline in real wages, falling living standards among Mexican workers, and massive unemployment. When default on foreign debt loomed, both the Zedillo administration and its supporters (primarily in the Clinton administration and the IMF) were seen to give priority to bailing out investors—especially those abroad—while ignoring the plight of the Mexican masses. Eventually NAFTA attracted the usual litany of opposition to liberalization rooted in trade dilemmas. Free trade benefits some at the expense of others. Free trade sacrifices other values in pursuit of growth for a segment of the population. Free trade creates reliance on foreigners, which diminishes national autonomy and threatens long-term development.

In Canada, the evaluation of NAFTA is colored by the experience of the previous five years with CUSTA (especially the deep recession that initially accompanied it), the long history of uneasy economic relations with the United States, and uncertainties about the future of the federal system of Canada itself. Anxieties about national sovereignty and the outlook for labor have weighed heavily in Canadian assessments of NAFTA; these assessments became a litmus test of attitudes toward the Conservative government, which negotiated both CUSTA and NAFTA. Antagonism toward free trade contributed to the October 1993 national election in which Conservatives were humiliated by losing all but two of their 169 seats in the 295-member Parliament and winning only 16 percent of the popular vote. New Liberal prime minister Jean Chrétien originally vowed to renegotiate NAFTA but later backed off from this position.

THE DILEMMA OF NATIONAL SOVEREIGNTY

International agreements that preclude certain national policies—as NAFTA prohibits most trade barriers—invariably involve some loss of national sovereignty. Although this dilemma has affected attitudes toward NAFTA in all three countries, the issue has arisen in a different way and with a different intensity in each nation.

In the United States, national sovereignty has been a minor concern, subsumed by greater apprehension about the environment and job issues though related to both. For example, NAFTA shifts some economic and environmental decisions away from national legislatures to binational review panels created to resolve trade disputes. Environmental and other groups that fear they will have less influence on these panels than they currently enjoy with Congress contend that the transfer of authority to supranational bureaucrats undermines national sovereignty and deprives citizens of rights of access to officials through elections, lobbying, and open public debates.[36] This same issue arose much more powerfully in the context of the WTO, apparently because Americans do not see Canada and Mexico as the grave threat to national sovereignty that a global institution might become.

Mexican concern about national sovereignty has produced one major concession in the NAFTA agreement: the exemption of Pemex, the Mexican national oil company, from its investment provisions. Pemex, though inefficient and corrupt, has become a Mexican symbol of independence and autonomy that has resisted privatization and retains protection against foreign competition in some areas.

The national sovereignty issue has acquired its greatest prominence in Canada, where closer trade with the United States has always triggered concern about maintaining national autonomy in matters of politics, economics, and culture. The continuing fear of U.S. domination is exemplified by the fate of the 1911 Canadian-American free trade treaty. During its ratification in the U.S. Congress, some proponents represented it as a first step toward the annexation of Canada, an outcome vehemently opposed by most Canadians. As a consequence, the Canadian government was denied reelection in a campaign dominated by the campaign slogan of the opposition, "No truck or trade with the Yankees."[37]

The source of these concerns is not hard to see. In economic terms, critics claim that NAFTA will increase American domination of Canada. Even before CUSTA, exports to the United States constituted 75 percent of Canada's trade and 20 percent of its total GNP.[38] American foreign direct investment in Canada is valued at $70 billion with 20 percent of Canada's 500 largest firms owned by Americans. About half of Canadian manufacturing is foreign-owned, most by Americans. Statements like that of U.S. trade representative Clayton Yeutter to a Canadian newspaper shortly after the CUSTA negotiations do not allay those fears: "The Canadians don't understand what they have signed. In 20 years they will be sucked into the U.S. economy."[39] The response is predictable; Shirley Carr, president of the Canadian Labour Congress, recently remarked, "It is in the interest of the United States to try to take over Canada. . . . They want to disrupt and disturb everything we have and bring us down to their level."[40] Of course, intensive trade with a more developed and more powerful nation has fed such anxieties since the days of Friedrich List, but regional integration can be especially troublesome in this regard. Indeed, the dilemma of declining national sovereignty has even dogged the EU, though Germany is much less dominant within the EU than the United States is within NAFTA.[41] American dominance has been especially striking in terms of culture: "Only 3 to 5 percent of all theatrical screen time in Canada goes to Canadian films; 97 percent of profits from films shown in Canada go out of the country, 95 percent to the U.S.; 95 percent of English-language TV drama is non-Canadian; Canadian-owned publishers have only 20 percent of the book market; 77 percent of the magazines sold here are foreign; 85 percent of record and tape sales are non-Canadian."[42]

In response to these concerns, CUSTA's Article 2005 states that "cultural industries are exempt from the provisions of this agreement," thus allowing a continuation of Canadian protection and promotion of cultural industries that has existed for most of the twentieth century.[43] It is interesting that this very same issue also arose in the Uruguay Round talks, with French negotiators eventually winning protection from Hollywood film producers they regarded as symbols of American cultural hegemony.

THE DISTRIBUTIONAL DILEMMA AND THE POLITICS OF LABOR ISSUES

In both Canada and the United States, however, the most controversial issue concerns the impact of NAFTA on jobs and wages. Unlike the Corn

Laws, which posed the distributional dilemma principally in terms of sectors of the economy, in NAFTA the dilemma has emerged as a class issue. Opponents have contended that NAFTA would produce a net loss of jobs, especially among the unskilled, who are least able to adjust; a decline in wages among the unskilled who remain employed; and a transition period involving disruption and risk that is excessive given the small and uncertain projected gains.[44]

Liberal trade theory makes a persuasive case for NAFTA's long-term benefits, including more job creation than job loss, though macroeconomic computer models generally show the net effect to be quite small. Opponents of NAFTA question outcomes derived from such computable general equilibrium (CGE) models because they require unrealistic assumptions such as full employment, balanced trade, and capital immobility.[45] It is especially noteworthy that the major fear—job loss—is assumed away by the CGE assumption of full employment. As one critic points out, "We might forgive the Ford employee for being less than convinced by a CGE model that crosses a deep ravine by *assuming* a bridge."[46] Arguments for free trade often appear most convincing to those who have no stake in their truth, but for the workers whose livelihood depends on the accuracy of the trickle-down models, the theories usually seem too flimsy to justify the risks.

Labor concerns arose from the recognition that NAFTA would destroy American jobs as some U.S. firms lost sales to Mexican firms and others moved production facilities to Mexico. Opponents emphasized dislocations from NAFTA-related job loss estimated in the range of 150,000 to 500,000.[47] The transition period can be long and painful: It is estimated that 40 percent of laid-off workers will remain unemployed a year later and that the remainder will suffer wage losses averaging 10 percent for service workers, 20 percent for manufacturing workers, and 30 percent for automobile and steel workers. Within five years, most workers will have recovered their previous wages; but 35 percent will never again make the same wages, and three-fourths of workers will not go back to the same type of job. The average cost of a job loss for a worker amounts to about $80,000 over a lifetime.[48] Proponents observe that NAFTA-related job-loss estimates are modest in relation to the 2 million Americans expected to lose their jobs every year for the next decade for reasons unrelated to NAFTA. Further, they note that job loss to low-wage countries is inevitable even in the absence of NAFTA. Finally, they point out that some job gains from NAFTA are just as inevitable as some job losses. It is no wonder that businesses emphasize their vision of an efficient, comparative advantage–based economy that would eventually result from NAFTA and that labor organizations emphasize the transition costs that would be borne before such a future could emerge.

Free trade always triggers labor's concern about employment, wages, and social dumping, but three considerations make the issue unusually

Smith-Corona, last US typewriter maker, moves to Mexico.

NAFTA fallout. Danziger—© *The Christian Science Monitor*

acute in the case of NAFTA. First, huge disparities in wage rates and working conditions between the United States and Mexico increase the pressure on American workers. With wages for unskilled labor roughly eight to ten times higher in the United States than in Mexico, American firms have a strong incentive to either abandon production requiring unskilled labor or move it to Mexico.[49] Negotiating under this kind of threat, American workers will be unable to resist a decline in wage rates and living standards. In fact, the factor price equalization theorem, an elaboration of Heckscher-Ohlin, states that free trade will cause all factor prices, including wage rates, to equalize across nations. Supporters hope that NAFTA will bring a growth boom to Mexico that results in Mexican wages rising to U.S. levels rather than American wages falling to Mexican levels, but that is unlikely. Mexico's very high unemployment rate precludes any upward pressure on wage rates from labor shortages for many years.[50] Furthermore, weak labor laws in Mexico make it difficult for labor to press for higher wages. As a result, NAFTA might lower wages in the United States without raising them in Mexico, which would be especially alarming because wages for unskilled labor are already declining in the United States. For example, during the 1980s the real wages of those without a high school diploma fell 10 percent, and a similar effect seems to be spreading to high school graduates.[51]

Second, capital mobility, which makes the relocation of labor-intensive production to Mexico easy, sharpens the competition between American and Mexican labor, especially by eroding productivity differences between them.[52] The factor price equalization theorem holds that wage rates will fully equalize only if the productivity of workers in the two countries is identical. Thus, the current gap in wage rates should persist so long as American workers remain so much more productive than Mexican workers, but the modernization of the Mexican economy fueled by the foreign direct investment (FDI) of American firms is likely to erode that difference, at least for unskilled labor. By the end of 1991, foreign direct investment in Mexico totaled about $33 billion, with nearly two-thirds of it originating in U. S. corporations.[53] In anticipation of NAFTA, capital inflows to Mexico were estimated at $18 billion in 1992, including $5 billion in foreign direct investment.[54]

The *maquiladora* program can be seen as a kind of pilot project for NAFTA, demonstrating the power of combining American capital with Mexican labor. Since 1965, firms on the Mexican side of the U.S. border, known as maquiladoras, have been permitted to import parts duty free from the United States and to export the assembled product back into the country, also duty free. By 1992, nearly 2,000 factories operating under

Wage bargaining at a maquiladora. Danziger—© The Christian Science Monitor

this program employed nearly 500,000 workers, about 20 percent of the total manufacturing labor force in Mexico.[55] Meanwhile, employment and wages for American unskilled labor had stagnated.

Third, unlike the EU, NAFTA contains very little provision for dealing with dislocations, and, unlike in Europe, the social welfare system in the United States provides less protection from structural unemployment. In Canada, where the welfare state is more advanced than in the United States, the left fears that dislocations may overwhelm its capacity and force the abandonment of prized programs of social insurance.

Partisan alignments reflect the Stolper-Samuelson expectation that free trade will benefit the abundant factor of production (capital, in the United States) and harm the scarce one (unskilled labor is scarce in the United States relative to the huge surplus of cheap labor in Mexico). These distributional implications of free trade explain why more than 75 percent of Republicans voted for final passage of NAFTA in the U.S. House of Representatives and why more than 60 percent of Democrats voted no even after heavy lobbying by Democratic president Bill Clinton.

THE DILEMMA OF VALUE TRADE-OFFS
AND ENVIRONMENTAL POLITICS

Most of the major American environmental groups also opposed NAFTA, especially the Sierra Club and Friends of the Earth, which (unsuccessfully) sought a court order to require the administration to file an environmental impact report. For three reasons, critics feared that a commitment to NAFTA's free trade principles would require a compromise with the value of environmental protection. First, the border region of Mexico could become an export platform for companies who want to sell products in the United States but evade American environmental standards. Second, the availability of the border region to polluting industries may produce social-dumping pressures on American state and local governments to save jobs by lowering environmental standards. Third, NAFTA opens American environmental regulation to foreign challenge because it can be interpreted as an illegal barrier to trade.

The direct environmental dangers are concentrated in the border area between Mexico and the United States, which hosts the maquiladora program. Countless reports and studies have documented it as an environmental wasteland with threats to the human population on both sides of the border, especially from water pollution. The Rio Grande, which serves as the U.S.-Mexican border for much of its length, is heavily polluted with metals and raw sewage. It provides drinking water for a million people and irrigation water for a large agricultural area, but its fecal contamination levels "regularly exceed, often by a factor of a hundred, standards to protect public health." The New River, which begins in Mexico and flows into the Salton Sea, California's largest lake, is known as the most polluted river in North America. Beaches within several miles of the outlet of the Tijuana River into the Pacific Ocean have been closed for ten years. In San Elizario, Texas, 90 percent of the population has contracted hepatitis by age thirty-five because of a polluted aquifer.[56]

This pollution originates largely in maquiladora firms, fully 10 percent of which admitted that they had migrated to avoid American environmental regulations and take advantage of the weaker environmental laws and notoriously lax enforcement in Mexico.[57] For example, the La Paz agreement of 1983 required that industries importing chemicals into Mexico return any resulting hazardous wastes to the country of origin, but a 1988 report of the U.S. EPA showed that only 1 percent of maquiladoras had done so. This record cannot be a surprise: In 1990, the Mexican federal government budget for environmental law enforcement was only $3.15 million.

Environmentalists also fear that NAFTA will trigger value trade-offs similar to those that have arisen from conflicts between various environmental policies and previous free trade agreements, including GATT. For example, the Bush administration successfully pressured British Columbia to end a government-funded tree-planting program because it was an "unfair subsidy" to the Canadian timber industry. Similarly, government payments to farmers to promote soil and water conservation could be interpreted as an unfair subsidy of agricultural exports. Export restrictions on lumber designed to enforce practices of sustainable forestry could be considered a violation of prohibitions against export restraints.[58] Restricting imports of food contaminated with pesticides now banned in America can be grounds for foreign governments to sue the United States for establishing nontariff barriers to trade.

The most dramatic recent episode occurred in the 1994 clash known as GATTzilla versus Flipper, in which a GATT tribunal ruled in favor of a complaint brought by the EU on behalf of European tuna processors who buy tuna from Mexico and other countries that use purse seine nets. The United States boycotts tuna caught in that way, since the procedure also kills a large number of dolphins, but GATT ruled that the U.S. law was an illegal barrier to trade because it discriminates against the fishing fleets of nations that use this technique.

Initial experience with CUSTA confirms that such environmental trade-offs will arise under NAFTA. "The first trade dispute under the free trade agreement involved a challenge by the U.S. to regulations under Canada's Fisheries Act established to promote conservation of herring and salmon stocks in Canada's Pacific coast waters." The provision to require reporting was struck down by the dispute panel.

Similarly, the Canadian government challenged the U.S. EPA's regulations that require the phaseout of asbestos, a carcinogen once frequently used as a building material.[59] A balance between environmental concerns and free trade principles could be achieved, but NAFTA, which lacks the EU's recognition of the social and political dilemmas of trade, does not do so.

CONCLUSION: LESSONS FROM NAFTA

Trade ties together the fate of nations. Prosperity in one country can be "exported" to another through trade, but dependence on others can also transmit less pleasing conditions. Trade is not equally desirable under all circumstances or with all possible partners, especially because its effect on value trade-offs, distributional patterns, and state concerns can vary dramatically. In this light, regional integration offers a cautious compromise between self-sufficiency and global free trade by allowing a nation to selectively choose its partners in destiny. Despite difficulties in the past and uncertainties about the future, the EU exemplifies the virtue of such an approach, taking advantage of the economic, political, and social compatibility of its members to forge an organization that can address common problems and achieve shared goals.

The early experience with NAFTA is less clear, and the decision to bind together the fate of all three North American nations cannot yet be definitively assessed. However, a major currency crisis that began less than a year after NAFTA's implementation in January 1994 has cast doubt on whether Mexico is yet stable enough to be a reliable member of a regional trade organization. That currency crisis, which was marked by a 40 percent decline in the value of the peso, not only disrupted regional trade and precipitated a deep recession in Mexico but also triggered concern about Mexico's ability to meet its foreign-debt obligation. In response, the Clinton administration, fearful of the consequences of a collapse in the Mexican economy, provided a $20 billion line of credit as part of a $50 billion international effort to rescue Mexico from imminent default.[60]

It is instructive to note that NAFTA both contributed to Mexico's economic problems and helped export them to the United States. The key role is played by the Mexican peso, which despite a temporary boost from NAFTA could not maintain its value under the pressure imposed by Mexico's trade liberalization. As trade barriers fell throughout the early 1990s, Mexican imports soared, producing a trade deficit that finally reached 8 percent of GDP in 1994. Ordinarily this deficit would have caused the peso to decline steadily until its equilibrium value was reached, but instead it was offset for a while by a huge—but temporary—inflow of capital from abroad, more than $60 billion in portfolio investment alone from 1990 to 1993. Much of this originated from foreign investors who were persuaded by enthusiastic supporters of liberalization that Mexico represented the next great investment opportunity, especially in anticipation of NAFTA.[61] Inevitably, this capital inflow began to decline, putting downward pressure on the value of the peso. The Salinas government recognized that a falling peso would produce domestic inflation, erode the confidence of foreign investors, and undermine the reputation of the PRI for financial management, all of which it wanted to avoid during the 1994 presidential election. Thus, it expended treasury funds to artificially support the peso (and pressured the central bank to expand the money supply by over 20 percent). With foreign reserves nearly exhausted—falling below $7 billion—the new president, Ernesto Zedillo, was forced to announce a 13 percent devaluation of the peso less than three weeks after his inauguration in December 1994. This became the last in a string of incidents—among them the Chiapas revolt, a contested election result, and a political assassination—that had alarmed foreign investors over the previous year. The devaluation effectively acknowledged an economic crisis, which drove frightened investors to react in panic. The peso declined by 40 percent, the Mexican stock market sank by a similar amount, inflation skyrocketed, and unemployment increased. With American economic interests now tied to the stability of the Mexican economy and NAFTA's prestige bound up with the success of the Mexican liberalization program, the Clinton administration arranged an emergency bailout with help from the IMF and other institutions. The changes in Mexican macroeconomic policy required by the crisis itself and those imposed as part of the bailout agreement guaranteed a sharp recession that, among other effects, would reduce the trade between Mexico and the United States that NAFTA was designed to boost. Recent reports show illegal immigration on the U.S.-Mexican border sharply increased, American export businesses suffering, and Mexican democracy teetering. As of late 1995, the dislocations associated with Mexico's trade liberalization and the NAFTA agreement meant to signify its permanence are more apparent than the benefits that remain projected for the future. Trade generates dilemmas that can overwhelm its advantages unless nations and organizations are prepared to respond to them.

SEVEN

□ □ □

Looking Ahead

This book has had two missions. First, I have attempted to explain the issues and problems that surround international trade, especially the dilemmas that arise from the opportunities it presents. Second, I have traced how perceptions of these dilemmas have shaped trade policy choices in several different nations, institutions, and time periods.

MISSIONS REVIEWED

Few would deny the contention of liberal theory that trade permits a higher level of aggregate consumption than would be possible if consumers were prevented from purchasing foreign products. It is hard to imagine modern life without the benefits of trade. However, this aggregate economic effect tells only part of the story; trade also carries with it important social and political implications. Trade shapes the distribution of income and wealth among individuals, affects the power of states and the relations among them, and constrains or enhances the ability of both individuals and nations to achieve goals built on other values. These other effects of trade are more equivocal and sometimes more ethereal than the aggregate economic effects. Empirically, they are more difficult to predict because they vary with circumstances; normatively, they are more difficult to assess because they touch values that are far from universal. They present dilemmas because no trade policy choice can avoid the negative consequences inherent in each alternative.

National governments select trade policies according to how these dilemmas have been understood and assessed. They have been viewed differently depending upon the efficiency of markets and the competitive

Life without international trade. Danziger—©*The Christian Science Monitor*

positioning of firms from different countries within them. An important role is also played by empirical theories that describe and predict the effects of trade and normative theories that elucidate the principles appropriate for judging the desirability of these outcomes and choosing among them. In the final analysis, the balance of political power among those with alternative views shapes the policy choices of governments.

It is striking how recurrently these themes appear in different contexts. Across several centuries, trade policy choices have been debated in the language of liberalism and mercantilism. The strengths and weaknesses of each intellectual tradition remain very much as they were when they were founded. The explanations for the choice between them exhibit similar continuity over time.

MERCANTILISM AND LIBERALISM: A SUMMARY PERSPECTIVE

Classical mercantile trade policy represented a distinctive response to the dilemmas posed by trade. Mercantilists advocated government control of markets, especially in international trade, in order to generate specific distributional outcomes, especially the protection of consumers and grain producers. They also pursued the values of social justice, national development, and self-sufficiency with greater zeal than the values of greater consumption and efficiency, which were associated with liberalism. They saw unregulated trade as more of a threat to state power and national defense than as a guarantor of international peace.

Mercantilism evolved in response to existing conditions in the economy and foreign affairs, in tune with prevailing currents of social and economic theory, and in recognition of the realities of the distribution of power. Inevitably, these foundations eventually crumbled: By the middle of the nineteenth century, the theories and values that sustained mercantilism, the conditions of markets that limited its alternatives, and the political power of its supporters and opponents had all changed.

In fact, mercantilism can be interpreted as a middle ground—a transition—between the sharp antagonism to the market characteristic of the Middle Ages and the modern era's acceptance of market principles. For most of Western history, social theory had favored the control of markets for the public purpose (especially by government), but a rapidly evolving economy began to offer material advantages too large to so easily dismiss on ethical grounds. Mercantilism sought to accommodate the material needs and opportunities of this changing economic order yet not fully abandon the commitment to manage economic affairs in accord with other values. Although this economic system was maintained by the predominant powers of the period—the Crown and the church—the growth of political challengers and the fading of their social views doomed classical mercantilism. By the middle of the nineteenth century, mercantilism was seen as a curious anachronism that was ill suited to meet the modern challenge.

No doctrine can escape the fate of obsolescence. Perhaps theories are mortal: Just as they are born, they must die. They can be "true" but they cannot be universal. Perhaps theories are more like endangered species: Though born to a habitat whose destruction they rarely survive unchanged, they can evolve and adapt to a new environment. In either case, it is wise to understand the roots of theories and the limits that are imposed by the values they assume and the material conditions to which they apply. But it would be a mistake to underestimate the adaptability of a viewpoint that has arisen in as many different times and places as mercantilism.

Certainly, the classical brand of mercantilism seems foreign today, but we dismiss its lessons at considerable peril. Mercantilism was neither as ignorant nor as ill advised as many contemporary commentators imply. Unfortunately, history is written by the victors. Too often, the wisdom of the losers is thus lost, denied its rightful place in our arsenal of weapons waiting to be applied should new challenges require. Mercantilism's lessons are eclipsed by self-congratulatory hubris, but our abandonment of the issues raised by this vision is as dangerous as our failure to appreciate the inner logic of mercantilism as a whole. The challenges faced by classical mercantilism reappear in the modern era: trade deficits, reliance upon other nations, the need for government revenues, the difficulty of initiating infant industries, the desire to provide security for all citizens, the use of trade for other foreign policy purposes, and the unfair practices of other nations. These issues are not dead but only recast. The protection of consumers and workers may no longer be seen principally as a Christian imperative, but it is just as surely mandated by democratic political systems erected to fulfill the modern values of justice and citizen welfare. Fear of dependence on others for food may no longer lead nations to policies of self-sufficiency in grain, but the Persian Gulf War reminds us of the alternative when other nations control trade in a vital product. We need no longer fret about the revenues of the Crown or accommodate the privileges of a landed aristocracy, but the government still needs revenue and some groups still command greater attention from the state than others.

So it should not be a surprise that mercantilists survive, fueled by the original logic even if rooted in a different soil or known by a different label. We need not be baffled or enraged by the Japanese system of import protection and export subsidies or the European Union's Common Agricultural Policy, both of which have more in common with the Anglo-American past than we may be prepared to admit. Nor are the mercantilist impulses in our own trade system extinguished; we call them fair trade rather than protection, but the distinction is elusive. Most unfortunately, we deny that trade raises many of the same dilemmas today that were confronted with more candor and vision by those whose names we can no longer recall.

Liberalism, too, represents a distinctive reaction to the dilemmas of trade. Though rooted initially in a particular historic period, liberalism has subsequently been adapted to a wide range of circumstances and remains of contemporary relevance. Liberalism resolved the dilemma over competing values by rejecting mercantilism's early Christian emphasis on communitarianism and social stability while embracing the aggregate consumption and individualism of secular utilitarianism. Liberalism resolved the distributional dilemma by accepting market-based outcomes over state-mandated ones, with clear benefits for industrialists and clear losses for landowners. Finally, liberalism resolved the dilemma over the effect of trade on the state by accepting interdependence and forsaking self-sufficiency.

The key to the acceptance of liberalism was the powerful theory of comparative advantage with Ricardo's memorable demonstration of the gains from trade: The standard of living of consumers improves under the efficient specialization unleashed by free trade. However, the seed of free trade had to be planted in ground made fertile by the dominance of values and social ideas compatible with liberalism. A theory that appealed to aggregate material interests and trusted the market to bring about acceptable social outcomes had to wait until the middle of the nineteenth century, by which time the liberal ideas of private property, materialism, individualism, and the division of labor had become familiar and ethically acceptable. The commercialization of agriculture, the rapid growth of towns and industry, change in church doctrine, and the growing influence of secular utilitarian social and political ideas doomed the village-based communal ethics of an earlier age.

At the same time, the market and the productive forces which it organized had developed sufficiently to play their appointed role in liberal theory. Britain's industries were the most competitive in the world, foreign agriculture had the capacity to both feed England and earn revenues to purchase British manufactures, and trade was easier and more reliable because of transportation improvements and relative peace among nations. Against this backdrop, optimistic estimates of transition costs and favorable assessments of short-term risks versus long-term gains are understandable.

Finally, the need for a political force capable of tending the crop with skill and enthusiasm was filled by the industrial class, which was growing in political strength and economic importance. The distributional implications of free trade—particularly when grain prices were so vividly apparent to consumers—operated to the advantage of free traders. After British industry's competitive dominance allowed it to forsake protection for itself, free traders were able to present a compelling case in broad national-interest terms.

However, the flowering of free trade that was symbolized by the repeal of the Corn Laws in 1846 was not lasting but was only one phase of a now familiar cycle in which any approach to trade generates the very forces that eventually bring about its reversal. The more extreme the policy approach, the more visible are the dilemmas it produces. The unbridled market of the early nineteenth century—though it generated rapid economic growth and technical progress—produced an ideological backlash and an alteration in social and political structures that together created market-interventionist states. The trade suppression of the 1930s—though it sought security for workers—produced a depression and war that led to renewed internationalism and restored faith in markets.

FUTURE CHALLENGES

It is hard to predict what form trade controversies will take in the immediate future—an extension of NAFTA, the refinement of the WTO, another round of trade talks, another skirmish in a trade conflict with Europe or Japan, the integration of new powers such as China into the heart of the global political economy. It is easier to predict the broad forces that will be at work in these specific instances—the dilemmas of trade—and how they will be resolved in line with prevailing theories and values, the condition of markets, and the balance of political power.

Perhaps the most striking characteristic of the global political economy in the 1990s is the extraordinary efficiency of its markets. Transportation and communication advances make the conduct of global trade cheaper, easier, and faster than previous generations could have imagined. Indeed, transportation costs are now so low that we have entered an era of global *production*. For example, the Ford Fiesta assembled in Europe contains major parts from Ford plants in more than a dozen countries.[1]

This development is also fueled by enormous capital flows between nations. The stock of foreign direct investment is now over $1,000 billion.[2] "The London Eurodollar market, in which the world's financial institutions borrow from and lend to each other, turns over $300 billion each working day, a volume at least twenty-five times that of world trade.... In addition, ... foreign currency transactions in the world's main money centres, in which one currency is traded against another, ... run around $150 billion a day."[3]

In economic terms, this extraordinary mobility of both productive capacity (capital and technology) and finished goods means that tiny differences in competitive advantage can be exploited without being eaten up by transportation costs. However, at the same time, residents of the new

Unemployment in the global market. Danziger—©*The Christian Science Monitor*

global village are becoming increasingly uneasy with the small margin of error between success and failure in the modern market. Workers, for whom security is a primary value, fear that comparative advantage will shift so quickly that no jobs will be secure. States, for whom power over other domestic actors and sovereignty against foreign ones are primary values, fear that they will lose the ability to control the national economy at the same time that electorates increasingly hold them responsible for it and just as economic power has begun to displace military power in foreign policy. Inevitably, this mobility for some actors—multinational corporations and other owners of capital and technology—affords them a bargaining advantage over actors with inherently less mobility, especially workers and nation-states. We can expect that both will respond to the sharpened dilemmas.

Indeed, states already have responded, by increasing the use of NTBs and by creating regional arrangements that give them a geographical range comparable to the actors they are trying to control. Increasing regionalism solves some problems and exacerbates others. In particular, the emerging pattern of regionalism amounts to a discriminatory trading system of superblocs that some fear could endanger international peace. The trade discrimination implicit in regionalism creates foreign policy tensions between blocs at the same time that conflict-dampening global interdependence, which otherwise might help contain it, declines.

Thus, the chief challenge for the global trading system is to reinvigorate the institutions that govern international trade without eroding the legitimate rights and responsibilities of national governments. Not only must the global system promote peace and prosperity, it must be seen to do so better than regional arrangements. All this must be accomplished in an era lacking the shared interests and values that made such progress easier in the case of Bretton Woods, lacking the conviction that global management is necessary (which was brought about by World War II and the Great Depression), and lacking a hegemonic leader committed to the process and capable of delivering a globally acceptable compromise. These goals must also be achieved during an era of slow global growth, especially in the developed nations, when competition is at its most heated.

In addition, a consensus must be achieved among nations that represent greater diversity than ever before. If accommodating Japanese trade policy has generated tensions, the dislocations implicit in dealing with the People's Republic of China (PRC), for example, loom even larger. The PRC is among the fastest-growing economies in the world and is quickly becoming a major force in global trade. Its vast potential market of 1 billion consumers represents a lure that has led the international community to tread lightly on Chinese violations of international norms even when they are dramatically visible. In esoteric trade matters between countries with vastly different values and institutions, where matters are seldom so clear, one can expect even greater reluctance to establish clear limits. To cite only the most extreme example, China, whose bilateral trade surplus with the United States is second only to Japan's, exports many products manufactured by slave labor. Not only does this offend the sensibilities of many foreigners, it creates an impossible competition problem for American workers. Already under threat from poor labor in Mexico, they are now being challenged to produce at lower unit cost than slaves.

For the nation, the greatest challenge will be to cope with the dilemmas of trade that become more binding as trade levels increase. In particular, states must deal adequately with distributional dilemmas without eliminating the beneficial trade that brings them about. In doing so, they must view the value underlying the theory of comparative advantage—the maximization of consumption—as only one policy goal among many components of what Max Corden has called the "conservative social welfare function." According to this function, nations avoid income declines for most groups even if they would be balanced by larger income gains among other groups. The reason is fourfold. First, it is regarded as unfair to diminish incomes via government policy. Second, because most individuals are risk averse, the knowledge that this function is being pursued provides security benefits to all. Third, social peace is endangered by sharp increases in income inequality. Fourth, for all of the previous reasons, governments are likely to fall if incomes decline.[4]

The most successful policies are likely to be those that create institutional structures that ease trade dilemmas rather than relying on either pure liberalism or pure mercantilism. This has been accomplished in very different ways in Europe and in Japan, where the challenges have been felt more acutely and for a longer time than in the United States

In Europe, regional regulation has sought to structure trade competition so as to minimize value clashes, especially by protecting the ability of the welfare state to ameliorate the distributional effects of trade. Of course, in the process of responding to trade dilemmas, regional organizations must cope with the competing priorities that cut across nations and political parties. The European right sees the slow growth of output and employment in recent years as evidence that a regional welfare state is not economically sustainable. The left counters with the observation that trade expansion without social protection to cope with the dislocations it produces is not politically sustainable.

In Japan, the effects of markets are muted by a variety of societal and governmental arrangements, including employment practices and private network structures, that purchase security at the expense of consumer benefits. Furthermore, aggressive foreign marketing shifts some of the dilemmas to foreign nations. Evidence increasingly suggests that resistance from both domestic consumers and foreign governments makes this solution only temporary.

These experiences should help to shape attitudes in the United States, where efforts to resolve these dilemmas are somewhat more recent in origin. The central lesson does not promote optimism: Trade dilemmas cannot be fully resolved because they inevitably require choices. High levels of trade promote distributional effects that are beneficial to some but harmful to others. Regulations designed to protect the environment and to meet other societal goals often constrain the benefits to be earned from free trade. When the role of markets are strengthened, the role of the state must decline. Nations must choose.

CONCLUSION: INDIVIDUAL CHOICES

For the individual, the challenge is to recognize the central role that issues of international political economy—especially trade—will play in determining the kind of society, polity, and economy in which one will live. Individuals must demand that advocates of different policies respond to the entire range of considerations that lurk beneath the dull surface of trade policy. They must insist upon comprehensive policy packages that address all the trade dilemmas rather than rely only upon narrow considerations. They must require that the universal and eternal truths of Smith and Ricardo be balanced with the messy reality of specific cases. They must weigh the dilemmas posed by trade for the individual in his or her various roles—as consumer, as worker, and as citizen. Choose wisely.

□   □   □

Discussion Questions

CHAPTER ONE

1. Should a consumer consider the social and political effects of trade when deciding whether to buy a domestic or foreign product?

2. Some imports produce social costs, such as unemployment of domestic autoworkers or the need to maintain military forces to protect oil routes around the Persian Gulf. Should governments apply a tax on foreign products equal to these social costs?

3. Why are some nations so much more reliant on foreign trade than others?

CHAPTER TWO

1. What foreign policy conditions made reliance on trade unattractive to Britain during the mercantile period? Have similar conditions existed for developed countries in the last half of the twentieth century?

2. What changes in ethical outlook fueled the rise of liberal economic ideas? Have there been any changes in values or philosophy since Bretton Woods that might have a comparable influence on economic policy? (Environmentalism, perhaps?)

3. What changes in political power balances led to the repeal of the Corn Laws? Have similar changes occurred in the twentieth-century United States?

CHAPTER THREE

1. Can you identify any recent changes in the operation of markets that would be comparable to the improvements in transportation systems in early England? What effect would you expect these changes to have on trade policy preferences?

2. What change would you expect in U.S. trade policy from an election that left either the Democrats or the Republicans fully in control? Why?

3. Why do you think U.S. consumers did not exert more political pressure to eliminate restrictions on imports of Japanese autos, which increased prices on all autos significantly?

4. It is an interesting exercise to attempt to explain why liberalism or mercantilism emerged as the policy choice of particular individuals, groups, and nations in

particular periods. Choose your own position. Why is U.S. organized labor more protectionist now than in the 1950s? Are Canadian farmers free traders or protectionists? French farmers?

CHAPTER FOUR

1. On balance, did Bretton Woods favor the United States at the expense of other nations?

2. Why didn't the United States assume leadership of the global political economy after World War I instead of delaying until after World War II?

3. On balance, is Bretton Woods primarily a liberal or a mercantilist system?

CHAPTER FIVE

1. Why hasn't the United States adopted an explicit industrial policy comparable to those in Japan and Europe?

2. Why hasn't the United States taken a harder line with Japan, threatening dramatic trade sanctions if the bilateral trade deficit doesn't diminish?

3. Why have American-Japanese trade tensions accelerated so dramatically since the early 1980s?

4. Does Japan's export of goods to other countries create a moral obligation for it to purchase foreign imports? If individuals choose not to do so, does the government have a moral obligation to force them?

CHAPTER SIX

1. What factors explain why the EU and NAFTA have a different balance between the economic and social dimensions of regional integration?

2. Why did President Bill Clinton so enthusiastically support NAFTA when Democratic candidate Bill Clinton did not?

CHAPTER SEVEN

1. What courses of action are available for individuals to register their attitudes toward the dilemmas of trade?

2. Should a consumer consider the social and political effects of trade when deciding whether to buy a domestic or foreign product?

3. Should the United States continue to extend MFN status to China?

Notes

CHAPTER ONE

1. John Marttila, "American Public Opinion: Evolving Definitions of National Security," in Edward K. Hamilton, ed., *America's Global Interests: A New Agenda* (New York: W. W. Norton, 1989), pp. 261–315.

2. Richard Lamm, "The Uncompetitive Society," in Martin K. Starr, ed., *Global Competitiveness: Getting the U.S. Back on Track* (New York: W. W. Norton, 1988), pp. 12–42.

3. Laura D'Andrea Tyson, "Competitiveness: An Analysis of the Problem and a Perspective on Future Policy," in Starr, *Global Competitiveness*. Emphasis added.

4. These are among the American institutions that Richard Lamm suggests that we must reform and revitalize. See his essay "The Uncompetitive Society," in Starr, *Global Competitiveness*.

5. However, Japanese auto companies evaded these restrictions by producing cars in the United States. Further, they increased revenues with the same number of imports by shifting from cheap cars to luxury models.

6. See Rene Schwok, *US-EC Relations in the Post-Cold War Era: Conflict or Partnership?* (Boulder: Westview Press, 1991), chapter 6.

CHAPTER TWO

1. The phrase actually originates in physiocracy, an eighteenth-century economic theory propounded by François Quesnay, an adviser to Louis XV of France. Although they advanced a very different conception of the economy than liberals—emphasizing agriculture to the near exclusion of industry—physiocrats were, like liberals, free traders. When asked how best the state might foster the creation of wealth in the economy, Vincent de Gournay, an associate of Quesnay, responded, "laissez faire, laissez passer," literally, "allow it to be made, allow it to be traded."

2. The term "corn" is synonymous with "grain" and includes wheat, oats, rye, barley, malt, peas, and beans, as well as maize (which Americans call corn).

3. There are also major differences among these strategies. Latin America de-emphasized eventual export success, whereas Japan encouraged cartels among multiple firms instead of granting monopolies.

161

4. See E. Lipson, *The Growth of English Society: A Short Economic History* (New York: Henry Holt, 1950), p. 54.

5. Taxes on international trade and transactions account for about 1.5 percent of U.S. federal government revenues, about average among developed countries. Among less developed countries it is typically between 20 and 40 percent.

6. See W. Cunningham, *The Growth of English Industry and Commerce in Modern Times, Volume 2: The Mercantile System* (Cambridge: Cambridge University Press, 1938), p. 503.

7. See N.S.B. Gras, *The Evolution of the English Corn Market* (Cambridge: Harvard University Press, 1915).

8. See Donald Grove Barnes, *A History of the English Corn Laws from 1660–1846* (London: George Routledge, 1930), pp. 5–6.

9. Adam Smith, *An Inquiry into the Nature and Causes of the Wealth of Nations* (London: J. M. Dutton, 1910), p. 408.

10. See Cunningham, *The Growth of English Industry.*

11. J. Russell Major, *The Western World: Renaissance to the Present* (Philadelphia: J. B. Lippincott, 1966), p. 235.

12. Quoted in Cunningham, *The Growth of English Industry*, p. 387.

13. Similar arrangements were common in Europe at various times. In Russia, for example, they survived virtually intact until the agricultural reforms of 1904.

14. It is tempting to glorify such an ethical stance, but it must be remembered that what was regarded as "suitable for his station" reflected contemporary standards that tolerated massive inequalities in economic standards of living and vast differences in political rights between those of one station and another.

15. See Lipson, *The Growth of English Society*, p. 142.

16. See Barnes, *A History of the English Corn Laws from 1660–1846*, p. 34.

17. R. H. Tawney, *Religion and the Rise of Capitalism* (New York: New American Library, 1954), p. 43.

18. See Lipson, *The Growth of English Society*, p. 145.

19. Only members of a craft guild—masters and journeymen—were permitted to be employed in the industry or to sell their goods. Membership in the guild could be attained only after a lengthy period of apprenticeship with a master who would train the newcomer.

20. See Lipson, *The Growth of English Society*, chapter 2.

21. In the middle of the eighteenth century, a coach took fourteen days to make the trip from Edinburgh in Scotland to London in the south of England, a journey now accomplished in six hours by train and under two hours by plane.

22. By the middle of the nineteenth century about a quarter of the land was owned by 1,200 individuals with about 6,200 owning another quarter. Only about an eighth of the land was worked directly by its owners; the remainder was farmed by rent-paying tenants.

23. R. H. Tawney, *The Agrarian Problem in the Sixteenth Century* (London: Longmans, Green, 1912), p. 409.

24. However, price gouging to take advantage of desperate buyers remains even now unethical and frequently illegal.

25. See Barnes, *A History of the English Corn Laws*, chapter 6.

26. Lipson, *The Growth of English Society*, p. 48.

27. Ibid., p. 182.

28. Smith, *Wealth of Nations*, p. 401.

29. Ibid., p. 400.

30. Ironically, the trade in Portuguese wine resulted more from political restrictions than market forces. French wine was preferred by English consumers, but for foreign policy motivations differential English tariffs were negotiated under the Methuen Treaty of 1703 to encourage the importation of port wine from Portugal. See Lipson, *The Growth of English Society*, p. 155.

31. Though effective early in the Corn Law debates, this argument had less power by the 1840s because by this time an industrial sector had already emerged in most of Europe.

32. Even if employment declines somewhat, later liberals have shown that protectionism is less efficient than combining free trade with a subsidy for the losers. In this period, however, the state did not maintain a social safety net to provide subsidies such as unemployment insurance.

33. Quoted in Lipson, *The Growth of English Society*, p. 315.

34. Ibid., p. 320.

35. One effect of working-class rioting was the conversion of some landowners to a free trade position, most notably Lord Milton, heir to one of the largest landed estates in the country.

36. Even after the Reform Bill of 1832, about 80 percent of the members of Parliament were landowners. See W. O. Aydelotte, "The Country Gentlemen and the Repeal of the Corn Laws," *English Historical Review* 82, 322 (1967):51. However, the landed gentry were becoming less reliant on the agricultural sector because they were rapidly investing in industry and transportation. See Cheryl Schonhardt-Bailey, "Specific Factors, Capital Markets, Portfolio Diversification, and Free Trade: Domestic Determinants of the Repeal of the Corn Laws," *World Politics* 43 (July 1991):545–569.

37. Quoted in Barnes, *A History of the English Corn Laws*, p. 119.

38. Smith, *Wealth of Nations*, pp. 411–412.

39. Ibid.

40. Quoted in Barnes, *A History of the English Corn Laws*, p. 119.

CHAPTER THREE

1. The average import duty tumbled from more than 50 percent in 1820 to 30 percent in 1846 and finally to under 10 percent by the 1870s.

2. See Charles Kindleberger, "The Rise of Free Trade in Western Europe," *Journal of Economic History* 35, 1 (1975).

3. Increasing demand for food was a greater factor, however, as the population grew from 9 million to 33 million during the nineteenth century.

4. Two-thirds of those imports came from the United States because of the advent of steam-powered shipping. In 1846, English farmers were largely insulated from American competition by transatlantic transport costs that added more than a third to the price of American grain in Britain, but by the 1890s, transport costs had fallen by 75 percent.

5. *Das Kapital*, published in 1867, was his classic statement on capitalism.

6. Given the conditions of the time, Marx himself was a free trader, but most subsequent Marxists have disagreed with him on this point.

7. E. Lipson, *The Growth of English Society: A Short Economic History* (New York: Henry Holt, 1950).

8. The regulation of industrial labor—especially the Ten Hours Act of 1847—was passed by a parliament still dominated by landed interests, partially out of revenge against industrial interests for their leading role in the demise of the Corn Laws.

9. Lipson, *The Growth of English Society*, p. 285.

10. Middle-class suffrage is not to be confused with working-class suffrage. Even after the Reform Act of 1832 increased the number of eligible voters by half, only about a seventh of the adult male population met the stringent requirements.

11. In the modern era, parties of the right include British Conservatives, American Republicans, and European Christian Democrats; parties of the left include British Labour, American Democrats, and European Socialists and Social Democrats.

12. For example, Labour was the party of free trade in Britain throughout the 1920s; it was the Conservatives who enacted the protectionist policies associated with the collapse of the trading system. Similarly, in the United States, Democrats were free traders and Republicans were protectionist during this key period.

13. The famous Leontief paradox shows that the United States after World War II did not fit the predicted pattern because American imports were more capital intensive than American exports. This paradox is hotly debated; most economists deny that the Leontief paradox constitutes a disconfirmation of Heckscher-Ohlin theory, arguing instead for a reformulation that encompasses other factors of production.

14. Geographic cleavages also occur, but these are largely the product of sectoral considerations.

15. See Gary C. Hufbauer, Diane T. Berliner, and Kimberly A. Elliot, *Trade Protection in the United States: Thirty-one Case Studies* (Washington, D.C.: Institute for International Economics, 1986).

16. Friedrich List, *The National System of Political Economy* (Philadelphia: J. B. Lippincott, 1956), p. 440.

17. Forrest Capie, *Depression and Protectionism: Britain Between the Wars* (London: George Allen and Unwin, 1983), chapter 4.

18. Armed with very steep tariffs enacted in 1931 and 1932, Britain did negotiate bilateral agreements with sixteen nations between 1932 and 1935 to improve British access to those markets. In the United States, the high Smoot-Hawley tariff of 1930 provided the leverage for eighteen bilateral treaties between 1934 and 1938.

19. John A. C. Conybeare, *Trade Wars: The Theory and Practice of International Commercial Rivalry* (New York: Columbia University Press, 1987), p. 241.

20. Michael Kitson and Solomos Solomou, *Protectionism and Economic Revival: the British Inter-war Economy* (Cambridge: Cambridge University Press, 1990), p. 4.

21. See Conybeare, *Trade Wars*, p. 242.

22. This was not unforeseen. The unsuccessful Labour campaign to retain free trade had cautioned, in vain, regarding the global consequences of rising British

protectionism, asking, "Will the British people take the responsibility for the setting up of a fascist despotism in a Germany, driven to despair?" See Gerhard Kumleden, *The Workers' Case for Free Trade* (London: International, 1932).

23. Barry Eichengreen and T. J. Hatton, eds., *Interwar Unemployment in International Perspective* (Dordrecht, Netherlands: Kluwer Academic, 1988), chapter 1.

24. For a survey, see Charles Kindleberger, *The World in Depression 1929–1939* (Berkeley: University of California Press, 1973).

25. Recent scholarship suggests that protectionism played a smaller role in the economic collapse than was generally assumed at the time. For example, it has been estimated that Smoot-Hawley and the resulting retaliation from other countries cost the United States only 0.44 percent of GNP. See Lawrence Brunner, "The Effect of Trade Restrictions on the U.S. Economy in the Great Depression," paper presented to the American Economic Association, New York, December 1985 (cited in Conybeare, *Trade Wars*). Moreover, Kitson and Solomou, *Protectionism and Economic Revival*, contend that the British tariff of 1932 was actually beneficial to the British economy.

26. Recall that the explosion of protectionist and anti-Japanese sentiment of the early 1990s and President Bush's defeat in his 1992 bid for reelection were triggered by an American unemployment rate that never reached 8 percent.

CHAPTER FOUR

1. See Charles Kindleberger, *The World in Depression 1929–1939* (Berkeley: University of California Press, 1973); and Robert Gilpin, *U.S. Power and the Multinational Corporation: The Political Economy of Foreign Direct Investment* (New York: Basic Books, 1975).

2. American leadership was long overdue. Britain's ascendance peaked around 1880 and its relative decline had been unmistakable since World War I. The United States surpassed Britain in total income by the middle of the nineteenth century, in per capita income by the beginning of the twentieth, and in volume of global trade and investment shortly after World War I.

3. See Stephen Krasner, "State Power and the Structure of International Trade," *World Politics* 28, 3 (April 1976):317–347.

4. This standard component of liberal theory appeared as early as 1808 in the work of Robert Torrens, who also developed the theory of comparative advantage a decade before Ricardo. See Fritz Machlup, *A History of Thought on Economic Integration* (New York: Columbia University Press, 1977).

5. For a concise statement of the theoretical arguments, see John A. C. Conybeare, *Trade Wars: The Theory and Practice of International Commercial Rivalry* (New York: Columbia University Press, 1987). For the empirical studies, see Michael Kitson and Solomos Solomou, *Protectionism and Economic Revival: The British Inter-war Economy* (Cambridge: Cambridge University Press, 1990).

6. American isolationism before World War II was manifested in rejection of the League of Nations, insistence on the repayment of World War I loans, refusal to cooperate during the London Economic Conference of 1933, and very high tariff rates even prior to Smoot-Hawley (Conybeare contends that the United States adopted a free-rider posture more often than any other nation).

7. See Richard N. Gardner, *Sterling-Dollar Diplomacy: Anglo-American Collaboration in the Reconstruction of Multilateral Trade* (Oxford: Clarendon Press, 1956).

8. Quoted in John H. Jackson, *The World Trading System: Law and Policy of International Economic Relations* (Cambridge: MIT Press, 1989), p. 10.

9. The ITO proposed commodity agreements to ensure prices that were fair to consumers and provided a reasonable return to producers. It also provided for governmental cooperation in a variety of areas only tangentially related to trade.

10. In 1994 it had a secretariat of about 300, and since 1952 it has been treated de facto as a specialized agency of the United Nations.

11. This may be because workers can organize more effectively than consumers to translate their interests into government policy. Or it may be because prevailing values favor maximizing employment rather than maximizing consumption when they come into conflict. Or it may be because employment growth in a sector usually signals profit growth as well.

12. For a brief overview, see Robert Baldwin, *Trade Policy in a Changing World Economy* (Chicago: University of Chicago Press, 1988), chapter 11.

13. Additional exceptions to the principals of nondiscrimination and reciprocity apply only to developing nations under the rubric of "different and more favorable (DMF) treatment." See Brian Hindley, "Different and More Favorable Treatment—and Graduation," in J. Michael Finger and Andrzej Olechowski, eds., *The Uruguay Round: A Handbook for the Multilateral Trade Negotiations* (Washington, D.C.: World Bank, 1987), chapter 10.

14. Some concessions involve no reduction in tariff rates but only a pledge never to increase an existing rate, which is called a binding.

15. There are many exceptions, which I will discuss shortly.

16. Even the MFN clause cannot eliminate discrimination if a tariff schedule contains categories that apply only to the products of one country. For example, the 1902 German tariff law charged a lower duty on "brown cattle reared at least 300 metres above sea level and having at least one month's grazing at least 800 metres above sea level." The practical effect was to give preference to Swiss cattle. See Richard Pomfret, *Unequal Trade* (Oxford: Basil Blackwell, 1988), chapter 1.

17. For similar reasons, the United States had been able to achieve a decrease in tariffs of about one-third in bilateral treaties with thirty-one nations between 1934 and 1945 under the U.S. Reciprocal Trade Agreements Act, which contained a similar MFN provision.

18. Of course, the very definition of import liberalization as a concession under GATT's reciprocity principle is a mercantilist, not a liberal, conception.

19. Quantitative restrictions such as quotas are prohibited because, unlike tariffs, they require government administration that can easily disguise discrimination.

20. Gardner, *Sterling-Dollar Diplomacy*, p. 376.

21. Because this book focuses upon trade issues, I can mention only in passing those monetary problems not linked directly to trade.

22. Jeffrey J. Schott, ed., *Completing the Uruguay Round* (Washington, D.C.: Institute for International Economics, 1990).

23. "Free Trade's Fading Champion," *Economist*, April 11, 1992, p. 65.

24. Quoted in Robert Dodge, "Grappling with GATT," *Dallas Morning News*, August 8, 1994, p. 1D.

25. Sutherland is quoted in Brian Tumulty, "U.S. Industry Confronts Cost of Implementing GATT," Gannett News Service, July 18, 1994.

CHAPTER FIVE

1. Louis Harris and Gallup polls cited in "The Fading of Japanophobia," *Economist*, August 6, 1994, p. 22.

2. Trade between the two grew about 50 percent between 1985 and 1992: Japanese exports to the United States increased about 40 percent, and U.S. exports to Japan doubled from a much smaller base.

3. "Japan Gives Its Answer," *Economist*, May 13, 1995, p. 36.

4. Because of the larger U.S. market, American dependence, in percentage terms, is smaller: In 1992, only 11 percent of U.S. exports went to Japan, and 19 percent of U.S. imports were from Japan. See C. Fred Bergsten and Marcus Noland, *Reconcilable Differences? United States Japan Economic Conflict* (Washington, D.C.: Institute for International Economics, 1993), pp. 54–55.

5. "On one estimate, between 1986 and 1993 [Japanese investors] lost more than $320 billion on their investments in American bonds, property and other financial assets." "The Fading of Japanophobia," p. 21.

6. Quoted in Steven Schlossstein, *Trade War: Greed, Power, and Industrial Policy on Opposite Sides of the Pacific* (New York: Congdon and Weed, 1984), p. 4.

7. David E. Sanger, "As Ugly Feelings Grow, It's Hard to Separate Fact and Friction," *New York Times*, January 26, 1992, sec. 4, p. 1.

8. Quoted in Jon Woronoff, *World Trade War* (New York: Praeger, 1984), pp. 144–145.

9. Some argue that these unusual bilateral imbalances simply reflect the comparative advantage in manufacturing inherent in Japan's unique factor endowment of abundant capital but few natural resources. Critics suggest that protectionism is responsible for the unusually small penetration of the Japanese manufacturing market by foreign firms (about 1 percent in the early 1990s).

10. Charlie Turner, *Japan's Dynamic Efficiency in the Global Market: Trade, Investment, and Economic Growth* (New York: Quorum Books, 1991), p. 104.

11. Although global production of automobiles nearly tripled between 1960 and 1990, American production was almost unchanged. Thus, the American share of global production fell from over 51 percent in 1960 to 19 percent in 1990. For greater details, see Peter Dicken, *Global Shift: The Internationalization of Economic Activity*, 2nd ed. (New York: Guilford Press, 1992).

12. Ibid. American resentment is intensified by the belief that Japan's economic growth was built on the American market and under cover of the U.S. military umbrella.

13. List also noted that a trailing nation typically feels bitterness toward the dominant nation, especially in response to its exhortation for more liberal policies. Given the reaction of the United States, it appears that a declining power accepts the loss of its preeminent position with even less grace than a trailing nation accepts its long-standing status as a second-rate power.

14. Adam Smith, *An Inquiry into the Nature and Causes of the Wealth of Nations* (London: J. M. Dutton, 1910), p. 439.

15. Ibid., p. 437.

16. In part under foreign pressure, Japan enacted two huge fiscal stimulus programs in 1992 and 1993, though their actual impact on the trade surplus is unclear.

17. Raw figures suggesting that Japan saves twice as high a percentage of national income somewhat overstate the real gap, but the exact magnitude is clouded by differences in accounting procedures.

18. One study estimates that reducing the budget deficit by about $60 billion would improve the U.S. trade balance by about $30 billion, of which about $3 billion would be in the bilateral balance with Japan. See Bergsten and Noland, *Reconcilable Differences?* pp. 54–55.

19. Quoted in Woronoff, *World Trade War*, p. 230.

20. In 1955, Japanese output per worker was one-tenth of the U.S. level, but it reached 65 percent by 1985. See Turner, *Japan's Dynamic Efficiency*, p. xi.

21. However, in the early 1990s the U.S. government funded more than twice as large a share of R&D as the Japanese government, 44 percent to 20 percent. Of course, the priorities were different: Sixty-six percent of that was for defense in the United States but only 5 percent in Japan.

22. Takatoshi Ito, *The Japanese Economy* (Cambridge: MIT Press, 1992), p. 203.

23. Bergsten and Noland, *Reconcilable Differences?* p. 7.

24. David B. Audretsch, *The Market and the State: Government Policy Toward Business in Europe, Japan, and the United States* (New York: New York University Press, 1989), chapter 4.

25. Ito, *The Japanese Economy*, chapter 7.

26. Ibid., p. 190.

27. Another result is that unemployment is very low in Japan, which may partially explain why fiscal and monetary policy tends to be less expansionary than in the United States, where slack demand causes businesses to lay off workers. Because unemployed workers spend less, aggregate demand falls further, which increases unemployment, depresses the entire economy, and generates strong political pressure for stimulative macroeconomic policy, including budget deficits.

28. Identification of these technical barriers involves a subjective component, however. For example, defenders argue that demanding safety standards are not deliberate protectionist devices but rather an appropriate adaptation to a Japanese legal system that makes product-liability lawsuits extremely rare.

29. Foreign firms also face strong barriers to direct investment. Less than 1 percent of the global stock of foreign direct investment is in Japan.

30. Cited by Charlene Barshefsky, deputy U.S. trade representative, in a hearing before the Subcommittee on International Trade of the Committee on Finance of the U.S. Senate, November 8, 1993.

31. Economies of scale are especially significant in small markets and where substantial learning occurs during production. For example, in the large commercial aircraft industry, production costs per plane decline by about 20 percent with every doubling of volume. But only one or two firms can benefit from these economies of scale because the total global market is less than 500 planes per year. See Gernot Klepper, "Industrial Policy in the Transport Aircraft Industry," in Paul

Krugman and Alasdair Smith, eds., *Empirical Studies of Strategic Trade Policy* (Chicago: University of Chicago Press, 1994), pp. 101–129.

32. For example, the American firm Boeing dominated the commercial aircraft market until challenged by Airbus, which could not have done so were it not subsidized (and partly owned) by European governments.

33. Of course, the United States also has an industrial policy, though it is less sophisticated, extensive, and coordinated than Japan's. Its elements include tied foreign aid, military sales abroad, subsidized power and water, government R&D, and government procurement policies.

34. American antitrust policy, initiated by the Sherman Act of 1890 and the Clayton and Federal Trade Commission Acts of 1914, prohibits price-fixing or the exchange of price information by competing businesses. So-called vertical restrictions that impede competition are also illegal. For example, a supplier cannot prevent a retailer from carrying the products of a competing supplier or from selling a product below the manufacturer's suggested price.

35. Governments could impose restraints on imports whenever domestic industries were threatened, but the standard of injury and the method of remedy they could use varied. If the increase in imports resulted from market forces, "serious" injury had to be proven and the nation increasing protection was required to compensate with reduced protection in other sectors. If trade results from subsidies offered by foreign governments, the injury must be only "material," and nations need not offer compensation for tariffs that balance the subsidies.

36. "Free Trade's Fading Champion," *Economist*, April 11, 1992, pp. 65–66.

37. Exporters usually prefer voluntary export restraints administered by the exporting government rather than quotas administered by the importing government. Both usually involve charging firms a fee for the privilege of exporting, but in the former case the revenue goes to the exporting rather than the importing government.

38. Cited in Bergsten and Noland, *Reconcilable Differences?* p. 71.

39. See Julio Nogues, Andrzej Olechowski, and L. Alan Winters, "The Extent of Non-tariff Barriers to Industrial Countries' Imports," in J. Michael Finger and Andrzej Olechowski, eds., *The Uruguay Round: A Handbook for the Multilateral Trade Negotiations* (Washington, D.C.: World Bank, 1987).

40. Turner, *Japan's Dynamic Efficiency*, p. 68.

41. See Bergsten and Noland, *Reconcilable Differences?* chapter 5.

42. See ibid.

43. Advisory Committee on Trade Policy and Negotiations, "Major Findings and Policy Recommendations on U.S.-Japan Trade Policy," 1993, Washington, D.C. Quoted in ibid., p. 19.

44. Ironically, the biggest loser would have been Mazda, which is partially owned by Ford, and the biggest beneficiaries Germany's BMW and Mercedes-Benz.

45. "Car Wars: Mr. Kantor's Outrageous Gamble," *Economist*, May 20, 1995, p. 59.

46. See Leon Hollerman, *Japan, Disincorporated: The Economic Liberalization Process* (Stanford: Hoover Institution Press, 1988).

CHAPTER SIX

1. Regional integration can take a variety of forms. In a preferential trade area, a group of countries establishes lower barriers to the import of goods from member countries than from outside countries. The free trade area is a special case of a preferential trade area in which trade barriers between members are reduced to zero. A customs union is a preferential trade area in which the members adopt a common external tariff. A common market allows the free movement of factors of production such as capital and labor as well as free trade in goods. Finally, an economic union or community occurs when the economic policies of common market nations are coordinated and harmonized under supranational control and a single currency.

2. Timothy M. Devinney and William C. Hightower, *European Markets After 1992* (Lexington, Mass.: Lexington Books, 1991), p. 21.

3. The Benelux customs union among Belgium, Luxembourg, and the Netherlands had been formed in 1948.

4. For convenience, I will use the label EU to refer to both the current European Union and its predecessor organizations.

5. The EU, whose trade constituted 15 percent of the global total in 1992, has a population of 375 million and a GDP of $5 trillion. NAFTA, with a similar level of trade, encompasses a population of 363 million and a GDP of about $6.3 trillion.

6. The United States has never fully accepted the EU's conformity with Article 24 because it has not eliminated tariffs on "substantially all" goods (failing, most notably, with respect to agriculture).

7. C. A. Primo Braga and Alexander J. Yeats, "The Simple Arithmetic of Existing Minilateral Trading Arrangements and Its Implications for a Post-Uruguay Round World," International Trade Division Working Paper, World Bank, Washington, D.C., 1992.

8. Jacob Viner, *The Customs Union Issue* (New York: Carnegie Endowment for International Peace, 1950).

9. As quoted in Phillip Revzin, "Welcome to Their Party," *Wall Street Journal*, December 30, 1988, p. A6.

10. From the 1960s through the 1980s, Europe was outpaced by growth in Japan and in the newly industrializing countries of Asia; during the 1980s, even the United States grew more rapidly.

11. Paolo Cecchini, *The European Challenge, 1992* (Aldershot, England: Gower, 1988).

12. Such arguments were especially influential because much of America's industrial success has been attributed to the economies of scale that its vast market has permitted.

13. Quoted in Devinney and Hightower, *European Markets After 1992*, p. 16.

14. Quoted in Richard Pomfret, *Unequal Trade* (Oxford: Basil Blackwell, 1988), p. 75.

15. Indeed, the UK, preferring a more limited objective, founded the European Free Trade Association (EFTA) in 1960 with Sweden, Denmark, Norway, Switzerland, Austria, and Portugal.

16. Beverly Springer, *The Social Dimension of 1992: Europe Faces a New EC* (New York: Greenwood Press, 1992), p. 27.

17. One study estimates that protecting a Detroit autoworker with trade barriers may cost as much as $105,000 per job. See Gary Hufbauer, Diane Berliner, and Kimberly Elliot, *Trade Protection in the United States: Thirty-one Case Studies* (Washington, D.C.: Institute for International Economics, 1986).

18. "The Slippery Slope," *Economist*, July 30, 1994.

19. Harmonization of VAT rates has been delayed as nations battle over whether the VAT should be collected in the producing or consuming country.

20. Commission of the European Communities, *Everything You Wanted to Know About Europe Without Frontiers*, vol. 6 (Brussels: CEC, January 1992), p. 117.

21. Margaret Thatcher, "Britain and Europe," speech delivered to the College of Europe, Bruges, Belgium, September 20, 1988.

22. The EU's legality under GATT also hinges on this issue because Article 24 requires that the level of protection created by a regional arrangement "shall not on the whole be higher or more restrictive" than the previous level. For tariffs, this standard is fairly clear, but nontariff barriers and complex rules of origin make ascertaining whether an agreement qualifies quite difficult. See Ernest H. Preeg, "The Compatibility of Regional Economic Blocs and the GATT," in Sidney Weintraub, ed., *Annals of the American Academy of Political and Social Science*, special volume, "Free Trade in the Western Hemisphere," (March 1993): 164–171.

23. This concern was expressed as early as 1942 in a study by the Council on Foreign Relations for the U.S. State Department: "The United States would favor economic unification of Europe only if steps were taken to avoid the creation of an autarkic continental economy. Positive American policy should aim at the interpenetration of Europe's economy with the rest of the world, as well as the lowering of barriers within Europe." Quoted by Boyd France, *A Short Chronicle of United States–European Community Relations* (Washington, D.C.: European Community Information Service, 1973), p. 6.

24. Congress had nearly blocked the initial negotiations for the less controversial CUSTA but failed to do so when the Senate Finance Committee deadlocked at 10 to 10.

25. Like all free trade areas that lack a common external tariff, NAFTA establishes rules of origin to define goods that are ineligible for preferential access. For example, textiles manufactured outside North America do not enjoy tariff-free access to the American market even if they are first exported into Mexico to evade the higher U.S. barriers and then transshipped into the United States. However, if those raw textiles are fashioned into completed garments in Mexico, the finished product might qualify as domestic and be eligible for tariff-free import into the United States. NAFTA's rules of origin contain complex domestic-content and tracing clauses to determine eligibility, which excludes about 20 percent of the goods currently traded among these three countries, chiefly in textiles, apparel, and autos. See Gary Clyde Hufbauer and Jeffrey J. Schott, *NAFTA: An Assessment* (Washington, D.C.: Institute for International Economics, 1993), p. 5.

26. NAFTA requires that all government contracts above $25,000 use competitive bidding open to foreign firms but excludes services and exempts state and local governments. Moreover, such clauses are notoriously easy to evade by stipulating conditions that can be met only by domestic firms.

27. These differences also make dispute resolution difficult because NAFTA relies on binational review panels to determine whether trade policy actions are in accord with national laws and regulations. This arrangement may not ensure fairness between countries with very different legal traditions, such as the United States and Mexico. See Joseph A. Greenwald, "Dispute Settlement in a North American Free Trade Agreement," in Weintraub, *Annals*, pp. 172–182.

28. Immigration laws, which were not addressed in NAFTA, also remain as barriers to bringing together American capital and Mexican labor.

29. In 1985, 80 percent of Canadian exports to the United States were already duty free and the remainder faced an average rate of only 3.3 percent; for U.S. exports to Canada the corresponding figures were 65 percent and 9.9 percent. See Paul Wonnacott, *The United States and Canada: The Quest for Free Trade* (Washington, D.C.: Institute for International Economics, March 1987), p. 3. However, the actual extent of protection—how much trade is prevented—is notoriously difficult to ascertain from how much trade is permitted. For example, if all tariff rates were either 0 percent or 1,000 percent, no trade at all would take place in those goods with the 1,000 percent tariff. To say that 100 percent of actual imports entered duty free, however, would falsely suggest an absence of protection.

30. Ignacio Trigueros, "A Free Trade Agreement Between Mexico and the United States?" in Jeffrey J. Schott, ed., *Free Trade Areas and US Trade Policy* (Washington, D.C.: Institute for International Economics, 1989).

31. Similarly, NAFTA was intended to prevent a return to the interventionist investment policies of Canada during the Trudeau period.

32. For a survey, see Drusilla K. Brown, "The Impact of a North American Free Trade Area: Applied General Equilibrium Models," in Nora Lustig, Barry P. Bosworth, and Robert Z. Lawrence, eds., *North American Free Trade: Assessing the Impact* (Washington D.C.: Brookings, 1992), pp. 26–68.

33. Hufbauer and Schott, *NAFTA: An Assessment*, p. 24.

34. Hufbauer and Schott, in ibid., p. 21, estimate that about a third of the increased imports from Mexico might be trade diverted from other previous exporters.

35. The net effects on migration are difficult to estimate because NAFTA will probably initially *increase* migration by displacing Mexican rural workers—perhaps by 100,000 annually for the first few years—but *decrease* it thereafter by generating growth and employment opportunities in Mexico. See ibid., p. 25.

36. NAFTA allows "snap-back" trade remedies, which reinstate existing barriers when industry profits are threatened by trade, but no similar provision is made with respect to labor or the environment.

37. Previous free trade plans have also foundered on strained political relations: An 1854 U.S.-Canadian free trade agreement was abrogated by the United States in 1866 over resentment of Canadian support for the Confederacy during the American Civil War.

38. About 70 percent of total Mexican trade is also with the United States, but America relies heavily on neither: Over two-thirds of American trade falls outside North America.

39. Cited in John Cavanagh, John Gershman, Karen Baker, and Gretchen Helmke, eds., *Trading Freedom: How Free Trade Affects Our Lives, Work, and Environment* (San Francisco: Institute for Food and Development Policy, 1992), p. 35.

40. Cited in Wonnacott, *The United States and Canada*, p. 15. This attitude stems from the considerable loss of Canadian manufacturing jobs from 1990 to 1992, which most Canadians attribute to CUSTA. It is testimony to perceptual differences in the two countries that a similar job loss also occurred in the United States, but few Americans attributed it to Canada: Canada fears the United States, but the United States largely ignores Canada. Both of those attitudes contribute to Canadian resentment of the United States—and to opposition to NAFTA.

41. The United States accounts for about 70 percent of the population and 85 percent of the regional output of the NAFTA nations; Germany makes up about 22 percent of the population and 25 percent of the regional product of the EC.

42. Rick Salutin, "Keep Canadian Culture Off the Table—Who's Kidding Who," in Laurier LaPierre, ed., *If You Love This Country* (Toronto: McClelland and Stewart, 1987), pp. 205–206. Quoted in John Herd Thompson, "Canada's Quest for Cultural Sovereignty," in Stephen J. Randall, ed., *North America Without Borders?* (Calgary: University of Calgary Press, 1992).

43. Ibid.

44. Mexican peasants who produce corn and beans may also lose to the greater efficiency of American agrobusiness. Canadian employment losses are less clear because economies of scale allow firms to find a profitable niche without abandoning a sector entirely. However, labor organizations in all three countries simultaneously argue that they will lose jobs to the other two. This perception may reflect the visibility of the concentrated job loss that occurs under free trade; the benefits are less dramatic because they are scattered in small increments across many firms.

45. James Stanford, "Continental Economic Integration: Modeling the Impact on Labor," in Weintraub, *Annals*, pp. 92–110.

46. Ibid., p. 109.

47. See Hufbauer and Schott, *NAFTA: An Assessment*, p. 21.

48. See David Rosenbaum, "Clinton Walks Thin Line on NAFTA," *Allentown Morning Call*, October 3, 1993, p. A4.

49. That disparity is about twice as great as the largest in the EU, between Germany and Portugal, which, of course, do not share a border. See Barry P. Bosworth, Robert Z. Lawrence, and Nora Lustig, "Introduction," in Lustig, Bosworth, and Lawrence, eds., *North American Free Trade: Assessing the Impact* (Washington D.C.: Brookings, 1992), p. 4.

50. In 1991, after decades of unprecedented export-led economic success, the average hourly compensation for production workers was only $3.58 in Hong Kong, $4.32 in Korea, and $4.38 in Singapore compared to $15.45 in the United States, $14.41 in Japan, and $22.17 in Germany. The comparable Mexican figure is $2.17. See Hufbauer and Schott, *NAFTA: An Assessment*, p. 13.

51. See Alan Madian, "A Free Trade Area with Mexico: Will U.S. Workers Lose?" in Weintraub, *Annals*, p. 87.

52. Nearly 30 percent of U.S. imports come from U.S. corporations abroad. See Cavanagh et al., *Trading Freedom*, p. 18.

53. Bosworth, Lawrence, and Lustig, "Introduction," p. 7.

54. That figure is about twice the previous record for FDI in a single year. See Hufbauer and Schott, *NAFTA: An Assessment*, p. 4.

55. See Kathryn Kopinak, "The Maquiladorization of the Mexican Economy," in Ricardo Grinspun and Maxwell Cameron, eds., *The Political Economy of North American Free Trade* (New York: St. Martin's Press, 1993), pp. 141–162.

56. Cavanagh et al., *Trading Freedom*, pp. 68–70.

57. Ibid., p. 74

58. Ibid., pp. 27–31.

59. Ibid., p. 42.

60. By comparison, the United States spends less than $14 billion per year on all foreign economic and military aid with about half going to Israel and Egypt.

61. Much of the capital inflow also represented the return of capital that Mexican citizens had sent abroad for safety during the instability and debt crisis of the 1980s.

CHAPTER SEVEN

1. Furthermore, more than half of the parts, by value, are produced outside Ford plants. See Peter Dicken, *Global Shift: The Internationalization of Economic Activity*, 2nd ed. (New York: Guilford Press, 1992), p. 300.

2. John Stopford and Susan Strange, *Rival States, Rival Firms: Competition for World Market Share* (Cambridge: Cambridge University Press, 1991), p. 17.

3. Peter Drucker, "The Changed World Economy," *Foreign Affairs* 64:782–783.

5. W. Max Corden, *Trade Policy and Economic Welfare* (Oxford: Clarendon Press, 1974), p. 107.

Suggested Readings

Audretsch, David B. 1989. *The Market and the State: Government Policy Toward Business in Europe, Japan, and the United States*. New York: New York University Press.

Barnes, Donald Grove. 1930. *A History of the English Corn Laws from 1660–1846*. London: George Routledge.

Bergsten, C. Fred, and Marcus Noland. 1993. *Reconcilable Differences? United States–Japan Economic Conflict*. Washington, D.C.: Institute for International Economics.

Capie, Forrest. 1983. *Depression and Protectionism: Britain Between the Wars*. London: George Allen and Unwin.

Cavanagh, John, John Gershman, Karen Baker, and Gretchen Helmke, eds. 1992. *Trading Freedom: How Free Trade Affects Our Lives, Work, and Environment*. San Francisco: Institute for Food and Development Policy.

Conybeare, John A. C. 1987. *Trade Wars: The Theory and Practice of International Commercial Rivalry*. New York: Columbia University Press.

Corden, W. Max. 1974. *Trade Policy and Economic Welfare*. Oxford: Clarendon Press.

Cunningham, W. 1938. *The Growth of English Industry and Commerce in Modern Times*. Cambridge: Cambridge University Press.

Devinney, Timothy M., and William C. Hightower. 1991. *European Markets After 1992*. Lexington, Mass: Lexington Books.

Dicken, Peter. 1992. *Global Shift: The Internationalization of Economic Activity*, 2nd ed. New York: Guilford Press.

Finger, J. Michael, and Andrzej Olechowski. 1987. *The Uruguay Round: A Handbook for the Multilateral Trade Negotiations*. Washington, D.C.: World Bank.

Gardner, Richard N. 1956. *Sterling-Dollar Diplomacy: Anglo-American Collaboration in the Reconstruction of Multilateral Trade*. Oxford: Clarendon Press.

Gilpin, Robert. 1975. *U.S. Power and the Multinational Corporation: The Political Economy of Foreign Direct Investment*. New York: Basic Books.

————.1987. *The Political Economy of International Relations*. Princeton: Princteon University Press.

Gras, N. S. B. 1915. *The Evolution of the English Corn Market*. Cambridge: Harvard University Press.

Grinspun, Ricardo, and Maxwell Cameron. 1993. *The Political Economy of North American Free Trade*. New York: St. Martin's Press.

Haggard, Stephen, and Chung-in Moon. 1989. *Pacific Dynamics*. Boulder: Westview Press.

Hufbauer, Gary C., and Jeffrey J. Schott. 1993. *NAFTA: An Assessment*. Washington, D.C.: Institute for International Economics.

Hufbauer, Gary C., Diane T. Berliner, and Kimberly A. Elliot. 1986. *Trade Protection in the United States: Thirty-one Case Studies*. Washington, D.C.: Institute for International Economics.

Ito, Takatoshi. 1992. *The Japanese Economy*. Cambridge: MIT Press.

Jackson, John H. 1989. *The World Trading System: Law and Policy of International Economic Relations*. Cambridge: MIT Press.

Kindleberger, Charles. 1973. *The World in Depression 1929–1939*. Berkeley: University of California Press.

————.1975. "The Rise of Free Trade in Western Europe."*Journal of Economic History* 35, 1.

Krasner, Stephen. 1976. "State Power and the Structure of International Trade." *World Politics* 28, 3 (April):317–347.

Lipson, E. 1950. *The Growth of English Society: A Short Economic History*. New York: Henry Holt.

List, Friedrich 1956. *The National System of Political Economy*. Philadelphia: J. B. Lippincott.

Lustig, Nora, Barry P. Bosworth, and Robert Z. Lawrence. 1992. *North American Free Trade: Assessing the Impact*. Washington D.C.: Brookings Institution.

Polanyi, Karl. 1944. *The Great Transformation*. New York: Farrar & Rinehart.

Pomfret, Richard. 1988. *Unequal Trade*. Oxford: Basil Blackwell.

Schott, Jeffrey J. 1990. *Completing the Uruguay Round*. Washington, D.C.: Institute for International Economics.

Smith, Adam. 1910. *An Inquiry into the Nature and Causes of the Wealth of Nations*. London: J. M. Dutton.

Springer, Beverly. 1992. *The Social Dimension of 1992: Europe Faces a New EC*. New York: Greenwood Press.

Starr, Martin K. 1988. *Global Competitiveness: Getting the U.S. Back on Track*. New York: W. W. Norton.

Stopford, John, and Susan Strange. 1991. *Rival States, Rival Firms: Competition for World Market Share*. Cambridge: Cambridge University Press.

Tawney, R. H. 1912. *The Agrarian Problem in the Sixteenth Century*. London: Longmans, Green.

————. 1954. *Religion and the Rise of Capitalism*. New York: New American Library.

Tyson, Laura D'Andrea. 1992. *Who's Bashing Whom? Trade Conflict in High-Technology Industries*. Washington, D.C.: Institute for International Economics.

Viner, Jacob. 1950. *The Customs Union Issue*. New York: Carnegie Endowment for International Peace.

Wonnacott, Paul. 1987. *The United States and Canada: The Quest for Free Trade*. Washington, D.C.: Institute for International Economics.

Glossary

Absolute advantage refers to the ability of a nation to produce more of a given commodity than another nation with the same quantity of resources (e.g., labor hours).

Balance of payments is the summary statement of a nation's financial transactions with the rest of the world, often divided into the **current account**, the **capital account**, and the **reserve account**.

Balance of trade is the value of a nation's exports minus the value of its imports. When imports exceed exports, it is said that the balance of trade is negative, unfavorable, or in deficit. When exports exceed imports, the trade balance is positive, favorable, or in surplus.

Beggar-thy-neighbor is a term used to describe policies designed to benefit one nation (or individual) at the expense of another, especially trade barriers and capital restrictions.

Bilateral actions are those that involve two states acting together.

Bretton Woods was the site of the 1944 conference that established the World Bank (IBRD) and the International Monetary Fund (IMF) and laid the groundwork for the General Agreement on Tariffs and Trade (GATT). The name is usually applied to these institutions and the international economic system that they govern.

Budget deficit describes the situation in which the expenditures of a nation's government exceed its revenues.

Buy America is a term applied both to various legislative acts mandating that governments (federal, state, or local) give preference to American products in their purchasing decisions and to public relations campaigns designed to convince citizens to give a similar preference in their own purchases.

Capital is a factor of production often divided into physical capital (plant and equipment, etc.) and human capital (e.g., skills of workers), both of which require the investment of financial capital (i.e., money).

Capital account is the portion of the balance of payments that records the volume of private foreign investment and public grants and loans.

Common Agricultural Policy (CAP) is the set of policies enacted by the EU (and its predecessors) to raise agricultural incomes through various subsidies and tariffs.

Comparative advantage refers to the ability of a nation to produce a given commodity at lower opportunity cost than another nation. That is, it must forgo less of an alternative commodity. A nation has a comparative advantage in that commodity in which its absolute advantage is greatest (or its absolute disadvantage the smallest).

Competitiveness is a term used to describe the ability of a nation's firms to produce goods at a price and quality enabling it to meet foreign competition.

The Corn Laws, which existed in England for centuries before their repeal in 1846, were a complex series of parliamentary acts designed to control the price of grains and the volume available to consumers. They consisted of barriers and subsidies to both imports and exports.

Countervailing duties are tariffs imposed on imports to offset subsidies by an exporting nation.

Currency markets are the sites where brokers buy the currency of one nation by selling that of another at exchange rates determined by supply and demand.

Current account is the portion of the balance of payments that records trade in goods and services as well as flows of income from investment.

Distributional dilemma refers to the inevitable choice implicit in trade policy between the pattern of income produced by trade and the pattern of income that would exist without trade. Whichever pattern is chosen, some individuals and groups will gain and others will lose.

Division of labor refers to the allocation of tasks among economic units (e.g., individual workers or national economies) in which each specializes in the task it performs most efficiently.

Economic liberalism is a doctrine that affirms a commitment to individualism, to the free market, and to private property; it opposes the intervention of government into markets. It advocates free trade and rejects mercantilism.

Economies of scale refers to the efficiency gains achieved by producing goods at the (large) volume that minimizes the production cost of each unit.

Efficient allocation of resources (or factors of production) refers to a situation in which production inputs (like land, labor, and capital) are employed in those sectors where they will produce the maximum output.

Embargo refers to a government order prohibiting the export of certain goods to certain nations.

Enclosure movement refers to the dissolution of agricultural commons and the communitarian economic and social patterns associated with them during the medieval era in Europe. It involved the conversion of commonly used land to private ownership, usually increasing the size and efficiency of plots but dispossessing peasants.

Entrepreneur is an investor who takes risks for economic gain.

European Community (EC) is a term used to refer to the various organizations that have facilitated regional integration in Europe, especially the European Economic Community (EEC), founded by the Treaty of Rome in 1957, and the European Communities, founded by the 1967 treaty that merged the EEC with EURATOM and the European Coal and Steel Community. All were forerunners of the European Union.

European Union (EU) is the organization created in 1993 to succeed the EC in furthering regional integration in Europe.

Export promotion is a government policy that encourages exports through direct and indirect subsidies.

Factors of production are the resources or inputs required to produce a good, especially land, labor, and capital.

Foreign exchange refers both to the currencies of nations and to the process of converting one to another through purchase.

Free rider refers to a nation (or individual) that benefits from a collective good without contributing to its provision, such as a nation that enjoys access to another nation's market but does not permit access to its own.

Free trade refers to a situation in which goods can be bought and sold on international markets without interference from barriers to trade enacted by governments, such as tariffs and quotas.

General Agreement on Tariffs and Trade (GATT) is an international treaty of 1947 that has facilitated trade by convening a series of negotiations to lower trade barriers, most recently the Uruguay Round.

Gold standard refers to the international monetary system in which gold was used as the reference point in valuing national currencies and as the ultimate medium for settling transactions, especially during the period from the 1870s to World War I.

Great Depression was the catastrophic downturn of the global economy in the 1920s and 1930s, marked by high unemployment, falling production, curtailed trade, and the social and political instability that followed.

Gross domestic product (GDP) is the total final output of goods and services produced by a nation's economy.

Gross national product (GNP) is the total output claimed by residents of a country. It consists of GDP plus net factor income from abroad.

Group of Seven is a consultative group consisting of the economic ministers of the seven largest industrialized democracies: the United States, Canada, Japan, Great Britain, Germany, France, and Italy.

Guilds were oligopolistic organizations of craftspeople (craft guilds) or merchants (trade guilds) that adopted common rules to govern their activities and protect their economic interests. Craft guilds, which were the forerunners of trade unions of workers, administered an apprenticeship system and quality standards.

Hegemonic leader (hegemon) is a dominant state that provides the leadership required to create and maintain the rules and organizations that manage the global economic system.

Hegemonic stability theory states that an open economic trading system (and most other forms of large-scale international cooperative arrangements) can be created and maintained only under the leadership of a single dominant state, without which trade is likely to decrease in volume and degenerate into discrimination, rivalry, and conflict.

Import-substituting industrialization (ISI) is a development strategy common to many less developed nations in which the state steers the domestic economy to produce industrial goods that were formerly imported, using trade barriers and sometimes subsidies of various kinds.

Industrial policy refers to any coordinated set of government policies designed to shape the composition of a nation's economy by targeting particular sectors or industries for growth. Usually, subsidies are provided to infant industries with the potential for growth, export success, or achievement of other important economic and political goals.

Infant industry refers to newly established firms that are targeted for import protection or export promotion, usually to enable them to better compete with established firms in other nations.

Interdependence refers to the situation in which various economic linkages between nations, especially trade and capital flows, make the welfare of citizens and the effectiveness of government policy in one nation contingent upon events, conditions, and policies in another nation.

International Bank for Reconstruction and Development (IBRD) is the largest of the international financial institutions that make up the World Bank group. Headquartered in Washington, D.C., it was originally created at Bretton Woods to provide capital for Europe after World War II.

International Monetary Fund (IMF) is the institution created at Bretton Woods to supervise exchange-rate policies of nations and encourage financial cooperation. It provides loans to nations experiencing balance-of-payments deficits and advice on how to correct them.

International Trade Organization (ITO) was the institution envisioned at Bretton Woods and designed at the 1948 Havana conference to coordinate trade policy and reduce trade barriers. Because it was never created, this role was partially filled by the GATT until the establishment of the World Trade Organization (WTO) after the Uruguay Round.

Iron law of wages states that in an unregulated market wage rates for unskilled labor will settle at the level required to keep workers barely alive.

Japan, Inc. is a term used to describe the close relationship between private business and governmental agencies like MITI, which foster Japanese exports, especially in the three decades after World War II.

Keiretsu is a network of Japanese firms that own shares in one another and cooperate in various ways.

Laissez-faire is the liberal doctrine that governments should refrain from interfering with markets in order to maximize efficiency.

(Economic) **liberal** is a term used to describe policies that feature minimal governmental interference with markets, especially trade policies with few barriers to imports.

Liquidity refers to an internationally accepted asset, for example, gold or the U.S. dollar, that can be used to settle payments between nations when national currencies are unacceptable because banks lack confidence in their future value.

Marshall Plan was the massive U.S. foreign aid program that helped to rebuild Europe after World War II.

Mercantilism refers to an eclectic mix of government policies that regulated trade before the advent of liberalism, especially through import barriers and export promotion, in pursuit of various national interests, including the power of the state. Its more modern versions are sometimes called neomercantilism.

Ministry of International Trade and Industry (MITI) is the powerful Japanese governmental organization that plays a central role in the industrial policy that plans and manages the Japanese economy, especially by providing credit, expertise, and regulatory relief for favored sectors of the economy.

Monopoly refers to a sector of the economy so dominated by a single firm that the lack of competition gives it the power to set prices that maximize its profits.

Most-favored-nation (MFN) **provision** is the nondiscrimination promise contained in GATT that each signatory will extend to every other signatory at least as favorable a treatment as it extends to any other nation.

Multilateral actions are those which involve many states acting together.

Multilateralism (multilateral liberalism) refers to a trading system in which nations refrain from negotiating lower trade barriers for some nations than others, relying instead upon the nondiscrimination principle such as the MFN provision of GATT.

National autonomy refers to the freedom of a nation-state from the coercion or constraints imposed by others so that it may actually exercise its right to national sovereignty.

National interest refers to the set of core goals said to motivate the foreign policy actions of nation-states, usually assumed to center around the maintenance of national security, sovereignty, and autonomy.

National safeguards refer to the various GATT escape clauses that permit nations to make exceptions to other GATT rules.

National sovereignty is the principle of international law that no state or supranational organization has legal authority within the boundaries of another nation, thus guaranteeing the right of a national government to adopt whatever laws or policies it wishes.

Navigation Acts were a series of parliamentary laws that regulated shipping as part of the mercantilist policy of early England. They included a requirement that British ships be used to transport British trade goods so as to strengthen the merchant marine and the navy as elements of national security.

Neomercantilism refers to the eclectic body of theory and policy advice that emerged after Smith and Ricardo to challenge liberal ideas and advocate government regulation of trade to achieve the national interest.

Nondiscrimination is the principle of equal treatment embodied in GATT's most-favored-nation clause. It prohibits a nation from maintaining different import barriers against the products of different nations (though there are many exceptions).

Nontariff barriers (NTBs) are import restrictions such as quotas and other regulations.

North American Free Trade Agreement (NAFTA) is the international treaty among the United States, Canada, and Mexico that provided for lower regional trade barriers beginning in 1994.

Oligopoly is a market structure in which a very small number of firms in a sector can together achieve a monopoly.

Optimum tariff is that rate of import taxation that will increase national welfare at the expense of others by inducing foreign producers to lower their export prices.

Orderly marketing arrangement (OMA) is a multilateral agreement whereby a nation establishes an individual import quota for each exporting nation.

Par value is the official exchange rate for a nation's currency established by that nation's government, often in conjunction with an international agreement such as the Bretton Woods fixed exchange-rate system.

Political economy refers to the interaction between the economic and political aspects of a national or international system, including the behavior of its actors and the structure of its institutions. This perspective questions the adequacy of studying either economics or politics without explicit recognition of the other.

Protectionism is the governmental practice of erecting barriers to imports for the purpose of allowing domestic firms greater market share.

Quota is a nontariff barrier to trade consisting of a limit a government places on the quantity of any given product that it will permit to be imported.

Reciprocity is the principle that a nation must extend to others trade benefits that are equivalent to those extended to them, with equivalence usually determined by negotiation.

Regional integration (or regionalism) refers to the practice of creating a regional group of nations each of which extends trade benefits to the others that are not available to nations outside the group.

Repatriation occurs when the profit from a foreign investment is returned to the nation of the investor.

Reserve account is the portion of the balance of payments recording changes in the level of a nation's reserve assets.

Social clause refers to provisions in trade agreements designed to offset the negative effects of trade-induced competition on the welfare of citizens, especially workers.

State goals dilemma refers to the choice that must be made when trade weakens the ability of the state to achieve some of its other goals.

Strategic trade theory describes how a government can help a firm benefit from economies of scale by adopting an aggressive industrial policy that promotes exports.

Subsidy is a direct payment or other benefit provided by the government to a firm to aid in the production or export of a particular good.

Tariff is a tax on imports.

Trade bloc refers to a group of nations that provide to one another trade benefits not available to outsiders, resulting in a great deal of trade within a bloc but little among blocs.

Trade deficit refers to the situation in a nation's balance of trade in which its imports exceed its exports.

Treasure was a term referring to precious metals, especially gold and silver, in the mercantilist period when they were the usual method of payment for imports.

Treasury bonds are certificates purchased by investors from the U.S. Treasury that entitle them to receive periodic interest payments and the return of their initial investment. The sale of bonds is the method used by the federal government to borrow money from investors to cover budget deficits.

Unilateral actions are those that involve one state acting alone.

Uruguay Round refers to the negotiations held under GATT auspices to lower trade barriers, implement trade rules, and create dispute-resolution mechanisms that began in Punta del Este in 1986 and concluded in Marrakech in 1994.

Usury laws place limits on the terms that may legally apply to loan agreements, such as those that place a ceiling on the interest rates that may be charged by credit card companies.

Values dilemma refers to the choice that must be made when trade achieves some goals at the expense of others.

Voluntary export restraint (VER) is a unilateral agreement under which a nation places a limit on the quantity of goods which it will export to another.

Voluntary restraint agreement (VRA) is a VER that has been reached on the basis of bilateral negotiations with the importing nation.

Welfare state is a term used to describe the system in which a government provides basic social protection to its citizens, such as unemployment insurance, income supplements to the poor, health care, and mandated employer practices such as minimum wage and benefits.

World Bank refers to the group of financial institutions including the International Bank for Reconstruction and Development (IBRD), the International Finance Corporation, and the International Development Agency. It provides loans for development projects all over the world, which are financed by the contributions of governments in developed nations.

World Trade Organization (WTO) is the international institution created by the Uruguay Round of GATT negotiations in 1994 to govern global trade.

Zaibatsu is one of the family-owned holding companies that were the predecessors of the *keiretsu* before World War II in Japan.

□ □ □

About the Book
and Author

In the Post–Cold War world, trade is the new arena for competition—between nations, between groups, between ethical and theoretical ideas. Political economist Bruce Moon puts contemporary trade events—NAFTA, United States–Japan controversies, the Uruguay Round of GATT, China's most-favored-nation status, the founding of the World Trade Organization—into historical and theoretical perspective with the British Corn Laws, the Great Depression, the Bretton Woods system, and the origins of the European Union. Economic theory, terms, and concepts are clearly explained and contextualized with those from international relations.

Throughout the book, three central dilemmas are examined: the unequal distribution of income and wealth created by international trade, the trade-off among competing values that trade requires, and the difficult interrelationship between economic and foreign policy goals within and among trading nations. Though internationally framed, each dilemma has ramifications at a variety of levels all the way down to the individual's role in the global economy—as a consumer, as a citizen, and ultimately as a moral agent.

Bruce E. Moon is associate professor of international relations at Lehigh University.

BOOKS IN THIS SERIES

Kenneth W. Grundy
**South Africa: Domestic Crisis
and Global Challenge**

□ □ □

David S. Mason
**Revolution in East-Central Europe
and World Politics**

□ □ □

Georg Sørensen
**Democracy and Democratization:
Process and Prospects in a Changing World**

□ □ □

Steve Chan
**East Asian Dynamism: Growth, Order, and
Security in the Pacific Region, second edition**

□ □ □

Barry B. Hughes
**International Futures: Choices in
the Creation of a New World Order**

□ □ □

Jack Donnelly
International Human Rights

□ □ □

V. Spike Peterson and Anne Sisson Runyan
Global Gender Issues

□ □ □

Sarah J. Tisch and Michael B. Wallace
**Dilemmas of Development Assistance:
The What, Why, and Who of Foreign Aid**

□ □ □

Ted Robert Gurr and Barbara Harff
Ethnic Conflict in World Politics

□ □ □

Fredric S. Pearson
**The Global Spread of Arms: Political Economy of
International Security**

187

Index